Advance Praise for *Information Rules*

"*Information Rules* is the indispensable battle manual for those on the front lines of the information revolution, and it is the first book to articulate practical strategies, tactics, and rules of engagement for surviving and winning standards wars. I needed this book in 1994 when EIT (Enterprise Integration Technologies Corporation) was battling Netscape and others for control of Internet security standards. Today, I depend on it to help Veo Systems survive the digital anarchy resulting from too many standards."

—**JAY M. TENENBAUM,** Founder and Chairman, Veo Systems,
and Founder and Chairman, CommerceNet

"This book develops excellent frameworks for a systematic analysis of the information economy. Shapiro and Varian explain key concepts such as lock-in, network externalities, and standards with great clarity and bring them to life through many fascinating and current examples. The reader emerges with a thorough understanding of the information economy. Full of powerful tools for strategic decision making, *Information Rules* is a valuable source for students, researchers, managers, and legislators."

—**PHILIPP AFÈCHE,** Assistant Professor of Managerial Economics
and Decision Sciences, J. L. Kellogg Graduate School of
Management, Northwestern University

Information Rules

Information Rules

A STRATEGIC GUIDE TO THE NETWORK ECONOMY

Carl Shapiro
Hal R. Varian

HARVARD BUSINESS SCHOOL PRESS
BOSTON, MASSACHUSETTS

03 02 01 00 99   5 4 3 2

Library of Congress Cataloging-in-Publication Data
Shapiro, Carl.
    Information rules : a strategic guide to the network economy /
Carl Shapiro and Hal R. Varian.
        p.   cm.
    Includes bibliographical references and index.
    ISBN 0-87584-863-X (alk. paper)
    1. Information technology—Economic aspects. 2. Information
society.   I. Varian, Hal R. II. Title.
HC79.I55S53 1998
658.4'038—dc21   98-24923
                                                            CIP

The paper used in this publication meets the requirements of the American National Standard for
Permanence of Paper for Printed Library Materials Z39.49-1984.

To Dawn, Eva, and Ben

To Carol and Chris

Contents

Preface

Luck led us to write this book.

Each of us became economists because we wanted to apply our analytical training to better understand how society functions. By our good fortune, the economics of information, technological change, game theory, and competitive strategy were emerging fields of inquiry when we started our professional careers. We jumped in and offered our own contributions in these areas. Never did we imagine that, twenty years later, we would find ourselves in the middle of an information revolution. What started as an academic exercise, centered on research and publishing, has evolved into speeches, consulting work, expert testimony, government service, and even a deanship.

As we strayed from academia, we often heard complaints that economics was not much use in today's economy. At first, we were perplexed by these complaints, since they often came from the very same people who sought our advice. Then we solved the puzzle: the complaints were directed at the classical economics most people learned in school, with its emphasis on supply and demand curves and perfectly competitive markets, like markets for agricultural commodities. We had to agree: to an executive rolling out a new software product or introducing the on-line version of a magazine, supply and demand curves just don't help much. Yet we knew that a sizable body of work in the field of economics speaks directly to current issues in the information economy.

Finally, we realized that our clients and friends were thirsty for knowledge about all manner of topics that we and our colleagues had been writing about for years but were rarely covered in most classes. They wanted to know how to set prices for different customer groups, how to design product lines for information goods, and how to manage their intellectual property. They wanted to know how to protect themselves from lock-in and how to take advantage of it when possible. We discovered great interest in the dynamics of software markets: why does a single company tend to dominate for a time, only to be displaced by a new leader? And we became more and more involved in the application of the antitrust laws to the information economy, with one of us heading off for a stint as the chief economist at the Antitrust Division of the Justice Department. In short, we lucked out: people actually wanted to know and use research results from our chosen fields.

At the same time, we kept hearing that we are living in a "New Economy." The implication was that a "New Economics" was needed as well, a new set of principles to guide business strategy and public policy. But wait, we said, have you read the literature on differential pricing, bundling, signaling, licensing, lock-in, or network economics? Have you studied the history of the telephone system or the battles between IBM and the Justice Department? Our claim: You don't need a brand new economics. You just need to see the really cool stuff, the material they didn't get to when you studied economics. So we wrote this book.

Our goal is to present insights from economics research and from our own experience applying economics in the network economy in a form suitable for the managers and policy makers who have to make strategic choices involving information technology. We believe that the ideas, the concepts, the models, and the way of thinking that we describe here will help you make better decisions. We also believe that our discussion will serve you well for years to come. Even though technology advances breathlessly, the economic principles we rely on are durable. The examples may change, but the ideas will not go out of date.

Of course, we are not saying that we know all the answers. Most of the time business solutions come down to "It depends." Our aim is to help you figure out *what* the solution depends on. And the best way to understand such dependencies is to have a framework that relates causes and effects. If you have a clear understanding of what's going on, and some examples of how other businesses have solved related problems, you will be better placed to make more informed and effective decisions.

Several of our friends and colleagues have contributed valuable suggestions to this book. We especially want to thank Erik Brynjolfsson, Randy Katz, David Messerschmitt, John Miller, Andrew Odlysko, Sherman Shapiro, Deepak Somaya, Doug Tygar, and Robert Wilensky for their valuable comments.

Finally, we want to thank our wives and children for their patience and good nature throughout this project.

1 | The Information Economy

As the century closed, the world became smaller. The public rapidly gained access to new and dramatically faster communication technologies. Entrepreneurs, able to draw on unprecedented scale economies, built vast empires. Great fortunes were made. The government demanded that these powerful new monopolists be held accountable under antitrust law. Every day brought forth new technological advances to which the old business models seemed no longer to apply. Yet, somehow, the basic laws of economics asserted themselves. Those who mastered these laws survived in the new environment. Those who did not, failed.

A prophecy for the next decade? No. You have just read a description of what happened a hundred years ago when the twentieth-century industrial giants emerged. Using the infrastructure of the emerging electricity and telephone networks, these industrialists transformed the U.S. economy, just as today's Silicon Valley entrepreneurs are drawing on computer and communications infrastructure to transform the world's economy.

The thesis of this book is that durable economic principles can guide you in today's frenetic business environment. Technology changes.

Economic laws do not. If you are struggling to comprehend what the Internet means for you and your business, you can learn a great deal from the advent of the telephone system a hundred years ago.

Sure, today's business world is different in a myriad of ways from that of a century ago. But many of today's managers are so focused on the trees of technological change that they fail to see the forest: the underlying economic forces that determine success and failure. As academics, government officials, and consultants we have enjoyed a bird's-eye view of the forest for twenty years, tracking industries, working for high-tech companies, and contributing to an ever-growing literature on information and technology markets.

> **Technology changes.**
> **Economic laws do not.**

In the pages that follow, we systematically introduce and explain the concepts and strategies you need to successfully navigate the network economy. Information technology is rushing forward, seemingly chaotically, and it is difficult to discern patterns to guide business decisions. But there is order in the chaos: a few basic economic concepts go a long way toward explaining how today's industries are evolving.

Netscape, the one-time darling of the stock market, offers a good example of how economic principles can serve as an early warning system. We're not sure exactly how software for viewing Web pages will evolve, but we do know that Netscape is fundamentally vulnerable because its chief competitor, Microsoft, controls the operating environment of which a Web browser is but one component. In our framework, Netscape is facing a classic problem of interconnection: Netscape's browser needs to work in conjunction with Microsoft's operating system. Local telephone companies battling the Bell System around 1900 faced a similar dependency upon their chief rival when they tried to interconnect with Bell to offer long-distance service. Many did not survive. Interconnection battles have arisen regularly over the past century in the telephone, the railroad, the airline, and the computer industries, among others. We wonder how many investors who bid Netscape's stock price up to breathtaking heights appreciated its fundamental vulnerability.

We examine numerous business strategies on both the information (software) and the infrastructure (hardware) sides of the industry. Software and hardware are inexorably linked. Indeed, they are a leading example of complements, one of the key concepts explored in our book.

Neither software nor hardware is of much value without the other; they are only valuable because they work together as a system.

INFORMATION

We use the term *information* very broadly. Essentially, anything that can be digitized—encoded as a stream of bits—is information. For our purposes, baseball scores, books, databases, magazines, movies, music, stock quotes, and Web pages are all *information goods*. We focus on the value of information to different consumers. Some information has entertainment value, and some has business value, but regardless of the particular source of value, people are willing to pay for information. As we see, many strategies for purveyors of information are based on the fact that consumers differ greatly in how they value particular information goods.

Of course, information is costly to create and assemble. The cost structure of an information supplier is rather unusual. Since the very nature of competition in information markets is driven by this unusual cost structure, we begin our overview of information strategy there.

The Cost of Producing Information

Information is costly to *produce* but cheap to *reproduce*. Books that cost hundreds of thousands of dollars to produce can be printed and bound for a dollar or two, and 100-million dollar movies can be copied on videotape for a few cents.

Economists say that production of an information good involves *high fixed costs* but *low marginal costs*. The cost of producing the first copy of an information good may be substantial, but the cost of producing (or reproducing) additional copies is negligible. This sort of cost structure has many important implications. For example, cost-based pricing just doesn't work: a 10 or 20 percent markup on unit cost makes no sense when unit cost is zero. You must price your information goods according to consumer value, not according to your production cost.

Since people have widely different values for a particular piece of information, value-based pricing leads naturally to differential pricing. We explore strategies for differential pricing in detail in Chapters 2 and 3. Chapter 2 is concerned with ways to sell an information good to identifiable markets; Chapter 3 examines ways to "version" information goods to make them appeal to different market segments which will pay different prices for the different versions.

For example, one way to differentiate versions of the same information good is to use *delay*. Publishers first sell a hardback book and then issue a paperback several months later. The impatient consumers buy the high-priced hardback; the patient ones buy the low-priced paperback. Providers of information on the Internet can exploit the same strategy: investors now pay $8.95 a month for a Web site that offers portfolio analysis using 20-minute delayed stock market quotes but $50 a month for a service that uses real-time stock market quotes.

> *Price information according to its value, not its cost.*

We explore different ways to version information in Chapter 3 and show you the principles behind creating profitable product lines that target different market segments. Each version sells for a different price, allowing you to extract the maximum value of your product from the marketplace.

Managing Intellectual Property

If the creators of an information good can reproduce it cheaply, others can copy it cheaply. It has long been recognized that some form of "privatization" of information helps to ensure its production. The U.S. Constitution explicitly grants Congress the duty "to promote the progress of science and useful arts, by securing, for limited times, to authors and inventors, the exclusive right to their respective writings and discoveries."

But the legal grant of exclusive rights to intellectual property via patents, copyright, and trademarks does not confer complete power to control information. There is still the issue of enforcement, a problem that has become even more important with the rise of digital technology and the Internet. Digital information can be perfectly copied and instantaneously transmitted around the world, leading many content producers to view the Internet as one giant, out-of-control copying machine. If copies crowd out legitimate sales, the producers of information may not be able to recover their production costs.

Despite this danger, we think that content owners tend to be too conservative with respect to the management of their intellectual property. The history of the video industry is a good example. Hollywood was petrified by the advent of videotape recorders. The TV industry filed suits to prevent home copying of TV programs, and Disney attempted to distinguish video sales and rentals through licensing arrangements. All of these attempts failed. Ironically, Hollywood now makes more from video than from theater presentations for most productions. The video sales and rental market, once so feared, has become a giant revenue source for Hollywood.

When managing intellectual property, your goal should be to choose the terms and conditions that maximize the *value* of your intellectual property, not the terms and conditions that maximize the protection. In Chapter 4 we'll review the surprising history of intellectual property and describe the lessons it has for rights management on the Internet.

Information as an "Experience Good"

Economists say that a good is an *experience good* if consumers must experience it to value it. Virtually any new product is an experience good, and marketers have developed strategies such as free samples, promotional pricing, and testimonials to help consumers learn about new goods.

But information is an experience good *every* time it's consumed. How do you know whether today's *Wall Street Journal* is worth 75 cents until you've read it? Answer: you don't.

Information businesses—like those in the print, music, and movie industries—have devised various strategies to get wary consumers to overcome their reluctance to purchase information before they know what they are getting. First, there are various forms of browsing: you can look at the headlines at the newsstand, hear pop tunes on the radio, and watch previews at the movies. But browsing is only part of the story. Most media producers overcome the experience good problem through *branding* and *reputation*. The main reason that we read the *Wall Street Journal* today is that we've found it useful in the past.

The brand name of the *Wall Street Journal* is one of its chief assets, and the *Journal* invests heavily in building a reputation for accuracy, timeliness, and relevance. This investment takes numerous forms, from the company's Newspapers in Education program (discussed in

Chapter 2), to the distinctive appearance of the paper itself, and the corporate logo. The look and feel of the *Journal*'s on-line edition testifies to the great lengths designers went to carry over the look and feel of the print version, thereby extending the same authority, brand identity, and customer loyalty from the print product to the on-line product. The *Wall Street Journal* "brand" conveys a message to potential readers about the quality of the content, thereby overcoming the experience good problem endemic to information goods.

The computer scientists who designed the protocols for the Internet and the World Wide Web were surprised by the huge traffic in images. Today more than 60 percent of Internet traffic is to Web sites, and of the Web traffic, almost three-fourths is images. Some of these images are *Playboy* centerfolds, of course—another brand that successfully made the move to cyberspace—but a lot of them are corporate logos. Image is everything in the information biz, because it's the image that carries the brand name and the reputation.

The tension between giving away your information—to let people know what you have to offer—and charging them for it to recover your costs is a fundamental problem in the information economy. We talk about strategies for making this choice in our discussion of rights management in Chapter 4.

The Economics of Attention

Now that information is available so quickly, so ubiquitously, and so inexpensively, it is not surprising that everyone is complaining of information overload. Nobel prize–winning economist Herbert Simon spoke for us all when he said that "a wealth of information creates a poverty of attention."

"A wealth of information creates a poverty of attention."

Nowadays the problem is not information access but information overload. The real value produced by an information provider comes in locating, filtering, and communicating what is useful to the consumer. It is no accident that the most popular Web sites belong to the search engines, those devices that allow people to find information they value and to avoid the rest.

In real estate, it is said that there are only three critical factors:

location, location, and location. Any idiot can establish a Web presence—and lots of them have. The big problem is letting people know about it. Amazon.com, the on-line bookstore, recently entered into a long-term, exclusive agreement with America Online (AOL) to gain access to AOL's 8.5 million customers. The cost of this deal is on the order of $19 million, which can be understood as the cost of purchasing the *attention* of AOL subscribers. Wal-Mart recently launched the Wal-Mart Television Network, which broadcasts commercials on the television sets lined up for sale at the company's 1,950 stores nationwide. Like AOL, Wal-Mart realized that it could sell the attention of its customers to advertisers. As health clubs, doctors' offices, and other locations attempt to grab our valuable attention, information overload will worsen.

Selling viewers' attention has always been an attractive way to support information provision. Commercials support broadcast TV, and advertisement is often the primary revenue source for magazines and newspapers. Advertising works because it exploits statistical patterns. People who read *Car and Driver* are likely to be interested in ads for BMWs, and people who read the *Los Angeles Times* are likely to be interested in California real estate.

The Internet, a hybrid between a broadcast medium and a point-to-point medium, offers exciting new potentials for matching up customers and suppliers. The Net allows information vendors to move from the conventional broadcast form of advertising to one-to-one marketing. Nielsen collects information on the viewing habits of a few thousand consumers, which is then used to design TV shows for the next season. In contrast, Web servers can observe the behavior of millions of customers and immediately produce customized content, bundled with customized ads.

The information amassed by these powerful Web servers is not limited to their users' current behavior; they can also access vast databases of information about customer history and demographics. Hotmail, for example, offers free e-mail service to customers who complete a questionnaire on their demographics and interests. This personal information allows Hotmail to customize ads that can be displayed alongside the user's e-mail messages.

This new, one-to-one marketing benefits both parties in the transaction: the advertiser reaches exactly the market it wants to target, and consumers need give their attention only to ads that are likely to be of interest. Furthermore, by gathering better information about what particular customers want, the information provider can design products that are more highly customized and hence more valuable. Firms that master this sort of marketing will thrive, while those that continue to conduct unfocused and excessively broad advertising campaigns will be at a competitive disadvantage. We'll examine strategies for customizing information in detail in Chapters 2 and 3.

TECHNOLOGY

We have focused so far on the information side of "information technology." Now let's turn to the technology side—that is, the infrastructure that makes it possible to store, search, retrieve, copy, filter, manipulate, view, transmit, and receive information.

Infrastructure is to information as a bottle is to wine: the technology is the packaging that allows the information to be delivered to end consumers. A single copy of a film would be of little value without a distribution technology. Likewise, computer software is valuable only because computer hardware and network technology are now so powerful and inexpensive.

In short, today's breathless pace of change and the current fascination with the information economy are driven by advances in information technology and infrastructure, not by any fundamental shift in the nature or even the magnitude of the information itself. The fact is, the Web isn't all that impressive as an information resource. The static, publicly accessible HTML text on the Web is roughly equivalent in size to 1.5 million books. The UC Berkeley Library has 8 million volumes, and the average quality of the Berkeley library content is much, much higher! If 10 percent of the material on the Web is "useful," there are about 150,000 useful book-equivalents on it, which is about the size of a Borders superstore. But the actual figure for "useful" is probably more like 1 percent, which is 15,000 books, or half the size of an average mall bookstore.

> *The technology infrastructure makes information more accessible and hence more valuable.*

The value of the Web lies in its capacity to provide immediate access to information. Using the Web, information suppliers can distribute up-to-date information dynamically from databases and other repositories. Imagine what would happen if the wine industry came up with a bottle that gave its customers easier, quicker, and cheaper access to its wine. Sure, the bottle is only infrastructure, but infrastructure that can reduce cost and increase value is tremendously important. Improved information infrastructure has vastly increased our ability to store, retrieve, sort, filter, and distribute information, thereby greatly enhancing the value of the underlying information itself.

What's new is our ability to manipulate information, not the total amount of information available. Mom-and-pop hardware stores of yesteryear regularly checked their inventories. The inventory information now captured by Home Depot, while surely more accurate and up-to-date, is not vastly greater than that of a generation ago. What is truly new is Home Depot's ability to re-order items from suppliers using electronic data interchange, to conduct and analyze cross-store demand studies based on pricing and promotional variations, and to rapidly discount slow-moving items, all with minimal human intervention.

Indeed, in every industry we see dramatic changes in technology that allow people to do more with the same information. Sears Roebuck popularized catalog sales more than a century ago. Lands' End does not have that much more raw information than Sears did. Like Sears, it has a catalog of products and a list of customers. What is new is that Lands' End can easily retrieve data on customers, including data on previous purchases, that allows it to engage in targeted marketing. Furthermore, Lands' End can use the telecommunications and banking infrastructure to conduct transactions in real time over the telephone and on-line.

Content providers cannot operate without infrastructure suppliers, and vice versa. The information economy is about both information *and* the associated technology.

Systems Competition

Systems show up everywhere in information technology: operating systems and applications software, CPUs and memory chips, disk drives and controller cards, video cassette recorders and the videotapes themselves. Usually, one firm cannot hope to offer all the pieces that make up an information system. Instead, different components are made by different manufacturers using very different production and business models. Traditional rules of competitive strategy focus on competitors, suppliers, and customers. In the information economy, companies selling complementary components, or *complementors,* are equally important. When you are selling one component of a system, you can't compete if you're not compatible with the rest of the system. Many of our strategic principles are specifically designed to help companies selling one component of an information system.

The dependence of information technology on systems means that firms must focus not only on their competitors but also on their collaborators. Forming alliances, cultivating partners, and ensuring compatibility (or lack of compatibility!) are critical business decisions. Firms have long been faced with make/buy decisions, but the need for collaboration, and the multitude of cooperative arrangements, has never been greater than in the area of infotech. We describe how firms must function in such a systems-rich and standards-rich environment in Chapter 8.

Focus not just on your competitors but also on your collaborators and complementors.

The history of the Microsoft-Intel partnership is a classic example. Microsoft focused almost exclusively on software, while Intel focused almost exclusively on hardware. They each made numerous strategic alliances and acquisitions that built on their strengths. The key for each company has been to commoditize complementary products without eroding the value of its own core strengths. For example, Intel has entered new product spaces such as chipsets and motherboards to improve the performance of these components and thereby stimulate demand for its core product: microprocessors. Intel has helped to create a highly competitive industry in component parts such as video cards, sound cards, and hard drives as well as in the assembly and distribution of personal computers.

Microsoft has its following of independent software vendors (ISVs), and both companies have extensive licensing programs with original equipment manufacturers (OEMs). And they each have each other, an extraordinarily productive, if necessarily tense, marriage. It's in the interest of each company to create multiple sources for its partner's piece of the system but to prevent the emergence of a strong rival for its own piece. This tension arises over and over again in the information technology sector; Microsoft and Intel are merely the most visible, and profitable, example of the complex dynamics that arise in assembling information systems.

Apple Computer pursued a very different strategy by producing a highly integrated product consisting of both a hardware platform and the software that ran on it. Their software and hardware was much more tightly integrated than the Microsoft/Intel offerings, so it performed better. (Microsoft recognized this early on and tried to license the Apple technology rather than investing in developing its own windowing system.) The downside was that the relative lack of competition (and, later, scale) made Apple products more expensive and, eventually, less powerful. In the long run, the "Wintel" strategy of strategic alliance was the better choice.

Lock-In and Switching Costs

Remember long-playing phonograph records (LPs)? In our lexicon, these were "durable complementary assets" specific to a turntable but incompatible with the alternative technology of CDs. In plain English: they were durable and valuable, they worked with a turntable to play music, but they would not work in a CD player. As a result, Sony and Philips had to deal with considerable consumer *switching costs* when introducing their CD technology. Fortunately for Sony and Philips, CDs offered significant improvement in convenience, durability, and sound quality over LPs, so consumers were willing to replace their music libraries. Quadraphonic sound, stereo AM radio, PicturePhones, and digital audiotape did not fare as well. We'll see how the new digital video (or versatile) disks (DVDs) will do in the next few years.

As the impending problem of resetting computers to recognize the year 2000 illustrates, users of information technologies are notoriously subject to switching costs and lock-in: once you have chosen a technology, or a format for keeping information, switching can be very expensive. Most of us have experienced the costs of switching from one brand of computer software to another: data files are unlikely to transfer perfectly, incompatibilities with other tools often arise, and, most important, retraining is required.

Switching costs are significant, and corporate information officers (CIOs) think long and hard about changing systems. Lock-in to historical, legacy systems is commonplace in the network economy. Such lock-in is not absolute—new technologies do displace old ones—but switching costs can dramatically alter firms' strategies and options. In fact, the magnitude of switching costs is itself a strategic choice made by the producer of the system.

Lock-in arises whenever users invest in multiple complementary and durable assets specific to a particular information technology system. You purchased a library of LPs as well as a turntable. So long as these assets were valuable—the albums were not too scratched and the turntable still worked—you had less reason to buy a CD player and start buying expensive CDs. More generally, in replacing an old system with a new, incompatible one, you may find it necessary to swap out or duplicate *all* the components of your system. These components typically include a range of assets: data files (LP records, COBOL programs, word processing documents, etc.), various pieces of durable hardware, and training, or human capital. Switching from Apple to Intel equipment involves not only new hardware but new software. And not only that, the "wetware"—the knowledge that you and your employees have built up that enables you to use your hardware and software—has to be updated. The switching costs for changing computer systems can be astronomical. Today's state-of-the-art choice is tomorrow's legacy system.

This type of situation is the norm in the information economy. A cellular telephone provider that has invested in Qualcomm's technology for compressing and encoding the calls it transmits and receives is locked into that technology, even if Qualcomm raises the price for its gear. A large enterprise that has selected Cisco's or 3Com's technology and architecture for its networking needs will find it very costly to change to an incompatible network technology. Whether the enterprise is locked in to proprietary Cisco or 3Com products or to an "open" standard with multiple suppliers can make a big difference.

Lock-in can occur on an individual level, a company level, or even a societal level. Many consumers were locked into LP libraries, at least in the sense that they were less inclined to purchase CD players because they could not play LPs. Many companies were locked into Lotus 1-2-3 spreadsheets because their employees were highly trained in using the Lotus command structure; indeed, Lotus sued Borland for copying the 1-2-3 command structure in its spreadsheet product, Quattro Pro, a dispute that went all the way to the Supreme Court. Today, at a societal level, most of us are locked into Microsoft's Windows desktop operating environment.

We explore lock-in and switching costs in Chapters 5 and 6. We'll examine the different kinds of lock-in, strategies to incorporate proprietary features into your product, and ways to coordinate your strategy with that of your partners. We'll explain how to exploit lock-in when you are offering an information system and how to avoid it, or at least anticipate it, when you are the buyer.

Positive Feedback, Network Externalities, and Standards

For many information technologies, consumers benefit from using a popular format or system. When the value of a product to one user depends on how many other users there are, economists say that this product exhibits *network externalities,* or *network effects.* Communications technologies are a prime example: telephones, e-mail, Internet access, fax machines, and modems all exhibit network externalities.

Technologies subject to strong network effects tend to exhibit long lead times followed by explosive growth. The pattern results from *positive feedback:* as the installed base of users grows, more and more users find adoption worthwhile. Eventually, the product achieves critical mass and takes over the market. Fax machines illustrate nicely the common pattern. The Scottish inventor Alexander Bain patented the basic technology for fax machines in 1843, and AT&T introduced a wire photo service in the United States in 1925, but faxes remained a niche product until the mid-1980s. During a five-year period, the demand for and supply of fax machines exploded. Before 1982 almost no one had a fax machine; after 1987, the majority of businesses had one or more.

The Internet exhibited the same pattern. The first e-mail message was sent in 1969, but up until the mid-1980s e-mail was used only by techies. Internet technology was developed in the early 1970s but didn't really take off until the late 1980s. But when Internet traffic did finally start growing, it doubled every year from 1989 to 1995. After the Internet was privatized in April 1995, it started growing even faster.

Positive feedback makes large networks get larger.

But network externalities are not confined to communications networks. They are also powerful in "virtual" networks, such as the network of users of Macintosh computers: each Mac user benefits from a larger network, since this facilitates the exchange of files and tips and encourages software houses to devote more resources to developing software for the Mac. Because these virtual networks of compatible users generate network externalities, popular hardware and software systems enjoy a significant competitive advantage over less popular systems. As a result, growth is a strategic imperative, not just to achieve the usual production side economies of scale but to achieve the *demand side* economies of scale generated by network effects.

We explore the implications of network externalities for business strategy in Chapter 7. The key challenge is to obtain critical mass—after that, the going gets easier. Once you

Network effects lead to demand side economies of scale and positive feedback.

have a large enough customer base, the market will build itself. However, having a superior technology is not enough to win. You may need to employ marketing tools such as penetration pricing to ignite the positive feedback.

The company that best understands information systems and complementary products will be best positioned to move rapidly and aggressively. Netscape grabbed the Web browser market early on by giving away its product. It lost money on every sale but made up for it in volume. Netscape was able to give away its browser and sell it, too, by bundling such critical components as customer support with the retail version and by selling complementary goods such as server software for hefty prices.

In competing to become the standard, or at least to achieve critical mass, consumer *expectations* are critical. In a very real sense, the product that is *expected* to become the standard *will* become the standard. Self-fulfilling expectations are one manifestation of positive-feedback economics and bandwagon effects. As a result, companies participating in markets with strong network effects seek to convince customers that their products will ultimately become the standard, while rival, incompatible products will soon be orphaned.

Competitive "pre-announcements" of a product's appearance on the market are a good example of "expectations management." In the mid-1980s, when Borland released Quattro Pro, a new spreadsheet, Microsoft was quick to counter with a press release describing how much better the next release of its comparable program, Excel, would be. It didn't take long for the press to come up with the term *vaporware* to describe this sort of "product." Microsoft played the same game IBM had played in an earlier generation, when IBM was accused of using pre- announcements to stifle competition. When network effects are strong, product announcements can be as important as the actual intro- duction of products.

Product pre-announcements can be a two-edged sword, however. The announcement of a new, improved version of your product may cut into your competitors' sales, but it can also cut into your own sales. When Intel developed the MMX technology for accelerating graphics in the fall of 1996, it was careful not to advertise it until *after* the Christmas season. Likewise, sales of large-screen TV sets in 1997 declined as con- sumers waited for digital television sets to arrive in 1998.

Because of the importance of critical mass, because customer expec- tations are so important in the area of information infrastructure, and because technology is evolving so rapidly, the *timing* of strategic moves is even more important in the information industry than in others. Mov- ing too early means making compromises in technology and going out on a limb without sufficient allies. Japan's television network NHK tried to go it alone in the early 1990s with its own high-definition television system, with disastrous consequences: not only has NHK's analog MUSE system met with consumer resistance in Japan, but it has left the Japanese behind the United States in the development and deployment of digital television. Yet moving too late can mean missing the market entirely, especially if customers become locked into rival technologies. We'll explore timing in Chapter 7 along with our discussion of critical mass, network externalities, standards, and compatibility.

Whether you are trying to establish a new information technology or to extend the lifetime of technology that is already popular, you will face critical compatibility decisions. For example, a key source of leverage for Sony and Philips in their negotiations with others in the DVD alliance was their control over the original CD technology. Even if Sony and Philips did not develop or control the best technology for DVD, they were in the driver's seat to the extent that their patents prevented others from offering backward-compatible DVD machines. Yet even compa- nies with de facto standards do not necessarily opt for backward com- patibility: Nintendo 64 machines cannot play Nintendo game cartridges from the earlier generations of Nintendo systems. We explore a range of compatibility issues, including intergenerational compatibility, in Chap- ter 8.

Another method for achieving critical mass is to assemble a powerful group of strategic partners. For this purpose, partners can be customers, complementors, or even competitors. Having some large, visible customers aboard can get the bandwagon rolling by directly building up critical mass. In November 1997 Sun took out full-page ads in the *New York Times* and other major newspapers reciting the long list of the members of the "Java coalition" to convey the impression that Java was the "next big thing."

Having suppliers of complements aboard makes the overall system more attractive. And having competitors aboard can give today's and tomorrow's customers the assurance that they will not be exploited once they are locked in. We see this strategy being used with DVD today; Sony and Philips, the original promoters of CD technology, have teamed up with content providers (that is, customers) such as Time Warner and competitors such as Toshiba to promote the new DVD technology. Both player manufacturers and disk-pressing firms are on board, too. The same pattern occurs in the emergence of digital television in the United States, where set manufacturers, who have the most to gain from rapid adoption of digital TV, are leading the way, with the Federal Communications Commission (FCC) dragging broadcasters along by offering them free spectrum for digital broadcasts.

Very often, support for a new technology can be assembled in the context of a formal standard-setting effort. For example, both Motorola and Qualcomm have sought to gain competitive advantages, not to mention royalty income, by having their patented technologies incorporated into formal standards for modems and cellular telephones.

If you own valuable intellectual property but need to gain critical mass, you must decide whether to promote your technology unilaterally, in the hope that it will become a de facto standard that you can tightly control, or to make various "openness" commitments to help achieve a critical mass. Adobe followed an openness strategy with its page description language, PostScript, explicitly allowing other software houses to implement PostScript interpreters, because they realized that such widespread use helped establish a standard. Nowadays, participation in most formal standard-setting bodies in the United States requires a commitment to license any essential or blocking patents on "fair, reasonable and non-discriminatory terms." We explore strategies for establishing technology standards in Chapter 8.

A go-it-alone strategy typically involves competition to *become* the standard. By contrast, participation in a formal standard-setting process, or assembling allies to promote a particular version of technology, typically involves competition *within* a standard. Don't plan to play the higher-stakes, winner-take-all battle to become the standard unless you can be aggressive in timing, in pricing, and in exploiting relationships with complementary products. Rivalry to achieve cost leadership by scale economies and experience, a tried and true strategy in various manufacturing contexts, is tame in comparison. Just ask

> *Standards change competition for a market to competition within a market.*

Sony about losing out with Beta in the standards war against VHS, or the participants in the recent 56k modem standards battle. We explore effective strategies for standards battles in Chapter 9.

POLICY

The ongoing battle between Microsoft and the Justice Department illustrates the importance of antitrust policy in the information sector. Whether fending off legal attacks or using the antitrust laws to challenge the conduct of competitors or suppliers, every manager in the network economy can profit from understanding the rules of the game. We explore government information policy in Chapter 10, including antitrust policy and regulation in the telecommunications sector.

Microsoft's wishes to the contrary, high-tech firms are not immune to the antitrust laws. Competitive strategy in the information economy collides with antitrust law in three primary areas: mergers and acquisitions, cooperative standard setting, and monopolization. We explore the current legal rules in each of these areas in Chapter 10.

Overall, we do not believe that antitrust law blocks most companies from pursuing their chosen strategies, even when they need to cooperate with other industry members to establish compatibility standards. Now and then, companies are prevented from acquiring direct rivals, as when Microsoft tried to acquire Intuit, but this is hardly unique to the information sector.

The Sherman Anti-Trust Act was passed in 1890 to control monopolies. Technology has changed radically since then. As we have stressed, the underlying economic principles have not. As a new century arrives, the Sherman Act is flexible enough to prevent the heavy hand of monopoly from stifling innovation, while keeping markets competitive enough to stay the even heavier hand of government regulation from intruding in our dynamic hardware and software markets.

HOW WE DIFFER

We've explained what this book is about. We also should say what our book is *not* about and what distinguishes our approach from others.

First, this book is not about *trends*. Lots of books about the impact of technology are attempts to forecast the future. You've heard that work will become more decentralized, more organic, and more flexible. You've heard about flat organizations and unlimited bandwidth. But the methodology for forecasting these trends is unclear; typically, it is just extrapolation from recent developments. Our forecasting, such as it is, is based on durable economic principles that have been proven to work in practice.

Second, this book is not about *vocabulary*. We're not going to invent any new buzzwords (although we *do* hope to resurrect a few old ones). Our goal is to introduce new terms only when they actually describe a useful concept; there will be no vocabulary for the sake of vocabulary. We won't talk about "cyberspace," the "cybereconomy," or cyber-anything.

Third, this book is not about *analogies*. We won't tell you that devising business strategy is like restoring an ecosystem, fighting a war, or making love. Business strategy is business strategy and though analogies can sometimes be helpful, they can also be misleading. Our view is that analogies can be an effective way to *communicate* strategies, but they are a very dangerous way to *analyze* strategies.

We seek models, not trends; concepts, not vocabulary; and analysis, not analogies. We firmly believe the models, the concepts, and the analysis will provide you with a deeper understanding of the fundamental forces at work in today's high-tech industries and enable you to craft winning strategies for tomorrow's network economy.

2 | Pricing Information

The *Encyclopedia Britannica* has been regarded as a classic reference work for more than two hundred years. And, as a classic, it has commanded a premium price: a few years ago a hardback set of the thirty-two volumes of the *Britannica* cost $1,600.

In 1992 Microsoft decided to get into the encyclopedia business. The company bought rights to *Funk & Wagnalls,* a second-tier encyclopedia that had been reduced to supermarket sales by the time of the purchase. Microsoft used the *Funk & Wagnalls* content to create a CD with some multimedia bells and whistles and a user friendly front end and sold it to end users for $49.95. Microsoft sold *Encarta* to computer original equipment manufacturers (OEMs) on even more attractive terms, and many computer manufacturers offered the CD as a freebie.

Britannica started to see its market erode and soon realized that it needed to develop an electronic publishing strategy. The company's first move was to offer on-line access to libraries at a subscription rate of $2,000 per year. Large libraries bought this service—after all, it *was* the *Britannica*—but smaller school libraries, offices, and homes found CD encyclopedias adequate for their needs and much more affordable. *Britannica* continued to lose market share and revenue to its electronic

opportunities. We said earlier that information is an experience good—you have to experience it to know what it is. Just as sellers of new brands of toothpaste distribute free samples via direct mail campaigns, sellers of information goods can distribute free samples via the Internet. The toothpaste vendor may pay a dollar or two per consumer in production, packaging, and distribution to promote its product; but the information vendor pays essentially nothing to distribute an additional free copy. For information goods, copies are free for the producer as well as for the consumer; we will investigate the implications of this fact in detail in Chapter 4.

Large fixed costs and small incremental costs—that is, substantial economies of scale—are hardly unique to information goods. Many other industries have cost structures that share these characteristics. It costs a lot to lay optical fiber, buy switches, and make a telecommunications system operational. But once the first signal has been sent, it costs next to nothing to send additional signals over the fiber, at least until capacity is reached. It costs United a huge amount to purchase and operate a 747, but the incremental cost of an additional passenger is tiny, so long as the plane is not full. The first-copy costs common to information goods are "merely" the extreme version of what we see in other industries where scale economies are powerful, which includes many high technology industries like chip fabrication.

COSTS AND COMPETITION

So far we've seen that:

- Information is costly to produce but cheap to reproduce.

- Once the first copy of an information good has been produced, most costs are sunk and cannot be recovered.

- Multiple copies can be produced at roughly constant per-unit costs.

- There are no natural capacity limits for additional copies.

These cost characteristics of information goods have significant implications for competitive pricing strategy.

The first and most important point is that markets for information will not, and *cannot,* look like textbook-perfect competitive markets in which there are many suppliers offering similar products, each lacking the ability to influence prices. Such a market structure may be a plausible description of the market for wheat or government bonds, but it has little relevance to information markets.

We've seen business plans for "information auctions," where digital content is sold to the highest bidder(s). That sort of market structure works well for goods in fixed supply, like stocks or airline seats, but it simply isn't viable for a good in which the incremental cost of production is zero. Selling a generic product—say, a digital map, for 10 cents—isn't viable when your competition can sell the same map for 9 cents and still make a profit.

When Information Is Commoditized

To see why "information commodity markets" don't work, let's examine the history of CD phone books.

CD phone books first appeared in 1986 when Nynex developed a directory of the New York area. Nynex charged $10,000 per disk and sold copies to the FBI, the IRS, and others. The Nynex executive in charge of the product, James Bryant, left to set up his own company, Pro CD, to produce a national directory. A consultant who worked on the project, Claude Schoch, had the same idea and created Digital Directory Assistance.

The phone companies wouldn't rent their computerized listings to the CD companies at a reasonable price, since they didn't want to cannibalize their $10 billion Yellow Pages services. So Pro CD hired Chinese workers to do the transcriptions in a Beijing factory, at a cost per worker of $3.50 per day. These Chinese workers typed in all the listings in every phone book in the United States—in fact, they typed them in *twice* to check for errors!

The resulting database had more than 70 million listings. These data were used to create a master CD, which was then used to create hundreds of thousands of copies. These copies, which cost well under a dollar a piece to produce, were sold for hundreds of dollars in the early 1990s and yielded a tidy profit.

But other producers caught on: within a few years competitors such as American Business Information adopted essentially the same business model, with minor variations. By now there are at least a half-dozen companies that produce CD telephone directories, and prices have fallen dramatically. You can buy CD phone directories for less than $20, and there are also several directory listings on the Internet that provide the same service for free, covering their costs through advertising.

The story of CD telephone directories is a classic one: once several firms have sunk the costs necessary to create the product—be it a CD or a rail line—competitive forces tend to move the price toward marginal cost, the cost of producing an "additional" copy.

To see why, consider a simple example. Suppose that Numbers R Us and Fone Your Friends each offer a CD telephone directory for $200 a disk. Imagine that these two CDs are essentially identical—they have the same amount of information and similar user interfaces, and they are both reasonably current.

What happens if Numbers R Us decides to cut its price to $189.95? Since the products are essentially identical, consumers gravitate to the cheaper product. In response, Fone Your Friends cuts *its* price to $179.95. Numbers R Us responds with a $169.95 price . . . and so it goes. This downward spiral of prices may be hard to prevent. Once the sunk costs have been sunk, there is no natural floor to the price except the cost of producing and distributing another CD, which is only a few dollars. Nowadays, CD telephone directories sell for $19.95 or less, a far cry from the heady days of the 1980s.

Competition among sellers of commodity information pushes prices to zero.

Commentators marvel at the amount of free information on the Internet, but it's not so surprising to an economist. The generic information on the Net—information commodities such as phone numbers, news stories, stock prices, maps, and directories—are simply selling at marginal cost: zero.

Market Structures for Information Goods

The high sunk cost, low marginal cost feature of information markets has significant implications for the market structure of information industries. In the final analysis, there are only two sustainable structures for an information market.

1. The *dominant firm* model may or may not produce the "best" product, but by virtue of its size and scale economies it enjoys a cost advantage over its smaller rivals. Microsoft is everyone's favorite example, since it controls the market for operating systems for desktop computers.

2. In a *differentiated product* market we have a number of firms producing the same "kind" of information, but with many different varieties. This is the most common market structure for information goods: the publishing, film, television, and some software markets fit this model.

Amalgams of the two models are not uncommon; many software markets involve both differentiated products and disparate market shares. Indeed, one can say that all products are differentiated, it's just a question of how much. TV listings are an interesting example. *TV Guide* is the dominant firm in this industry, selling nearly a billion copies a year and offering some differentiated content. However, there are many local advertiser-supported guides, distributed for free as standalones or with hundreds of Sunday newspapers, that compete with the commodity information in *TV Guide*. After a period of relative calm, the TV listings market is gearing up for a heated battle with GIST TV and other on-line TV listing services. On-line listings are likely to give the print media a run for their money, especially if Web TV takes off.

Your basic strategy will depend on what kind of industry you are in. At the most fundamental level, we have the classic time-tested principles of competitive strategy:

- **Differentiate your product.** If you are in a differentiated products industry, you must add value to the raw information, thereby distinguishing yourself from the competition.

- **Achieve cost leadership.** If you are in a dominant firm industry, your strategy should be to achieve cost leadership through economies of scale and scope.

These classic prescriptions are just as valid as they ever were, but the unique characteristics of information markets offer new opportunities to implement them.

Pricing policies are central to successfully implementing either strategy. To succeed, you must either become the price and cost leader based on your scale, or you must create a unique information resource and charge for it based on the value that it offers to consumers.

Even if you have the good fortune to dominate a market and don't have to worry about competitors, you still have to worry about pricing, since you need to price your products in ways that maximize their value. Stockholders naturally want high returns on their investments and can be just as difficult to deal with as competitors.

Differentiation

The lesson of the CD phonebook example is clear: don't let your information product become a commodity. Do everything you can to make sure there are no close competitors by differentiating your product from others that are available.

We opened this chapter with a description of the *Britannica* and *Encarta* battle. The latest strategy in that competition involves product differentiation. As we indicated earlier, *Britannica*'s product is far more complete and authoritative than Microsoft's. Simply on the dimension of quantity, *Britannica*'s 44 million words dwarf *Encarta*'s 14 million.

Britannica's price cuts have certainly had an effect on *Encarta*'s sales: Microsoft's share of unit sales of multimedia encyclopedias was 27.5 percent in 1996, down from 44.8 percent in 1995. But Microsoft is striking back. It increased the word count in the most recent release of *Encarta* by 30 percent and has purchased rights to use content from *Collier's*, a highly respected print encyclopedia.

It now looks like the market might be shaking out into two or three segments: a multimedia, bells-and-whistles market, an educational market, and an authoritative reference market. However, these market segments are still being contested. Whichever industry player wins these various market segments, consumers are likely to be the ultimate winners. Despite the intense competition and steep price declines, industry revenues surged 32 percent last year to about $60 million.

Even information commodities can be successfully differentiated if you exploit the unique features of the Internet. Bigbook is one of several business directories available on the Internet. These directories are essentially nationwide Yellow Page servers that allow the user to look up businesses by name or category. But Bigbook has a gimmick that differentiates it from its paper-based competitors. It has linked a geographic information system with its database of phone numbers and addresses, allowing it to display maps showing the location of each business the user looks up. These maps help to differentiate Bigbook's product from other business directories. However, even this clever idea isn't immune to competition—there are other sellers of geographic information systems, and competitors have already started to copy the idea.

One way to avoid such copying is to assert intellectual property rights to protect information commodities. West Publishing offers a good example of this strategy. Historically, only a few firms went to the trouble of collecting and publishing statutes and legal opinions. With high sunk costs, there was only room in the market for a limited number of competitors. But now, because these materials can be scanned and put onto a CD and are available in electronic form from the government, the fixed costs of collecting the information has fallen and several new suppliers have entered the market. CDs containing huge amounts of valuable legal information became available at bargain-basement prices. Fortunately for West, it was able to differentiate its product, notably through its copyrighted key number system, so as to protect its margins and survive, at least for a time. In the fall of 1996, U.S. Judge John S. Martin ruled that West could not claim copyright in its citation system, allowing rivals to cross-reference West numbers. West, seeking to protect an important source of product differentiation, appealed this ruling, hoping to maintain its primary competitive advantage.

Cost Leadership

If it is hard to differentiate your product, you can at least try to sell a lot of it. If you can sell more than others, your average costs will be the lowest, allowing you to make money when others cannot. But be careful—to sell a lot you will need to lower your price (at least to match any discounts offered by others) and so will necessarily earn a smaller amount on each unit sold. To win, you have to make up for it in volume. You also have to prevent others from capturing the inside track by selling more than you do. This can be a dangerous game; if two or more firms discount heavily, counting on the scale economies that come with market leadership, both cannot succeed. When Microsoft priced *Encarta* at $49.95, it was betting that it could move a lot of CDs at that price and drive competitors out of the mass market. Distribution skills, marketing expertise, and channel control are critical in this type of pricing game.

In traditional industries, reducing your average cost of production usually means focusing on unit costs of production: using supply chain management, workflow analysis, and other tools to cut costs of parts, assembly, and distribution. With information goods, unit costs of production are negligible and supply chain management and related techniques usually don't help much with the first-copy costs. The key to reducing average cost in information markets is to increase sales *volume*.

One great thing about information is that you can sell the same thing over and over again. Think of how a TV show is marketed. It's sold once

Reduce average cost by increasing volume through reuse and resale.

for prime time play in the United States. Then it's sold again for reruns during the summer. If it is a hot product, it's sold abroad and syndicated to local stations. The same good can be sold dozens of times. The most watched TV show in the world is *Baywatch,* which is available in 110 countries and has more than 1 billion viewers. In the United States, *Baywatch* isn't even broadcast on national networks; it is available only via syndication. The shows are cheap to produce, have universal appeal, *and* are highly reusable.

One company that is trying to exploit this strategy in the information industry is Reuters. Its core business is financial information; Reuters provides data to more than 255,000 terminals around the world, more than twice as many as its nearest competitor. It currently controls about 68 percent of the information market for foreign exchange, 33 percent of the equity market, and 24 percent of the fixed income market.

Reuters also provides news stories as a complement to its data services. Though its managers would be loathe to admit it, this is pretty much a commodity business. Several other news services, such as Associated Press, Bloomberg, and Dow Jones, sell similar material.

Despite the commodity nature of the news product, Reuters has managed to do well at this business. One of the reasons is that it has been able to package news items that are of interest to particular industries. This packaging adds value to the product by providing filtering and sorting services—services that are highly valuable to customers suffering from information overload.

For example, if you are in the shipping industry, you can purchase a news service from Reuters that will send you news that is relevant to shipping. Currently, these customized news services also cover foreign exchange, money, securities, fixed income, commodities, and energy.

Much of the news in these industries overlaps, allowing Reuters to sell many of the *same* pieces of information over and over again. The company avoids the trap of having its prime product commoditized by *organizing* it in ways that are useful to customers, thereby differentiating its product from the competition.

Reuters has been experimenting with Internet news services for several years. It has been a long-time supplier to ClariNet, an early on-line news provider. Recently Reuters has begun selling news feeds to Web-based news providers, such as Pointcast. Pointcast is a combination Web browser/screensaver that displays noteworthy headlines in categories chosen by the user. When a user clicks on a headline, the whole article appears. Furthermore, users can customize the browser/screensaver so that only information about certain industries, cities, or sports teams is displayed. Since Reuters already classifies its news items as a matter of course, it is easy for Pointcast to organize them for its users.

As of 1996, Reuters was the dominant news service on the Internet, supplying stories to thirty-five Web sites and making a profit doing so. This example shows that a volume-based strategy of cost leadership must be rooted in adding value to raw information to broaden appeal and fully exploit the economies of scale and scope.

Not surprisingly, Reuters' success has caught the attention of other information providers, most notably Michael Bloomberg, who has forged agreements with @Home, CNet, and AOL to provide on-line content. Bloomberg makes no secret of the fact that he wants to become "the business-news site for a very large percentage of the world's Internet users." Reuters has a head start, but it will have to fight hard to keep its market share.

First-Mover Advantages

We have suggested that market leadership through aggressive pricing can be a successful strategy in the presence of the scale economies endemic to information industries. However, such leadership may not be worth winning if victory only comes after a bloody price war. The best way to secure such a leadership position is through an early presence in the market, combined with a forward-looking approach to pricing.

As the *Encyclopedia Britannica* example shows, historical leaders in many information markets are at risk today of losing their leadership positions, as new technologies arise that vastly reduce the cost of creating or distributing the information that has been their mainstay. Reuters has responded by filtering and sorting its information to add value; West has protected its position by using its copyrighted key number system of legal references. Differentiation strategies such as these are often enabled by the very same new technologies that threatened to dethrone the industry incumbents.

Even if differentiation is difficult or limited, incumbent information providers are well placed to adopt a cost leadership position, so long as they are not rigidly wedded to their historical pricing practices. Owing to strong economies of scale, the market leader often tends to be the cost leader. If you have the good fortune to be the historical market leader, and if you are on par with a newcomer in terms of cost and technical prowess, you should be able to find a pricing strategy to retain your leadership position. Indeed, if you are alert, scale economies should work to your advantage, not against you. After all, you have the scale to start with. Just don't think you are entitled to continue to set selling prices as high as you have in the past.

A two-pronged approach offers the best chance for the historical leader in an information category to make money, even if it cannot prevent its information from becoming a commodity.

First, don't be greedy. Even while the incumbent remains the sole supplier of certain types of information, the threat of entry by look-alike information providers is very real for most information. Recognizing this, incumbents should be willing to sacrifice some of their short-term margin by dropping prices to make their markets less attractive to would-be entrants. This is what economists call *limit pricing:* set prices as high as you can without encouraging others to invest the sunk costs necessary to enter your market. If the information you sell is durable, like a piece of computer software or a reference tome, more aggressive pricing today can slow down or prevent entry tomorrow by taking some customers out of the market for a time: your sales today reduce demand for similar information in the future. Sales today may also serve the function of locking in customers who find it costly to switch from one supplier to another as they update their information (see Chapter 5). For all of these reasons, it pays to sacrifice some current profits through lower prices when facing a real threat of entry.

Play tough. Turn the threat of commoditization on its head and use it to your advantage. The key is to find a way to send a credible signal that entry will be met with aggressive pricing. After all, who would invest in duplicating the information you provide if convinced that you would lower prices aggressively to meet any new competition? One way to establish this reputation, painful though it may be in the short run, is to fight tooth and nail when faced with me-too entries for specific information products, both to hold your ground on the threatened product and to send a signal to companies who might otherwise attack you in other product areas. If you can convince potential entrants that you will respond with dramatic price cuts if they enter, then you won't have to lower prices now to discourage entry. A credible threat of price cuts after entry may be enough to convince would-be competitors that they won't be able to recover their sunk costs and thus discourage them from entering the market in the first place.

It's true that cutting prices in the wake of entry can precipitate a price war—so you should do it only if you think you can win. When trying to estimate the benefits of price cutting, it is important to realize that you are investing not only in eliminating a potential competitor but also in establishing a reputation as a formidable opponent. This investment will be amply repaid down the road by discouraging potential entrants.

In our experience, information providers with established brand names often hesitate to drop prices quickly enough to warn off potential entrants, perhaps because they think their brand name shields them from competition. Sure, a valuable brand name will allow you to command *some* premium, but it will not guarantee you the same prices or margins you enjoyed before new information technologies arrived that caused per-copy and distribution costs to fall.

Companies slow to accept the inevitability that new technologies will force lower prices for basic information may find themselves losing market share

To discourage entry, avoid greed and play tough.

rapidly on all fronts. Competitive advantages based on access to raw information are under siege; the trick is to migrate incumbency and scale advantages into value-added aspects of information, where advantage is more sustainable.

If you think your position as a market leader is totally secure, try reciting the following mantra three times: "CP/M, WordStar, VisiCalc." Each of these products had, at one time, a 100 percent market share. But because their producers failed to respond to the competition quickly enough, each is now history.

PERSONALIZING YOUR PRODUCT

If you are successful in creating a unique source of information and avoiding commoditization, you have some breathing room in terms of both pricing and product design—that is, how you package and present your information. But how do you make the most of that room? How do you extract the most value from the information you have created? The answer comes in two parts: First, personalize or customize your product to generate the most value for your customers. Second, establish pricing arrangements that capture as much of that value as possible.

Personalize your product and personalize your prices.

A good example of how information technology can be used to personalize information services and thus add value is the previously mentioned news provider Pointcast. The news stories that a user sees are highly *personalized.* If you are interested in the Boston Red Sox, the computer industry, international business, and the weather in New England, you can instruct Pointcast to show you news headlines and stories on those topics.

What is even more interesting is that Pointcast will show you ads that are personalized in the same way—ads having to do with baseball, fast food promotions, discount travel agencies, and Boston restaurants. This ability to customize and personalize advertising is a very powerful marketing tool that Internet businesses are only beginning to understand and exploit. Intermediaries like DoubleClick and Softbank Interactive Marketing sell ads targeted by day of week, time of day, continent, country, state, or operating system, and they are adding more capabilities each day.

Table 2.1. Bulk versus Targeted Ad Rates for Web Search Engines (Cents per View)

Site	Bulk	Targeted
DejaNews	2.0¢	4.0¢
Excite	2.4	4.0
Infoseek	1.3	5.0
Lycos	2.0	5.0
Yahoo!	2.0	3.0

Source: Michael Lesk. "Projections for Making Money on the Web." In Deborah Hurley, Brian Kahin, and Hal Varian, eds., *Internet Publishing and Beyond*. (Cambridge, Mass.: MIT Press, 1998).

Search engines such as Yahoo! provide another example of this kind of personalization: when you search for Web sites about, say, "fishing," you will be shown a list of sites having to do with fishing . . . along with an ad for some fishing-related product. When we tried this recently, we saw an ad for the Florida Keys touting the great deep sea fishing in the area.

Yahoo!, like other search engine companies, sells ads linked to search terms ("hot words") for a premium price. Table 2.1 shows some rates search engine companies charge for bulk and targeted ads. Note that targeted ads sell for about 50 percent more than bulk ads. The reason is simple: consumers of the targeted ads likely put a higher premium on the product being advertised and hence are more likely to buy.

"Search engine spamming" is a variant on this theme. For example, one Web site selling children's clothing added hidden tags containing the words "child care." The operators of the site figured that people looking for child care would also be interested in children's clothing. The search engine operators are fighting this practice, since it reduces the value of their product. Several refuse to index invisible words. In September 1997 the U.S. District Court in San Francisco issued an injunction against a Web site that used the invisible words "playboy" and "playmate" in its Web site, upholding *Playboy*'s claim of copyright infringement. Being invisible was no defense!

KNOW YOUR CUSTOMER

If you want to personalize your information product, you have to know something about your customers. The hoary injunction "Know Thy

Customer" is as important in the information economy as in the industrial economy, if not more so. What has changed is that the two-way communication offered by the Web greatly increases the opportunities for information providers to learn about their customers. While cable television companies know where their subscribers live and what channels they subscribe to, information providers on the Web have the ability to know what Web surfers are actively looking for, where they spend their time, and more. Those companies that are first, and best, at figuring out how to use the unique customer information available on the Web stand ready to reap substantial rewards.

Consumer information is valuable, however you seek to generate revenues: by subscription, by pay per use, or by advertising. If you require users to pay, you need feedback on what they like and dislike. If you are supporting your content with advertising, you need feedback on who your users are and whether they are likely to buy the products that your advertisers want to sell. The two main ways to get user information are (1) registration and billing, through which you can ask for demographic information, and (2) observation, which allows you to get information about customer behavior by means of their search queries and clickstream (both to be explained shortly).

Registration and Billing

The *New York Times* Web site doesn't charge users for content but does require them to register. This allows the *Times* to collect information on the demographics and reading habits of 2.1 million users, which can then be used to set ad rates. The *Times* asks for the classic information used in the paper-based subscription business, the ZAG: zip code, age, gender.

Zip code information is an automatic requirement for mail-based subscriptions. These numbers convey a lot of information about the customer, which makes it easy for a publication to describe the demographics of their subscribers to advertisers. Web sites, on the other hand, have had a very difficult time getting users to provide information about themselves. Remember the joke about the two dogs at the computer, where one says to the other, "On the Internet no one knows you're a dog"? Well, no one knows your zip code either—unless you tell them.

Sites that require payment, such as the *Wall Street Journal,* ask for your zip code as part of the billing process. This number can be checked against credit card records, which makes it pretty reliable.

Registration and billing are fine for major sites such as the *New York Times* or *Wall Street Journal.* But many Web sites don't require registration, either because of the nature of the content they provide or because of user resistance. But Internet services providers (ISPs) such as AOL do have access to this critical piece of information about their customers. Since AOL bills users and authenticates them at log-in, AOL can provide advertisers with information on user demographics. This gives ISPs a big advantage in marketing and allows them to charge a premium for hosting Web sites. Remember the AOL-Amazon.com deal described in Chapter 1? Part of that $19 million is payment for customer demographics.

Obviously, content providers would prefer to have direct access to their users' demographics rather than pay AOL a premium for that information. Their strategy should be to bribe users to give them the appropriate demographics, which can in turn be passed on to advertisers. One way to do this is with promotional offers: send out a coupon that will be honored only if the user returns it with the requested demographic information. Reliable demographics will become more and more valuable as the on-line advertising market heats up. Another way to get this kind of information is to offer a valuable service in exchange. Recall the example of Hotmail, described in Chapter 1, which offers free e-mail services in exchange for responses to its questionnaire.

Consumers are often reluctant to provide information about themselves since they don't know how it will be used. According to a study by Donna Hoffman, Tom Novak, and Marcos Peralta of Vanderbilt University, 94 percent of Web users surveyed have refused to provide information to a Web site, and 40 percent have given fake information. There are two interesting developments in this area, one technological, the other institutional.

The technological development is the open profiling standard being developed by the W3 group. This is a way for consumers to store information about themselves, such as name, address, buying habits, interests, etc., and release it on a controlled basis. Such a standard should make it both easier and safer for individuals to manage their personal information.

The institutional development is the creation of "privacy auditors," such as TrustE, that will verify that firms' claimed privacy practices are in fact followed. Such neutral auditing may play a critical role in inducing consumers to give content providers the information they want. With reasonable safeguards, we expect that many consumers will be happy to sell information about themselves for a nominal amount, in part because consumers value receiving well-targeted information, especially via asynchronous communication channels that allow consumers to control *when* they receive the information.

Observation

The other primary way to learn about your customers is by observing their on-line behavior. Most Web sites now allow users to search their contents. But the Web hosts rarely save the users' queries. Knowing what your users are looking for—and whether they find it—is extremely valuable information; save it and analyze it.

In addition to monitoring searches, you should also monitor your customers' "clickstream," the sequence of actions they take while visiting your site. Web log files contain much useful information about user behavior, but they are difficult to analyze for several reasons. First, there is simply a lot of data—sorting through it all takes time and effort. Second, the HTTP protocol that underlies the Web is "connectionless." The protocol treats each request (or hyperlink click) from each user as a separate transaction: there is no explicit concept of a series of transactions with a particular user.

This means that the Web developer has to build in support for recognizing a series of interactions with a given user. This information can be stored on the server side (in memory for short transactions, or on disk for extended ones) or on the browser side in the form of "cookies," files stored on the user's hard drive that contain information about the browser-server interaction.

Neither of these options is as powerful as one would like, however, since the design of the HTTP protocol makes it difficult to observe a lot of useful information about user behavior. For example, psychological studies have shown that user ratings of "interesting items" are very highly correlated with how long they look at the item. (Think of how you read the newspaper.) But the standard browser-server interaction makes it very hard to collect this information.

Java offers a very promising solution to this problem. With Java, you can write your own browser and measure every aspect of user behavior that you want—including time spent inspecting each item. This allows you to collect a much, much richer set of information about your users.

How can this information be used? Consider an on-line shopping service such as Peapod. Peapod, whose slogan is "Smart shopping for busy people," allows you to order groceries over the Internet, which are subsequently delivered to your home. Peapod gives you significantly more information about products than is available at the supermarket. For example, you get the price per unit, to enable comparison shopping, as well as detailed nutritional information. Imagine how useful it would be to marketers to know what aspects of product information people really look at and care about. Such information is valuable to any on-line retailer, whether in the business of selling computer components or automobiles. When you know more about your customer, you

The Internet makes it easy to personalize information products, thereby adding value.

can design and price products in ways that better match consumer needs. Obtaining and using such customer information is essential to maximizing the value of your business.

PRICING YOUR PRODUCT

In addition to making it easy to personalize your product, the Internet also makes it easy to personalize your price. If the information products you sell are highly tuned to your customers' interests you will have a lot of pricing flexibility, since you won't have to worry as much about generic competitive products.

The purest example of tailored goods are research reports, such as those produced by Gartner Group, Forrester Research, the Research Board, and other similar organizations. The Research Board, for example, sells research reports to CIOs that are highly targeted to their interests and needs. In exchange, member companies pay subscription fees of $50,000 to $70,000 per year for this information, simply because it is hard to find such detailed and personalized information elsewhere.

But it isn't only high-priced information that can be personalized. You can do much the same thing with mass-market consumer information goods. To see the basic trade-offs, put yourself in the place of the marketing director at Intuit, who is trying to decide how to price the company's next release of its home accounting software, Quicken. The company recognizes that consumers have different values for this software: some can't function without it, others are only casual users.

If you set your price at $60 only the zealots will buy. If you set your price at $20, you will sell to lots of casual users but will pass up the potential profits from selling at a high price to the zealots. Which way should you go? Answer: It depends on how many customers of each type there are. If there are 1 million zealots and 2 million casual users, you would sell to a million people if you set a price of $60 and 3 million people (the zealots plus the casual users) if you set a price of $20. In this example you make the same revenue either way, but if there are more than 2 million casual users, the $20 price generates more revenue.

This simple calculation gives us the revenue picture; to figure out which price is more profitable, we would have to know something about the production, distribution, and support costs. In the interests of simplicity, we will ignore these costs for the moment and focus just on revenues.

We can use the numbers in this simple example to plot a bar chart showing the relationship between price and sales in Figure 2.1. Panels A and B show the revenue trade-off just examined: set a high price, and sell only to the consumers who place a high value on your product, or set a low price and sell to lots of consumers.

Now this story has an implicit assumption. It assumes that there is only *one* price being charged for Quicken. Wouldn't it be nice—for

Figure 2.1. *High, Low, and Differential Pricing*

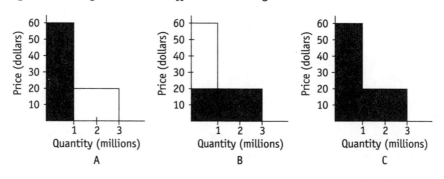

Intuit—if it could charge several prices? Then it could sell Quicken to each different consumer at that consumer's maximum willingness-to-pay. In the simple example described above, Intuit could sell a million copies at $60 and 2 million at $20, yielding a total revenue of $100 million. As shown in Panel C of Figure 2.1, this is much more than the company could get by selling at any single price. Charging each customer just what he or she is willing to pay is what economists refer to as "perfect price discrimination." As the modifier "perfect" suggests, it's rare to be able to discriminate to this extent in the real world. (We discuss Intuit's solution to this pricing problem in Chapter 3.)

There are many reasons why it is hard to achieve perfect price discrimination, but one of the most obvious is that it is awfully hard to determine what is the maximum price someone will pay for your product. And even if you do know what someone is willing to pay for your product, how can you offer it at a low price to those unwilling to pay more without allowing more eager buyers to take advantage of the same favorable terms?

If you sell goods for a posted price on a store shelf, you're pretty much stuck with the "one price fits all" model, augmented perhaps by coupons and occasional discounts. But if you sell goods to people using a "point-to-point" technology, as is possible on the Internet, you can sometimes arrange for multiple, and even personalized, prices. The current buzzword for this strategy is "one-to-one marketing," but it was first described by the economist A. C. Pigou in 1920 under the admittedly less catchy phrase "first-degree price discrimination."

Pigou distinguished three types of differential pricing, which he called first, second, and third degree, but we'd like to use more descriptive terms:

- **Personalized pricing:** Sell to each user at a different price.

- **Versioning:** Offer a product line and let users choose the version of the product most appropriate for them.

- **Group pricing:** Set different prices for different groups of consumers, as in student discounts.

We'll discuss personalized and group pricing in this chapter and devote the entire next chapter to versioning.

PERSONALIZED PRICING

Personalized pricing is being used today in traditional print media. Mail-order catalogs, for instance, often arrive with a stapled insert announcing "special offers" of one form or another. What is not widely known is that these special offers often involve prices that differ across consumers: your "special offer" might just be a premium price!

The vendor may offer different consumers different prices as a form of market research. The consumers can differ by location, by demographics, or by past purchase behavior. Sometimes the vendor has a good idea of what the price responsiveness of the different groups might be, and sometimes it is conducting market research to discover price responsiveness. (When the *Encyclopedia Britannica* wanted to determine consumer demand for its CD offering, it used a direct mail campaign, with prices ranging from $70 to $125.) Whatever the motivation, the vendor selling via catalog can charge different prices to different consumers because it is able to personalize the price.

But think how much *more personal* prices can be with intelligent use of information technology. Remember our fishing example? If your on-line travel agency knows that you are interested in deep-sea fishing, and it knows that deep-sea fishermen like yourself are often wealthy, it may well want to sell you a high-priced hotel package. On the other hand, if the travel agency knows that you like snorkeling, and snorkelers prefer budget travel, then they can offer you a budget package.

In these examples, the provider can design a package that is optimized for your interests and charge you accordingly. But be careful about those premium prices for deep-sea fishermen: even wealthy deep-sea fishermen can change travel agencies.

Personalized Pricing in Traditional Industries

Airlines are, of course, masters of differential pricing; they often have dozens of different fare classes on a particular flight. Your fare may depend on when you book, what restrictions you are willing to accept, and what your travel history has been.

Other participants in the travel industry have followed the airlines' lead. When customers call travel franchiser HFS to make a hotel reservation, they are invited to listen to a pitch for a "great travel service" that offers a variety of discounts. About 25–30 percent of the people who listen to the ad accept, which is twice the number the company would get from cold calls. By using the discount card, customers identify themselves as price-sensitive, travel-loving consumers; sellers of travel services can then offer them attractive personalized prices.

Information is also sold at highly personalized prices. The on-line database provider Lexis-Nexis sells to virtually every user at a different price. The price that you pay may well depend on what kind of enterprise you are (corporate, small business, government, academic), the size of your organization, when you access the databases (during the day or during the evening), how much you use the databases (volume discounts), which databases you use, whether you print the information or just view it on the screen, and so on and so forth. Just as with the airlines, almost every customer pays a different price.

The "smart" cash registers now being deployed in supermarkets provide another example of personalized pricing. With these machines in place, stores can offer you discounts (cents-off coupons) if they think you are price-sensitive. For example, suppose you buy a lot of guacamole and tortilla chips. The business that wants you to buy its salsa may well offer you some cents-off coupons. Even better: it can offer you the cents-off coupons only if you are currently buying a *competitor's* salsa. This is great from the viewpoint of the salsa producer, who can effectively sell at two prices—a high price to people who are willing to buy his product anyway, and a lower price to those who aren't currently consuming it.

Such techniques have been a boon to the grocery industry. From 1993 to 1996, the net profit margin rose from 0.49 percent of sales to 1.2 percent of sales, a new high in this $400 billion a year industry. According to industry analyst Brian Woolf, a frequent shopper program can add as many as two percentage points to gross margins within two years. Calmetta Coleman describes some of the strategies used by the supermarket chain Dorothy Lane:

> Club DLM enabled Dorothy Lane to stop running item-price ads. Now, much of the $250,000 it used to spend each year on newspaper advertising is plowed into the card program. Price discounts go only to club members. Direct mail is customized, based on individual shopping

habits: Buy a lot of bread and you get bread coupons. Monthly newsletters are sent to the top 30 percent of card holders, who account for about 82 percent of the company's sales. Their loyalty is rewarded: Dorothy Lane gives them a free Thanksgiving turkey.[1]

Dorothy Lane had to invest heavily in expensive infrastructure for gathering and analyzing scanner data about consumer purchases. But on-line businesses already have the information technology in place—the big challenge they now face is to use it effectively.

Personalized Pricing on the Internet

Because it is even more individualized and interactive than catalogs, the Internet offers even more attractive pricing opportunities. Catalog producers know your zip code and your buying history and can condition their offers on these variables, but they can't easily offer you prices based on what you are buying *now*. But this is a snap on the Internet.

Virtual Vineyards tracks the clickstream of each user and can instantaneously make them special offers based on their behavior. Amazon.com tracks the purchases of each consumer and recommends additional, related books the next time the user logs on. And these are just some of the marketing advantages that the Internet offers.

Catalog writers have to commit to a particular price for a printing of the catalog. Items that are the "wrong" color or style pile up in their inventories. They can address overstock problems in special supplemental catalogs, but these are expensive to produce and distribute. If your prices are all on-line, you can mark down items in excess supply immediately. Airlines already do this with their seats, using sophisticated yield management programs. More and more companies are acquiring the capability not only to track their inventory in real time but to adjust prices just as fast.

The Internet offers unique marketing opportunities that are extremely difficult to pursue via other media. American Airlines and Cathay Pacific have run several successful auctions for seats on their flights, and cruise lines are beginning to fill up empty cabins with last-minute sales using similar techniques.

Offering sales, close-outs, and other forms of promotional pricing is incredibly easy on the Internet since prices can be changed instantaneously. These promotions are attractive in moving your product, but they are even more attractive in terms of estimating market response to price changes. It's easy to offer a price reduction to every twentieth person who logs onto your site; if this price reduction increases your revenue from those customers, it may make sense to extend these low prices to all your customers. The Internet offers a *very* inexpensive form of market research, which will become of greater significance as the volume of on-line commerce grows.

In fact, the auctions for airline seats mentioned above play a dual role: they sell off unused seats, and they also help the airlines estimate the demand for their product. Computer retailers such as Egghead and CompUSA are using e-mail to push special offers at attractive prices for the same reason: to sell overstocked merchandise and to discover the price points that move their products.

Lessons in Personalized Pricing

Here are the lessons to take away from our discussion of personalized pricing:

- **Personalize your product and personalize your pricing.** This is easier to do on the Internet than on virtually any other medium since you communicate with your consumers on a one-to-one basis.

- **Know thy customer.** You can learn about your customer demographics by registration and about their interests by tracking their clickstream and search behavior. Analyze this information to see what your customers want.

- **Differentiate your prices when possible.** Different consumers have different values for your product. You can offer different consumers different prices based on their buying habits and other characteristics, as the supermarkets have done.

- **Use promotions to measure demand.** Promotions to estimate price sensitivity are very easy on the Internet, which makes market research a snap.

GROUP PRICING

In the previous section we talked about selling directly to individuals at personalized prices. But the prices weren't really perfectly individualized. Instead, people who had certain purchase histories, zip codes, or behavior patterns were offered different prices. People who shared a particular set of characteristics would be offered the same terms.

Sometimes you can base prices directly on group identity, a strategy economists refer to as "third-degree price discrimination." In this section we explore this kind of group pricing.

There are four reasons why you might want to sell to groups rather than directly to end users:

- **Price sensitivity:** If members of different groups systematically differ in their price sensitivity, you can profitably offer them different prices. Student and senior citizen discounts are prime examples.

- **Network effects:** If the value to an individual depends on how many other members of his group use the product, there will be value to standardizing on a single product. Microsoft has exploited this desire for standardization with its Microsoft Office suite.

- **Lock-in:** If an organization chooses to standardize on a particular product, it may be very expensive for it to make the switch owing to the costs of coordination and retraining. Again, Microsoft serves as the obvious example.

- **Sharing:** In many cases it is inconvenient for the individual user to manage or organize all information goods that he or she will want to consume. Information intermediaries such as libraries or system administrators can perform this coordination task.

Price Sensitivity

Student discounts and senior citizen discounts are popular forms of group pricing. Why do sellers offer such discounts? The standard answer is price sensitivity. It is a common exercise in any undergraduate economics or marketing course to show that a profit-maximizing seller will want to charge a lower price to consumers who are more sensitive to price.

This pricing strategy is commonly used for information goods that are sold internationally. A textbook that sells for $70 in the United States sells for $5 in India. True, it is printed on cheaper paper and lacks color illustrations, but it is essentially the same information. The price is lower in India because Indian customers simply cannot afford the U.S. price. The same holds for U.S. movies shown in India—they are priced at a fraction of the price paid in the domestic market.

This sort of market segmentation is quite well understood, so we won't devote much space to it. However, it is worth noting a potential problem: as more and more material becomes available on-line, differential international pricing will become more difficult.

Take the textbook example. If a U.S. publisher wants to sell a textbook on-line, it will probably have to set a single price, and this will likely be the high domestic price rather than the low Indian price. This means that the Indian market would not be served, depriving the Indian students the benefit of the U.S. textbook and the publisher of an extra source of revenue.

One way to deal with this problem is to try to localize the information, so that different versions of the book are targeted to different countries. An economics textbook that used examples in rupees and GDP figures from India wouldn't be very appealing to the U.S. market but would be highly welcome in India. Differentiating the product in this way allows for differential prices and has the potential to make all parties to the transaction better off.

It is common to see localized versions of software and dubbed versions of movies. The global Internet will localize all sorts of information goods because this will benefit producers in two ways: it allows them to sell to a larger market, and it prevents inexpensive foreign sales from cannibalizing domestic sales.

Network Effects

We're going to talk a lot more about network effects in Chapter 7, so we will just mention the basic idea here. As we said in Chapter 1, network effects arise when the value one user places on a good depends on how many other people are using it.

Such effects can arise for a variety of reasons (which we will describe later), but the reason that is most relevant here is the desire for standardization within an organization. It's a lot easier to get work done if your employees can share their files and experiences.

Sellers of software can exploit this desire for standardization and make it attractive for organizations to choose their product by offering them quantity discounts or site licenses. Typically, site licenses have applied to members of an organization or business at a particular physical location, but the Internet may well change this practice since geographic proximity is not as important as it used to be.

Software companies offer a plethora of licensing arrangements, based on the number of concurrent users, number of workstations, number of servers, geographic site, and type of industry to which they are selling. License management software can measure use along a variety of dimensions; the critical question is which dimensions to use.

There is no general answer. Everything depends on the specifics of the product. The guiding principle is to base pricing on the dimensions that are most closely correlated with the value of the software to the enterprise. This will generally mean offering a variety of pricing menus, allowing organizations to pick the one most appropriate for them.

A powerful photo-editing tool like Adobe's Photoshop might be used by one person in a small production house and by hundreds in a large one, so a quantity discount is a natural strategy. A statistical package may be used monthly in an accounting division but daily in a forecasting division. In this case, a concurrent licensing arrangement may be appropriate for the accountants, but a flat per-seat fee would make more sense for the forecasting division.

Lock-In

We said earlier that student discounts are attractive because students are very sensitive to price. But that's not the only reason for student discounts: another reason can be summarized by the slogan "Get 'em while they're young." If you are selling a good that has big switching costs (to be discussed in Chapter 5), then it pays you to offer deep discounts to get consumers "addicted" to your product. Although software producers don't hang around outside of schoolyards pushing their products (yet), the motivation is much the same. If you can get someone to use your product when he or she is a student, you've got a good chance of building a loyal customer down the road.

The *Wall Street Journal* has used this strategy very effectively. One of the paper's major assets is its reputation as the premier source for business and economic news. To maintain this reputation, the *Journal* has created a Newspapers in Education program that offers inexpensive subscriptions to students in business and economics classes. Not only does the paper offer very attractive prices to the students, but it offers *free* subscriptions to the faculty members whose students purchase subscriptions. This has two effects. It gives faculty members the incentive to require, or at least encourage, the students in their class to subscribe to the *Journal,* and it encourages the professors to refer to *Journal* articles in lectures. Both effects have helped to maintain and enhance the *Wall Street Journal*'s reputation.

The network effects discussed above are a common source of switching costs. If your product becomes ubiquitous in an organization, so that it is very costly to switch to something new, you will enjoy a lot of power in setting prices and contract terms.

Microsoft originally offered Microsoft Office using a variety of arrangements, including per-seat and concurrent-user licenses. Recently they dropped the concurrent licensing policy, reasoning that their product was used by virtually everyone in the organizations that adopted it. Will this lose a lot of customers? Probably not, says Mary Welch, a research director at the Gartner Group. "When considering the cost of retooling, redeploying, retraining and rewriting custom applications built on top of Microsoft products, most companies will simply dig deeper into their pockets for the extra cash."[2] We'll have a lot more to say about this sort of lock-in in Chapter 5.

Sharing Arrangements

Site licenses are only one example of what we might call "sharing arrangements." Academic journals that sell at a high price to libraries and a low price to individuals are another example. Libraries are willing to pay the higher price since the material is shared among many users. Videotapes are another good example: some videos, especially children's videos, are priced for household purchase, but some are clearly priced for rental store use only. The consumers then "share" the rental store copy. In these cases the library and the video store serve as "information intermediaries" that organize and manage the information for the end users.

One of the early appearances of "pricing for sharing" were the so-called "circulating libraries" in eighteenth-century England. During this period novels became a highly popular form of entertainment, so popular that printers had a difficult time keeping up with demand. In desperation, retail bookstores started "renting" out the latest hit novels. Many booksellers found this practice so lucrative that they dropped the selling side of their business and went entirely to the rental side, becoming, in effect, for-profit libraries.

Transaction costs determine whether it is better to sell or rent information.

Video stores in the United States followed much the same pattern. In the late 1970s, video machines were a rich man's toy, selling for more than $1,000. Prerecorded tapes were also expensive, often costing nearly $100. Just as books in the eighteenth century were initially available only to an elite, videos were only accessible to the rich.

The history of these two industries makes fascinating reading, shedding light on issues facing content owners today; we'll examine it in depth in Chapter 4. Here we want to consider the practical question of how to determine whether to price a good for individual or group purchase. The primary consideration is transaction costs: is it cheaper for the intermediary or the end user to manage the information?

Consider videos. The major consideration in pricing a video is whether the video warrants repeat viewing. It's no accident that the best-selling videos are generally children's videos. Children watch videos over and over again, and every parent quickly learns the value of *owning* popular kid vids rather than making daily trips to the rental store. The primary question facing those who set video prices is estimating the desire for the repeat viewing. Ten years ago, the Hollywood marketing wizards used seat-of-the-pants intuition, but the industry has now moved to focus groups, which sometimes reveal surprising effects.

For example, Disney executives were surprised to learn that there was a significant desire for repeat viewing of *Good Morning Vietnam,* with Robin Williams. This is not a children's movie, but people still showed a strong desire for ownership. Further investigation showed that the desire arose from the fact that there were so many rapid-fire wise-cracks in the film that people missed a lot the first time through. They wanted to watch it several times so they could get all the jokes.

The same issues come up when selling to libraries, schools, and other intermediaries. Items that are read only occasionally are often accessed via libraries: more than 70 percent of public library circulation is fiction, a figure that has remained constant for 200 years or more. Households commonly purchase books that people will use repeatedly, such as dictionaries and other general reference works.

The library and video examples show that rental and purchase arrangements coexist. By offering the product both for sale and for rental, the producer can segment the market. We discuss segmentation strategy in detail in Chapter 3, but the basic idea in the context of books and videos is to sell the good to the people who value it highly and allow the good to be shared among those with lower values. If you're a big Stephen King fan, you may want to buy his latest book in hardback when it first comes out. If you're not quite such a big fan, you'll get on the waiting list at the library. The producer sells at a high price to the avid Stephen King fans and sells at a much lower price to those who are willing to wait.

The Electric Library

One Internet company that has struggled with the buy/share issue is Infonautics, which offers a product called the Electric Library. The Electric Library offers full text of 150 newspapers, hundreds of magazines, international newswires, radio transcripts, and many other high-quality sources of information. The product has a user friendly, natural language interface for full-text searches. The individual subscription price for the service is $9.95 for one month or $59.95 for one year, and the company has won a number of educational and industry awards for the quality of its product.

Infonautics originally planned to market the Electric Library to high school and college students who were writing term papers. However, this turned out to be tough going: it had to sell to the parents, who naturally wondered why their kids couldn't just go to their local or school library. Since term-paper writing is episodic (at best!), the subscription model was problematic. The advent of large amounts of free content on the Web has made this business model even more difficult. Like the battle between the *Encyclopedia Britannica* and *Encarta* described at the beginning of this chapter, purveyors of high-quality content can find it difficult to compete with lower-quality but lower-priced content.

Infonautics has had much more success with its site license program for schools and libraries. School teachers and librarians can judge the quality of the Electric Library's offerings more effectively than most parents, and the product can be used in the context of other complementary products, which makes for an easier sell. Furthermore, school and library use presents the potential to market the product to individual users: once users experience the product at libraries, the authority conveyed by the library subscription and the merits of the product itself may well convince users to purchase an individual subscription.

LESSONS

- **Analyze and understand how much you invest in producing and selling your information.** Information is costly to produce but cheap to reproduce. Large up-front sunk costs, minimal capacity constraints, and low incremental cost allow for only a few viable market structures. Understanding how your industry will shake out is critical to formulating an effective long-run strategy.

- **If you are forced to compete in a commodity market, be aggressive but not greedy.** If you are one of many firms selling similar information, grab market share and exploit economies of scale to become a low-cost producer. Find ways to add value to the information by means of superior organization, user interface, or timeliness.

- **Differentiate your product by personalizing the information and the price.** Create a product with few close substitutes so that you can base your price on the value you offer to the consumer rather than on the prices set by the competition.

- **Invest in collecting and analyzing data about your market, using focus groups, statistical analysis, promotions, and other marketing techniques.** Conducting market research in real time is much cheaper to do on the Internet than with conventional channels, so exploit the information in your log files and clickstreams.

- **Use the information about your customers to sell them personalized products at personalized prices.** You can use buying histories, search choices, and clickstream behavior to differentiate prices and products.

- **Analyze the profitability of selling to groups.** Site licenses or rental plans may be more attractive than direct sales to individuals. Price sensitivity, desire for standardization, repeat use, and market segmentation are relevant considerations.

3 | Versioning Information

We've seen that a key aspect of pricing information is to use value-based pricing: sell your product at different prices to different consumers, according to how much they are willing to pay for it. We looked at two approaches to value-based pricing in Chapter 2: personalized pricing and group pricing.

Personalized pricing requires knowledge about individual customers. The best intelligence about customers comes directly from them, as when customers communicate their needs and indicate the products they would like to see or the categories of information of interest to them.

We certainly encourage companies to develop and exploit two-way communications with customers. However, you can still get valuable data about customers without customer-provided profiles, without expensive marketing data, and even without consumers' active involvement. How? Answer: You can learn a great deal about your customers by offering them a menu of products and seeing which one they choose.

For example, if you offer a product line with one product targeted for professional users and one product for amateur users, you can simply observe your sales figures to see how your market splits. We call this strategy "versioning." It means offering your information product in different versions for different market segments.

In this chapter we show you how to design your "product line" to capture the greatest profit from the information you are selling. Your profits will depend on both the *total* value you create for your customers and the *fraction* of that value which you are able to extract through the fees you charge for the information. To maximize your profits, you want to make the total value created as large as possible and then extract as much of that value as you can. This observation leads to the two basic principles for designing a product line of information goods.

- Offer versions tailored to the needs of different customers. A full line of information products will maximize the total value of the information you are providing.

- Design these versions to accentuate the needs of different groups of customers. Emphasizing customer differences allows you to extract more of the value you have created, as each customer selects the version that best meets his or her needs.

Economists call the second principle *self-selection*. You don't have to figure out what value the customer puts on your information product, because the customer reveals that value through the version that he or she selects.

Consider the Quicken example in Chapter 2. How did Intuit actually solve its pricing problem? It created two versions of the software, Basic Quicken, which sells for about $20, and Quicken Deluxe, which sells for about $60. The Deluxe version has a variety of extra features that appeal to the power users but aren't that attractive to the occasional user.

Let's see how the two above principles have been applied to one of the oldest forms of mass-market information provision: the book. How can a publisher such as Viking make the most money selling the newest Stephen King novel? Viking would *like* to sell the novel at a high price to the avid fans who will pay a lot for their favorite author's most recent book. But a high price would no doubt discourage purchases by those who are less enthusiastic readers of Stephen King. Ideally, the publisher would like to sell every copy of the book at a different price—that is, engage in the kind of personalized pricing that we described in the previous chapter.

The problem is, the publisher has no way to tell what any given individual is willing to pay for the book. Politely asking those customers who place the highest value on the latest Stephen King book to pay extra because they like it so much will not do the trick for obvious reasons. (Even if Viking or its distributors could keep track of readers who had rushed out to buy prior Stephen King books, attempting to charge more to this group would only encourage them to hide their identity or buy the book through another channel.) So it appears that the best the publisher can do is to differentiate the price by groups: sell at one price to the book club members, say, and at another price to retail book stores.

In fact, the publisher can do much better by applying our second principle: designing versions to emphasize customer differences. Here, high-value customers are impatient to get the book, while lower-value customers can more easily wait. The main difference here involves patience. Thus, the key to versioning books is to *delay* before offering less expensive versions. This is precisely what publishers do. After selling hardback copies to the intense fans, libraries, and book clubs, Stephen King's publisher then releases the book in paperback—so all those *other* fans can purchase it. And finally, after a few years, the book might even be remaindered and sold at an even lower price to those who scrounge around on the bargain tables. The book example is no doubt familiar to you. But our extraction principle applies widely to the sale of information of all types.

When you think about it, releasing different versions over time is a pervasive strategy for selling information. Movie producers initially release their productions in first-run theaters. After a few months they move to the hotel and airline market. A few months after that, they sell to the home video market. All those young, impatient people go to the movies. Parents with small children and empty nesters stay home and watch the videos a few months later.

DESIGNING YOUR PRODUCT LINE

So how can you use versions of your information in a way that induces self-selection? The key is to identify dimensions of your information product, such as timeliness, that are highly valued by some customers yet of little importance to others. Then offer versions that differ noticeably in ways designed to appeal selectively to each type of customer. The fact that different types of customers value these dimensions differently is what provides the basis for successful sorting.

Delay

Information is like an oyster: it usually has the greatest value when it is fresh. This is especially true of "strategic" information, such as information about stock market or interest-rate movements, where individuals possessing the information have a strategic advantage over those lacking it. But the principle applies more broadly, since we all like to think of ourselves as being up-to-date.

The fact that your information customers want the latest information means they will pay more for fresh information, making it worth your while to acquire and deliver information in a timely fashion. What does it say about versioning? Following the principle of looking for ways in which consumers *differ,* the key point is that consumers differ widely according to how eager they are for various types of information. This observation underlies the common versioning tactic of *delay.*

> **Information is like an oyster: it has its greatest value when fresh.**

Delay is a tried and true tactic for companies selling various services, not just information. Federal Express, not known for "delay," offers two classes of service, a premium class that promises delivery before 10 A.M. and a "next day" service that only promises delivery some time the next day. To encourage the senders to self-select, Fed Ex will make *two* trips to an address rather than deliver nonpremium packages before 10 A.M. They realize, quite correctly, that providing premium service for "ordinary" packages would reduce the value of premium service. Similarly, it has been claimed that the U.S. Postal Service has slowed down first-class service to make more money off of its premium overnight delivery product, Express Mail.

In the same way, information providers can offer early delivery of information at a premium. For example, PAWWS Financial Network charges $8.95 per month for a portfolio accounting system that measures stock values using twenty-minute delayed quotes. For $50 per month they will use real-time quotes. We don't know how they buy these quotes, but it would make sense for them to purchase real-time quotes, which they immediately forward to the high-paying customers, then delay the release of those same quotes for the other customers. PAWWS is willing to incur the extra costs of delay to get customers to self-select, just as Federal Express does when making two visits to an establishment rather than one.

User Interface

Another possibility is to provide high-paying customers with more powerful search capabilities. It often makes sense to offer different search interfaces to experienced and inexperienced users. In many cases, experienced users tend to be users with high willingness to pay; they are the customers who first signed on to purchase the information and generally use it most intensively. Allowing high-paying users more elaborate search capabilities makes sense in this case, even though there is little or no incremental cost associated with a more elaborate interface.

Smart design of user interfaces supports the idea of a more elaborate interface for more experienced users. Casual users typically welcome a stripped-down interface, while advanced users can handle additional capabilities. This makes the search interface an ideal candidate for versioning. (Also, as we'll see in Chapter 5, a simple user interface makes it easy for customers to start using your product, while later on a more involved, proprietary interface can make it more difficult for these same customers to drop your product for that of a rival.)

The Knight-Ridder company Dialog uses this strategy in its Web-accessible databases. One product, DialogWeb, is offered to "information professionals, on-line searchers, researchers, and other professionals." Another much cheaper and less powerful product, DataStar, offers a subset of the full Dialog database, with a much simplified user interface. DataStar advertises that "no training is required," which is attractive to nonprofessional searchers. But DataStar lacks the power of the full Dialog, making it *unattractive* to professionals. By versioning its product with different user interfaces, Knight-Ridder can simultaneously maximize the value of its database to customers *and* capture a large fraction of that value for itself.

Convenience

A versioning strategy that is closely related to delay is control of convenience by restricting the time or place at which an information service is used. Before the Web became popular, Dialog used to offer Dialog after Dark, a database searching service that was restricted to use after 5 P.M. Video rental stores now offer overnight, two-day rentals, and five-day rentals. Divx, which we will discuss in more detail in Chapter 4, offers DVDs that can be viewed only during a particular forty-eight-hour period.

Companies can also restrict access by location rather than time. For example, some on-line database providers have offered libraries licenses that allow unlimited use by patrons within the library but restrict use by off-site patrons.

Image Resolution

You can also use visual resolution to discriminate between users. For example, PhotoDisk has a library of photographs on the Web. Professional users want high-resolution images that can be printed in commercial journals; non-professionals want medium- or low-resolution images for newsletters. PhotoDisk sells different size images for different prices; at the time this chapter was written, it sold 600K images for $19.95 and 10Mb images for $49.95. Its on-line catalog offers small, thumbnail images called "comping images" that potential purchasers can examine. Once users choose the image they want using the low-resolution version as a guide, they can then download a medium- or high-resolution version, depending on their needs.

Speed of Operation

When selling software, a common strategy is to sell versions with different capabilities. Wolfram Research sells Mathematica, a computer program that does symbolic, graphical, and numerical mathematics. At one time, in the student version of Mathematica, the floating-point coprocessor was disabled, slowing down mathematical and graphical calculations. To implement this strategy, Wolfram had to add a floating-point library to the package at additional cost to itself, even though the software package with the floating-point library sold for a much cheaper price.

This same strategy shows up in hardware. The IBM LaserPrinter Series E was functionally identical to the standard LaserPrinter, but printed five pages per minute rather than ten pages per minute. A leading consumer testing lab for computer equipment found that the difference in speed was due to a chip that inserted wait states to slow down the printer! Why did IBM deliberately degrade the performance of its printer? Company managers realized that if they made the performance of the Series E *too* good, it would cut into the sales of their standard model. By versioning their product, they were able to sell to the home-office market at an attractive price without cannibalizing the sales of their professional model.

Intel followed much the same strategy with its 386SX chip, designing the chip with an integrated mathematical coprocessor that was then disabled. That allowed Intel to sell a low-priced chip to those who didn't need floating-point calculations while still maintaining a relatively high price for the math-enabled CPU.

Flexibility of Use

Another important dimension of information that can form the basis for versioning is the ability to store, duplicate, or print the information. Back in the days of copy-protected software, some software companies (such as Borland) sold two versions of their software—a low-priced version that could not be copied and a high-priced version without the copy protection. Nowadays, Lexis/Nexis imposes charges on some users for printing or downloading information. If customers differ significantly in their willingness to pay for storing, copying, or transferring information to other media, this, too, can form the basis for profitable versioning.

Capability

Table 3.1 summarizes the product line of Kurzweil, a software producer of voice recognition products. The products are distinguished by the total size of the vocabulary included and by the addition of vocabulary appropriate to specific professions. Note the dramatic differences in prices: the high-end version for surgeons is a hundred times more

Table 3.1. Kurzweil's Effective Versioning by Capability

Product	Price	Description
VoicePad Pro	$ 79	Vocabulary of 20,000 words
Personal	295	Vocabulary of 30,000 words
Professional	595	Vocabulary of 50,000 words
Office Talk	795	General office staff
Law Talk	1,195	Legal vocabulary
Voice Med	6,000	Medical offices
Voice Ortho	8,000	Special purpose medical vocabulary

expensive than the entry-level software! Kurzweil has correctly recognized that different market segments have different needs—and that the high-end will pay handsomely for the enhanced capability.

Features and Functions

Intuit's versioning of Quicken, discussed at the beginning of the chapter, is an example of how to use the feature set of a product to segment a market. The Quicken Deluxe version offers a mutual fund finder, a mortgage calculator, an insurance needs estimator, and other features valued by high-powered users. The basic version of the software offers only the core checkbook software. Intuit has pursued the same strategy with TurboTax, selling both a stripped-down and a deluxe version.

Comprehensiveness

In some cases, comprehensiveness is a crucial dimension: some customers will pay a big premium for more complete information. Information completeness varies a great deal, depending on the context. Consider how people use Dialog. Public affairs specialists and journalists like the fact that they can now search newspapers around the country or around the world. Scholars and students writing in-depth articles will place great value on historical depth. For marketing purposes, managers often value information that is broken down by customer or offers lots of details about historical purchasing patterns. The difference between DialogWeb and DataStar rests partly on these distinctions, which are a natural dimension along which any database provider can base different versions.

Annoyance

A prime example of this is "nagware," a form of shareware that is distributed freely but displays a screen at the start or end of the session encouraging you to pay a registration fee. Public television stations use this strategy in their fundraising drives. During one recent campaign, our local PBS station announced that it would stop breaking into the musical performances if users would just donate another $10,000 to meet the station's goal!

Support

The final dimension that we consider is technical support. Netscape originally made its browser available for free in a download over the Internet and for a price on a CD that came with a manual and access to technical support. Of course, by offering a downloadable version for free, Netscape gets around the "experience good" problem we described in Chapter 1: anyone can try the product with little or no risk to see if they like it.

McAfee Associates, which we discuss in more detail in Chapter 4, offers its virus detection software in a free, shareware version or as part of a subscription service that provides professional advice, notification, and technical support.

This strategy is somewhat dangerous for two reasons. First, if your customers really need technical support, they may decide your product is of low quality. Second, technical support is very costly to provide. Promises to offer support that are not delivered can be disastrous in terms of public relations.

In Table 3.2 we list the various dimensions we've discussed alongside a list of users or uses for which these dimensions have meaning. This list is not meant to be complete, and the examples should only be taken as illustrative. There are as many dimensions on which to version as there are dimensions to your product. Versioning is thus very product-specific.

ADJUSTING PRICE AND QUALITY

Your goal in versioning your information product is to sell to different market segments at different prices. By creating low-end and high-end

Table 3.2. Product Dimensions Susceptible to Versioning and Their Likely Users/Uses

Product Dimension	Likely Users/Uses
Delay	Patient/impatient users
User interface	Casual/experienced users
Convenience	Business/home users
Image resolution	Newsletter/glossy uses
Speed of operation	Student/professional users
Format	On-screen/printed uses
Capability	General/specific uses
Features	Occasional/frequent users
Comprehensiveness	Lay/professional users
Annoyance	High-time-value/low-time-value users
Support	Casual/intensive users

versions of your product, you can sell the same thing to customers with significantly different levels of willingness to pay.

If your premium-price, high-end product attracts some low-end customers, that's great: you're getting more revenue from them than if they had stuck to the low-end product. So, it pays to make your high-end product as attractive as possible. The problem arises at the other end of the product line: if your low-end version is too attractive, it may attract some customers who would otherwise pay a premium price for the high-end version.

> *Reduce the price of the high-end version and the quality of the low-end version.*

There are two ways to avoid this cannibalization. First, reduce the price of the high-end product to make it relatively more attractive. Second, reduce the quality of the low-end product to make it relatively less attractive.

Discounting Your High-End Product

When you create low-end information products, you may have to cut the price of your high-end product to keep your high-value customers happy. You should think about this choice the same way you think about pricing to meet the competition. Do your high-end products really offer sufficient value to your customers? If you discount the high-end price, will the increase in sales compensate you for the price reduction? Don't lose track of the fact that high-end sales lost to your low-end product still contribute to your revenues. What's important is the *difference* in the revenue you get from the high and low ends of your product line.

Value-Subtracted Versions

As we've indicated, versioning works for all kinds of goods. But versioning information has some special features.

For physical goods, it is usually more expensive to produce an extra unit of the high-quality versions. A Lexus costs more to build than a Camry, and a nineteen-inch TV is more costly to build than a fifteen-inch TV. But with information, it generally costs just about as much to distribute the fancy version as the plain version. In many cases, in fact, production of the low-quality version incurs additional costs, since it is often a degraded form of the high-quality version.

Think about delay. A financial service firm that offers real-time and delayed stock prices needs added storage capacity to offer the delayed service. Or resolution: the images have to be scanned using a high resolution and then degraded to produce the low resolution. Or speed: Wolfram Research had to build or purchase a floating-point emulation library in order to produce the student version of its software.

With information you usually produce the high-quality version first, and then subtract value from it to get to the low-quality version. This isn't universally true: versioning based on technical support costs more. But it is true often enough to formulate a basic design principle: if you add a fancy new feature to your software or information product, make sure there is some way to turn it off! Once you've got your high-value, professional product, you often want to eliminate features to create a lower-value, mass-market product.

PITFALLS—AND HOW TO AVOID THEM

Although customers may not like some of the practices we have suggested, it is important to remember that the low willingness-to-pay market often would not be served at all unless producers can "degrade" the product in a way that discourages high-willingness-to-pay consumers from purchasing it. Without the ability to offer distinct versions, your best strategy may be to offer the high-end product only, and offer it at a premium price. In dealing with customers, you should emphasize that the cheaper versions enhance consumer choice; indeed, customers picking them are revealing that they value the option to buy a low-end version of the product at a discount.

Make sure users can't easily turn the low-end version into the high-end version.

The key issue in designing an information product line is to pick the right dimensions on which to adjust the quality *and* to make sure that the quality adjustment cannot be undone by clever consumers or intermediaries.

For example, Microsoft offers two versions of its Windows NT software: the Windows NT Workstation, which sells for about $260, and the Window NT Server, which sells for $730–$1,080, depending on configuration. Workstation NT can run a Web server but accepts only ten simultaneous sessions; the server version will accept any number of simultaneous sessions. According to an analysis by O'Reilly Software, the two operating systems are essentially the same. In fact, the kernel (the core component of the operating system) is identical in the two products and relatively minor tuning can turn Workstation NT into Server NT. In response to O'Reilly's analysis, Microsoft claimed that the two operating systems differ on more than 700 counts. According to one reporter:

> "While the Big 'M' folks in Redmond maintain the products are vastly different, critics allege Workstation can be switched into the Server version with a few easy tweaks. An official Microsoft marketer suggests that's like arguing the only difference between men and women is a Y chromosome. We think it's more akin to discovering your date is in drag."[1]

Microsoft's marketing strategy made sense. The problem was that some sophisticated consumers were able to turn the low-cost version into the high-cost version. The danger for Microsoft was that system administrators could easily upgrade Workstation NT into Server NT, thus defeating Microsoft's strategy.

ON-LINE AND OFF-LINE VERSIONS

Our discussion of market segmentation brings up an interesting point about on-line information: it is often also available off-line. In many cases, off-line information is actually more convenient to use. For example, many readers feel that it is easier to read text on paper than on a screen. Similarly, music probably sounds better on your stereo than on the tiny speakers that came with your computer.

This quality difference cuts two ways: on the one hand, the fact that text quality is poorer on the screen than on paper means that you can sometimes offer documents on-screen for free and then sell them on paper. Ed Kroll's famous book, *The Whole Internet,* could be downloaded on-line at no cost at the same time it was sold in bookstores for $24.95.

In a similar vein, as mentioned earlier, Netscape Navigator can be downloaded for free or purchased on disk. Many users are willing to pay for the disk version since they find it more convenient to use, not to mention the fact that it comes with printed documentation and user support. We are told that Netscape was quite surprised by the success of the retail product since the people in the company all had high-speed Internet connections and disdained printed documentation. They didn't appreciate the position of the home dial-up user with a 4,800 bps modem. But once Netscape realized a market was out there, the company was more than happy to sell into it.

The difference between on-line delivery and off-line delivery cuts the other way, too. It is much cheaper to sell information on-line since there are no production or distribution costs. If you *want* consumers to buy the on-line product, you should try to figure out ways to make it more attractive to the consumer than the off-line version.

Esther Dyson offers a useful way to think about this. She suggests that you treat your on-line content *as if* it were free. This way, you focus your mind on ways to add value to your product. Dyson's Dictum is great advice, since it makes you think about information provision as a *service* rather than a good.

A practice of the National Academy of Sciences Press is a good illustration of this principle. It offers both on-line and printed versions of its books. Because the on-line version of a book is great for browsing and the printed copy is great for actual reading, the on-line version adds value because it gives the reader a way to browse *without* cannibalizing the sales of the hard copy.

In many ways, selling information on-line and off-line is like selling physical products through two separate channels of distribution. In deciding which "channel" to promote, and how to price into each channel, you need to consider not only the costs associated with that channel and the character of demand through it but also the extent of channel spillover or cannibalization. If an on-line download of information displaces a hard-copy sale, revenue may well be lost. On the other hand, if today's download enhances demand tomorrow for both on-line and off-line information, sacrificing some current revenue to make more in the future may make good business sense.

The key question to ask yourself is whether the on-line version is a complement or a substitute for the off-line version. If it is a substitute for the off-line version, then you'll want to charge for it, recovering costs through fees or advertising, or version it so that it doesn't directly compete with your off-line version. If it complements your off-line version, then you want to promote it as aggressively as possible, since it adds to the bottom line by encouraging sales of the off-line product.

> *Understand whether the on-line version stimulates sales or steals them from the off-line version.*

Often, providing information on-line enables the supplier to add value in ways that would not be possible off-line. This in turn creates opportunities for new versions. Perhaps most obvious and important fact is that on-line information can be searched, sorted, or filtered electronically. On-line information can also provide cross-references through hyperlinks to further information. West Publishing sells CDs containing legal reference materials with hyperlinks to its on-line subscription service. These CD sales thus promote West's subscription revenues.

Merely posting something that is available in print on-line doesn't add value to it, so you won't be able to sell it for a premium price (although you may reach more customers). And, even more important, if you don't come up with ways to add value to *your* on-line content, your competitors will surely come up with a way to add value to their content.

When you get right down to it, it is very rare to find someone who has truly unique (versus merely differential) content. AP, UPI, and Reuters all sell newswire stories. Reuters managed to gain a competitive advantage by using the strategy described earlier: bundling news stories into packages targeted at specific industries. Reuters saw the wisdom in Dyson's Dictum—treat your content *as if* it were free. The company's strategy focused on adding value to its on-line services, not just providing the same content on-line as off.

HOW MANY VERSIONS?

When you start to think about versioning your software or information services, the first issue that comes up is how many versions you should offer. The answer is highly context dependent, but we can offer some guidelines.

First, one version is too few, for just the reasons we have described earlier in this chapter. Everyone who sells information should think about what they might do to segment their market. On the other hand, you can have too many versions in your product line. On the supply side, there are costs to maintaining several different products. On the demand side, you run the risk of creating user confusion. You must make it crystal clear to your users which version you think is appropriate for them.

Kurzweil's menu, shown in Table 3.1, is a good model: customers know their own line of business so there is little confusion between the medical and legal versions. There is no reason not to create additional versions targeted toward finance, agriculture, and so on.

Dialog's segmentation into casual and professional users is natural, but the names (DialogWeb and DataStar) are not particularly descriptive. However, trying to subdivide this market further runs the risk of user confusion, especially if Dialog doesn't come up with better names.

But what dimensions should you vary to construct different versions? There are two general strategies: analyze your market and analyze your product.

Analyze Your Market

Think about whether your market naturally subdivides into different categories of consumers *and* whether their behaviors are sufficiently different that they *want* (or are willing to tolerate) different quality classes of product.

Airlines recognized early on that there were basically two classes of travelers: those who traveled for pleasure and those who traveled on business. Tourists normally planned in advance and stayed for several days, typically including a weekend. Business travelers had quite different patterns of behavior: their trips were short and during the week. They also often had to change routes on short notice. These key differences allowed the airlines to segment their markets by offering two fare classes: advanced purchases, with Saturday-night stayover and penalties for changing the fare, and ordinary Y-class travel.

The business/tourist distinction is a natural one for airlines, and it is a good place to start thinking about your market. Are there professional and amateur users? If so, what distinguishes them? Your low-end information product should be lacking the key attributes that high-end customers uniquely crave. If you understand your market well enough, you will be able to come up with versions that both give value to your customers *and* raise revenues.

Analyze Your Product

You should take a hard look at your product and identify its key attributes, with an eye on segmenting the market according to one or more of these attributes. Look at the list in Table 3.2. Can you use delay, user interface, resolution, speed, format, capability, or features to segment your market? A good starting point is to consider offering a high-end and a low-end version for each key attribute for which there are clear differences in customer value.

As we suggested earlier, a common strategy is to produce the high-end product and then degrade it in some way to get the low-end version. You should think carefully about how this approach might apply in your market.

Look at Table 3.2 and see if these dimensions apply to your product. Choose the resolution of your images for your professional art market, build your search capabilities for the most sophisticated group of users, design the speed of your downloads for your most demanding users, and so on. Add features until the incremental value of those features *to your most demanding customers* just equals the incremental development cost.

Then, when you are ready to develop the product for the lower-end markets, just start turning features off. Take the high-resolution images and produce low-resolution versions. Put wait states in your program to slow it down. Remove the buffering. Do whatever it takes to make the product relatively unattractive to the high willingness-to-pay users but still attractive to the next group down.

Designing your product from the top down offers two advantages. First, it's easy to meet the competition if it arises. Suppose your "premium" version uses high resolution and your "standard" version uses medium resolution.

Design the high-end product first, then remove features to make the low-end version.

If your competition comes out with a high-resolution product at mass-market prices, you can respond by repositioning your high-end product for the mass market. Since your premium product is already available, this will usually just involve some new packaging and promotion.

The hard part is coming up with new features for the high-end version. But this is what your R&D group is supposed to be doing—designing new features for your most demanding customers. These should go into your high-end product first, and then diffuse down to the lower-end products as competitive upgrades.

The second advantage is that you can use the low-end version of your product as a way to "advertise" the high-end product. Just as 72 dpi comp images on the Web offer a sample of the high-resolution images that PhotoDisk can provide, the student version of Mathematica serves as an advertisement for the professional version. You should make sure that your low-end users know how much better or faster the high-end version will work.

PAWWS, mentioned earlier in the chapter, is facing competition from other firms offering portfolio analyses, among them RiskView, a joint venture involving Dow Jones, IBM, and Infinity Financial Technology. A press release describing the system explains the motivation of these firms:

> By offering free access to its databases, Dow Jones said it hopes to create wider demand for its indexes from the investment community and academics. Infinity believes the new product will stimulate demand for risk analysis from brokerage firms, prompting them to turn to companies

like itself to design more sophisticated systems. And IBM gets to demonstrate its Internet capability in the financial risk and management arena. IBM can also link the new product to other services it provides that give investors additional information.[2]

Each of these companies indicates that it is willing to give away the services of RiskView to encourage individuals and firms to make use of other services for which they charge: Dow Jones wants people to buy customized data, while IBM and Infinity want people to buy more sophisticated services from them. This is potentially formidable competition for PAWWS. On the other hand, PAWWS has a significant advantage in being first to market and having a knowledge base of experience in dealing with its customers.

GOLDILOCKS PRICING

If you can identify many different constituencies for the information you sell, and there is little likelihood of user confusion, there is no reason not to offer many different versions. Consider the industry news feeds offered by Reuters and other on-line services. There is little risk of confusing an airplane manufacturer with a fast-food business, so why not divide the market as finely as possible? Indeed, in many cases, less information can be more valuable: by filtering and sorting the information, so the airplane manufacturer does not need to flip past pages describing fast-food franchising practices, the information service becomes more valuable.

On the other hand, mass-market software is often offered in just one or two versions. There are two reasons for this. One is the network effects mentioned in Chapter 2. Users want to be able to exchange electronic documents, and it is much more convenient if there is only one version of the product. Look at all the flak Microsoft got by changing the file formats for Office 97. (Of course, Microsoft's strategy of one-way compatibility probably accelerated the adoption of Office 97; we'll talk more about this in Chapter 7.)

The other reason is that naive users often have trouble identifying which product is appropriate for them. However, this problem can be turned around and even used to your advantage. For example, if you buy a new digital camera, you are likely to get a stripped-down version of Adobe's Photoshop software called PhotoDeluxe bundled with your camera. As a first-time purchaser of the camera, you are likely to be a new user of digital photography and can use the PhotoDeluxe out of the box. As you become more sophisticated, there is a good chance you will upgrade to Photoshop, the professional version of Adobe's software.

But what can you do if you can't figure out what the "natural" user classes are? While lots of organizations decide to produce two versions—"professional" and "standard"—we think this is probably not the best choice. A better policy, we believe, is to produce a "standard," a "professional," and a "gold" version. That is, we suggest adding a high-end package targeted toward users with very high value for the product.

The rationale for this suggestion derives from a psychological phenomenon known as "extremeness aversion." Consumers normally try to avoid extreme choices—it leaves them out on a limb. It's perceived as risky to go for the top or the bottom of the product line for most consumers, and much safer to choose something in the middle. Positioning a product so that it represents a compromise will end up getting you extra purchasers. Just like Goldilocks, most consumers don't want to choose between "too big" or "too small." They want the product that is "just right."

Consider a fast-food restaurant like McDonald's and imagine that it offers just two sizes of soft drink: small and large. Some users are sure of the size they want, but others will be uncertain. They will agonize over the choice, and some will come down on the side of the smaller, cheaper size, generating less revenue for the restaurant.

Now suppose that the restaurant offers three sizes of soft drink—small, medium, and large. Those who can't make up their mind now have an easy out: choose the medium size. This will happen even if the medium size in the three-choice example is the same price and size as the large size in the two-choice example! By adding a jumbo size that almost no one consumes, the producer can end up selling more than he would with only two choices, in part because the median product looks attractive in comparison with the expensive, jumbo version.

This effect can be significant. Itamar Simonson and Amos Tversky describe a marketing experiment using microwave ovens.[3] When the choice set consisted of a bargain-basement oven at $109.99 and a midrange oven at $179.99, customers chose the midrange oven 45 percent of the time. When a high-end oven at $199.99 was added to the choice set, the same midrange oven was chosen 60 percent of the time! As Smith and Nagle point out: "Adding a premium product to the product line may not necessarily result in overwhelming sales of the premium product itself. It does, however, enhance buyers' perceptions of lower-priced products in the product line and influences low-end buyers to trade up to higher-priced models."[4]

Extremeness aversion is used all the time in marketing. Every restaurateur knows that the best selling wine is the one with the second-lowest price on the menu. A common practice is to offer an obviously low quality wine at the bottom end, and set the price of the next wine up to be only slightly higher. This makes it seem like a really good deal, virtually guaranteeing significant sales.

If you can't decide how many versions to have, choose three.

How can extremeness aversion be used for information goods? The important thing to recognize is that the product you really want to sell is the middle product—the high-end product is there only to push people toward the compromise choice. If you are selling a newsletter, consider offering an immediate notification service of news events. If you are selling images, offer a superhigh-resolution version that would exceed the needs of most users. If you are versioning based on different feature sets, add features that almost no one would use but that give the high-end product a distinct identity.

One important strategy is to offer premium quality technical support as the main differentiator of the "gold class." This might be something like an "immediate response" line that connects users to technical support people without delay. This costs very little to offer. As long as too many people don't choose the gold version, the cost of adding this kind of support will be small.

CUSTOMIZING BROWSER AND CONTENT

In Chapter 2, we argued that Java could be used to customize information you collect about user behavior, allowing you to assemble a much richer set of information. Java can also help you in versioning information, since it can be customized to display the particular type you are selling in an optimal way.

For example, if you are selling bit-mapped images of text pages, you can optimize the viewer for black-and-white textual material. If you want to display objects in 3D that allow users to choose different viewpoints, this is also relatively easy to accomplish.

You can exploit the characteristics of how people view these images in order to add value to your product. For example, if you are looking at page 17 of an on-line article, it is likely that the next thing you will want to view is page 18, so the Java-based viewer can download page 18 in the background.

There are dozens of other forms of customization that *could* be done. Users of MovieLink want to view their favorite theaters first. Users of financial information services might want to highlight certain stocks. This kind of personalization *can* be done on the server side, but it is much more scalable if done on the browser side. By using Java (or programs like Java) the producer of the information can optimize the browser to display that information in more useful and effective ways.

But more subtly, you can also use Java to version your information. If you have some nice feature that makes your information more valuable to the user, you can also *turn that feature off* for some classes of users. You can offer professional access to your information (with page buffering), then offer access to the *same* information with the buffering turned off. Users with high willingness to pay pick the system that displays more quickly; users with low willingness to pay make do with the other one. This trick allows you to segment the market in very creative ways. Java-based viewers allow you to vary the ways in which consumers can access your information and give you a new tool to induce self-selection.

BUNDLING

Bundling is a special form of versioning in which two or more distinct products are offered as a package at a single price. A prominent example in the software industry is Microsoft Office, a product that bundles together a word processor, a spreadsheet, a database, and a presentation tool. Each of these products is also offered separately. This is what distinguishes bundling from tying, in which the individual products are offered *only* in the package.

Microsoft Office has been phenomenally successful, capturing over 90 percent of the market for office suites. There are several reasons for its success. First, the products are "guaranteed" to work well together: material can be cut and pasted or linked from one document to another with some confidence. Furthermore, the component parts use shared libraries so that the Office applications take up less disk space and work together more effectively than would be the case if you installed separate versions of the applications.

Even without these benefits flowing from integrating the different pieces of the bundle, bundling can be attractive and profitable. Since the price of the bundle is usually less than the sum of the component prices, a bundle of two products is effectively a way of offering one to customers who would buy the other product at a smaller *incremental price* than the stand-alone price. If each of two components sells for $70, and the bundle goes for $100, the incremental price of the second component is $30, less than the stand-alone price of $70. Dun & Bradstreet follows precisely this approach in selling detailed information about the consumer purchases of branded products, information obtained from scanner machines at the supermarket checkout counters and other retail locations. Manufacturers purchasing Dun & Bradstreet data in one geographic area get a discount on data obtained in other areas.

In considering bundling, you need to determine whether you would like to offer a targeted discount on one product to customers who would purchase the other product anyway. For example, if customers who value current-year information highly also are likely to value year-old information highly, it makes little sense to offer a discounted bundle containing information from both years. The on-line *Wall Street Journal* offers a discount to the subscribers of its paper version, since the people who already read the paper version get less value from the on-line version than nonsubscribers. But note that the *Journal* does not offer the paper subscribers a discount for the archives. They correctly realize that the on-line version is worth less to the paper subscribers, but the archives, if anything, are more attractive to paper readers, so there is no need to discount the price. Of course, you may be forced to offer such discounts if competitors do so as a way of attracting the most lucrative customers.

Dispersion in Customer Value

Bundling software applications can also allow you to significantly increase the value you extract from your customers when it reduces the dispersion in their willingness to pay. Let's consider a simple example.

Table 3.3 illustrates Mark and Noah's willingness to pay for two pieces of software. Mark works in the marketing department, where he uses a word processor most of the time and has occasional need for a spreadsheet. Noah works in accounting, where he mostly uses his spreadsheet but occasionally makes use of a word processor.

How should the software vendor price the word processor and spreadsheet to generate the most revenues? It is easy to see that there are only two sensible prices for their products: either $100 or $120. At $120 for each program, Mark will buy only the word processor, and Noah will buy only the spreadsheet. So, if each piece of software sells for $120 the vendor will earn total profits of $240. In contrast, if each program sells for $100, Mark and Noah will each buy both programs, and the software vendor makes $400. Clearly, pricing each product at $100 is the preferred strategy in this example.

But consider what happens if the software producer *bundles* the word processor and the spreadsheet together. Let's make the conservative assumption that the willingness to pay for the bundle is just the sum of the willingnesses to pay for the components. In this case, Noah and Mark would each be willing to pay $220 for the "office suite," resulting in a total revenue of $440 for the software vendor!

Bundling increases revenues in this example because the willingness to pay for the bundle is *less dispersed* than the willingness to pay for the components. This will happen when the consumers with a high willingness to pay for one component tend to have low willingness to pay for another component, that is, when there is a negative correlation across components in consumer value. Remember, if you set a flat price, you can only charge as much as the most reluctant purchaser is willing to

Table 3.3. Willingness to Pay for Software Applications

	Word Processor	Spreadsheet
Mark	$120	$100
Noah	$100	$120

pay—in our example, $100. So, if you do charge a flat price, techniques that *reduce* dispersion of willingness to pay will tend to increase revenues. Bundling can serve this function.

Of course, if you can use differential pricing, you can charge users with high values high prices anyway, so dispersion is not as much of a concern. Dispersion only matters if you are forced to use flat prices.

Bundling can reduce dispersion even when consumer values are positively correlated simply because the sum of a large number of values will tend to be less dispersed than any single value. As long as values are not *perfectly* positively correlated, you will typically get some reduction in dispersion by bundling.

Other Reasons for Bundling

There are many other reasons to bundle information goods such as computer software. One important consideration is *option value.* A consumer may find Microsoft Office an attractive purchase even if she doesn't currently use a spreadsheet, since she *might* use a spreadsheet in the future.

If the consumer *does* decide to use a spreadsheet in the future, she will naturally choose the one that is "free" in the Microsoft Office bundle. Of course, the spreadsheet really isn't free—the consumer paid for it when she purchased the bundle—but it does have a zero incremental cost once the bundle has been purchased.

> **Use bundling to introduce new products to consumers.**

Microsoft has exploited this sort of pricing in another interesting way. Back in the days when Microsoft faced competition in the operating systems market, it licensed DOS to clone manufacturers using a sliding scale that depended on the number of machines that the manufacturer *produced,* whether or not DOS was installed on them. This was called a *per-processor license,* because Microsoft's OEM customers paid royalties to Microsoft for their DOS license depending on how many processors (machines) they sold. Note that the pricing was based on the *production* of machines, not on the number of machines in which DOS was installed. This meant that when the manufacturers installed an OS on the machine prior to shipping, the natural choice was DOS, since it had already been paid for by virtue of the licensing policy. DOS had zero incremental cost of installation, making it very attractive relative to the competition. The Justice Department challenged this pricing structure in 1994, and Microsoft agreed to abandon it; see our discussion in Chapter 10.

Information Bundles

Information is commonly sold in bundles now: magazines are bundles of articles, and subscriptions are bundles of magazines. This makes good sense: there is often considerable variation in how much users would be willing to pay for different articles in a magazine. One reader of the *Economist* may read only the articles about America but get a lot of value out of them. Another reader might read only the articles about Europe and feel the same way about her choice. By bundling these articles together, the *Economist* reduces the dispersion in willingness to pay for the collection of articles it sells. If the publisher had to sell each article on a pay-per-read basis, it would likely get significantly less revenue.

The same thing holds true for subscriptions. Owing to lack of interest or lack of time, you probably don't read every issue of every magazine to which you subscribe. But you may still be willing to pay for the subscriptions because there are *some* articles in *some* issues that are valuable to you.

Certainly there are other reasons to bundle articles together into issues. There are economies of scale in printing, binding, shipping, and marketing. But even if many of these economies of scale were reduced—as they are for electronic publications—it may still pay to sell articles bundled together into subscriptions for just the reason described above: bundling will generally reduce the dispersion in willingness to pay, thereby enhancing revenue.

Customized Bundles

Information technology allows for some interesting twists on bundling. Currently, pop music is sold on CDs, which are typically bundles of individual songs. This is in accord with the rationale described above: people have different favorites, and bundling the songs together reduces dispersion in willingness to pay.

Technologies are now becoming available that will allow users to create their *own* CDs. MusicMaker allows you to choose from its database of 30,000 different tracks and create your own customized CD for less than $20. This is a great example of *mass customization* of information.

Another example is the so-called "personalized newspaper." Here the user chooses a set of categories and a software agent assembles articles in those categories for delivery. This technology allows a user to create his or her *own* bundle of articles. Customized textbooks are also available.

How should such products be priced? To get a hint, look back at the example of Noah and Mark that we used to introduce the idea of bundling. Think of their willingness to pay for the software packages as willingness to pay for individual pieces of music that can be laid down on a personalized CD. (To get the right order of magnitude, think of the numbers as denoting cents rather than dollars.) If we priced each piece of music at $1, we would make $4 off of Noah and Mark. But suppose that we used *nonlinear* pricing and said that the *first* song you chose would cost $1.20 and each additional song would cost $1. In this case, both Noah and Mark would chose both songs, and we would end up with $4.40, just as if we bundled the products ourselves. This example shows that quantity discounts can play the same role as bundling. In fact, quantity discounts can be thought of as a generalized form of bundling and are useful for much the same reasons that bundling is useful. MusicMaker, the custom CD site mentioned above, uses just this form of quantity discounts: the minimum order is five songs for $9.95, with additional songs costing only $1 each.

PROMOTIONAL PRICING

Promotional pricing is a commonly used marketing strategy. Promotions take many forms: firms can use sales (limited-time reductions in price), coupons (which require the consumer to bring in pieces of paper that then allow them discounts), rebates (in which consumers must mail in a piece of paper to get some money back), and so on. All of these marketing techniques have one feature in common: they impose some inconvenience cost on the consumer.

In the case of sales, the consumer has to watch for the sales to occur. In the case of coupons, the consumer has to clip the coupon and remember to take it to the store. In the case of rebates, the consumer has to remember to fill out the rebate form and mail it in.

Between 80 and 90 percent of adults use coupons at one time or another, but only 2 percent of all coupons produced are ever redeemed. This suggests that people use coupons very selectively: some people use them for food, others for computer software. Clearly, coupons wouldn't be a worthwhile marketing strategy if *everybody* used them. If everybody used them, the seller may as well cut the price and eliminate the cost of dealing with the coupons.

The coupons are worthwhile only if they segment the market. A coupon says, "I'm a price-sensitive consumer. You know that's true since I went to all this trouble to collect the coupons." Economists say that a coupon is a *credible signal* of willingness to pay. It is "credible" because only people who have a low willingness to pay tend to use coupons.

The same sort of thing goes for sales. The people who show up when you have a temporary price reduction are the people who find it worthwhile to watch for sales. These tend to be people who are price sensitive. People who buy even when your price is high aren't very price sensitive, almost by definition. Sales and other forms of promotions are often ways to segment the market into price-sensitive and nonprice-sensitive components.

What does this have to do with information pricing? Well, suppose that information technology lowers search costs so that *everyone* can "costlessly" find the lowest price. This means that sales are no longer a very good way to segment the market. Or suppose that software agents can costlessly search the net for cents-off coupons. In this case, the coupons serve no useful function.

Promotional pricing is valuable only if it segments the market.

Promotions of this sort are useful only if they are costly to the consumer, because it is only by imposing costs that they can identify price-sensitive consumers. If the computer costlessly does the searching or coupon clipping, the marketing technique loses its function.

Bargain Finder is a case in point. Brian Krulwich, a researcher at Andersen Consulting, designed a little program that would search on-line CD stores for the best prices for music CDs. Bargain Finder was an immediate hit on the Web: it had more than 100,000 uses in the first two months it was available. But after a few months of use, three of the eight stores that Bargain Finder searched decided to prevent it from accessing their price lists.

Remember the first lesson in Chapter 2? Avoid commoditization. The on-line CD stores didn't want to compete on price alone. They wanted to compete on service and value added. By allowing Bargain Finder to look only at one dimension of what the stores offered, they ended up commoditizing their product.

This sort of commoditization may be hard to avoid with Internet shopping. Services like PriceScan compile lists of advertised prices for computer equipment and consumer electronics. This is a great service for consumers, but it will make the retailing market even more cutthroat than it already is.

LESSONS

- **Adjust the characteristics of your information products to emphasize differences in what customers value.** You can offer different versions that have differential appeal to different groups, adjusting the price if necessary to sort the consumers.

- **You can version your products along a variety of dimensions.** Delay, user interfaces, image resolution, speed of operation, format, capability, features, comprehensiveness, annoyance, and support are some examples.

- **Add value to on-line information to differentiate it from hard copy.** Don't just put text on-line—do something with it that you can't do with the print version. At the very least, make it searchable and use links for cross-references.

- **If your market segments naturally, design your information product line to match.** For example, if there are professional and amateur users, offer versions that are designed and priced to appeal to each of these market segments.

- **If your market does not segment naturally, choose three versions (just like Goldilocks).** If you don't know how many segments there are, three versions is a good default choice. Plan to make most of your money off the middle version.

- **Control the browser.** Controlling the browser by using Java or similar technologies helps you modify the way you display your information, which helps you version and price your market.

- **Bundling makes sense if it reduces variation in willingness to pay.** Combining complementary goods increases revenue if it decreases the variation across customers in their willingness to pay.

- **Nonlinear pricing can also be used to let consumers build their own bundles.** Quantity discounts can increase usage and revenues at the same time.

- **Promotional pricing makes sense if it helps you segment the market.** Design your promotions to elicit different responses from different types of customers. Such targeted promotions help support versioning.

4 | Rights Management

Copyright owners continue to be ambivalent about the Internet. On the one hand, it represents a fantastic new medium for distribution; on the other, many in the publishing industry see it as one "giant, out of control copying machine."

The traditional protections offered by intellectual property law seem powerless to deal with many of the issues raised by digital media. In a widely quoted article, John Perry Barlow asserted that "Intellectual property law cannot be patched, retrofitted, or expanded to contain digitized expression. . . . We will need to develop an entirely new set of methods as befits this entirely new set of circumstances."[1]

Is Barlow right? Is copyright law hopelessly outdated? We think not. As in the other cases we have examined in this book, many of the tried and true principles are still valid. What has changed is that the Internet, and information technology in general, offers new opportunities and challenges in applying these principles.

The very technological advances that make rights management more difficult—the dramatic reduction in costs of copying and distribution—also offer a fantastic opportunity for owners of intellectual content. Just as owners of mineral rights in the nineteenth century welcomed the arrival of the railroad, which allowed them to transport their precious ore to market, so should the owners and creators of intellectual property rights in the twenty-first century view the digital revolution as a great opportunity to broaden their reach and distribution by orders of magnitude. Every new reproduction technology, from the printing press to the VCR, has brought forth dire predictions that it would destroy an industry, but somehow this has never happened. We are confident that owners of intellectual property can overcome the threats raised by digital reproduction just as they have overcome the threats raised by other reproduction technologies in the past.

In this chapter we will examine how digital technology affects the management of intellectual property. We think today's rights owners can learn some very important lessons from the history of intellectual property, so we examine some periods in which similar technological and institutional changes took place. Our message is an optimistic one: sure, some of the old business models are broken, but there are a lot of new models waiting to be discovered and implemented. The new opportunities offered by digital reproduction far outweigh the problems.

PRODUCTION AND DISTRIBUTION COSTS

Digital technology changes two significant costs faced by a publisher of content:

- **Reproduction costs.** Digital technology dramatically reduces the cost of making perfect reproductions.

- **Distribution costs.** Digital technology allows these reproductions to be distributed quickly, easily, and cheaply.

The impacts of these two cost changes often get confounded, but it is important to keep them separate. In other technological advances, the cost distinctions were more clear cut: some technologies made copying easier, and others made distribution easier. Consider the following two examples:

- A tape recorder offers a cheap way to copy music, but it is just as expensive to distribute a copy of a cassette as it is to distribute the original cassette. The tape recorder lowers the cost of copying, but not the cost of distribution.

- An AM broadcast of a classical recording is a cheaper way to distribute the music than a high-quality CD, but the sound fidelity is poor, and, even worse, listeners have no control over when they listen. Similarly, a black and white photocopy of an art book about the Sistine Chapel may be a cheaper method of distribution, but it is not nearly as valuable to potential users as the original full-color book. In these cases, the distribution costs are reduced, but the quality of the reproduction is much worse than the quality of the original.

Digital technology is uniquely potent precisely because it sharply lowers *both* copying and distribution costs. Each of these new capabilities offers a different set of challenges to rights management and requires a different set of responses.

MAKING LOWER DISTRIBUTION COSTS WORK FOR YOU

Don't fight against lower distribution costs; take advantage of them. Reduced distribution costs offer you a significant advantage by allowing you to promote your products more effectively.

Giving Away Your Content

We said in Chapter 1 that one of the defining characteristics of an information good is that it qualifies as an "experience good": consumers don't know what it is worth to them until they experience it. This has always been the case for information goods, no matter how they are packaged or delivered, and sellers of information have always had to come up with ways to deal with this problem.

Bookstores typically allow their customers to browse through their collection. As authors, we have read a lot of books standing up, especially those written by our competitors. Nowadays, you don't have to stand up. You can sit in a comfortable chair and sip a capuccino while absorbing the latest thought in business strategy. The book superstores have made it more comfortable to browse because they've discovered that it helps them sell more books. By "giving away" at least part of their content, they end up making a lot more money.

The Internet is a wonderful way to offer free samples of information content. People have debated the right advertising model for the Internet for several years, but the answer has been staring them in the face all along: the Internet is ideal for "infomercials." You can tell people about your product, and even give them pieces of it, while they remain comfortably at home. But there is a problem with Internet infomercials.

Give away free samples to sell your content.

Producers of physical goods don't worry about infomercials cutting into sales: an image of a shirt is quite different from a shirt. But an image of a photo *is* the photo, for most purposes, and owners of photo libraries are reluctant to post their photos on the Web for obvious reasons: how can they make money if they give away their product?

The obvious answer is: you give away only *part* of your product. This is like the old marketing tactic of offering free samples of consumer products, but updated for the digital age. The beauty of information is that it is particularly easy to give free samples of something that has zero marginal cost of distribution. The trick is to break your product up into components; some you give away, others you sell. The parts that are given away are the advertisements—the infomercials—for the parts you sell.

This rights management strategy is a twist on the versioning strategy described in Chapter 3. There we argued that you should offer a whole product line of information goods. The cheap versions (which can even be free) serve as advertisements for the high-priced versions.

Consider, for example, the case of books. No one wants to read a book, or even a long magazine article, on-line; it's just too painful given the limitations of the current technology. Studies have shown that most Web users will read only about two screens of material before they click off.

The ergonomic costs associated with on-line reading mean that large amounts of content can be posted without cutting into sales of hardcopy. In fact, in many cases, posting the on-line content can *increase* the sales of the physical version of the information good. The National Academy of Sciences Press put more than a thousand of its books on-line and found that the availability of the electronic versions has boosted sales of hard copies by two or three times. The MIT Press had much the same experience; it claims that making electronic books available on its Web site approximately doubles their sales.

But watch out: if the on-line version is too easy to print out, then hardcopy sales could suffer. The best thing to do is to make the on-line version easy to browse—lots of short screens, lots of links—but hard to print out in its entirety.

Demand for Repeat Views

For some sorts of information—music, for instance—repeated plays are very important. If you hear a song on the radio that you like, you may want to hear it again right away. But if you read a novel—even one that you enjoy very much—you are unlikely to want to read it again in the near future. The radio broadcast of a song is an ad for itself—or, more accurately, it's an ad for a more conveniently packaged version of itself. It's a free sample, but presented in an inconvenient form: the sample is provided when the DJ wants to broadcast it, not necessarily when you want to hear it. The value added by the CD version of the song is that it can be played when, where, and how you want it to be played. The CD has what economists call *option value:* you can exercise the option to play it where and when you want, unlike the radio broadcast of the same music. This is much like the versioning strategy we advocated in Chapter 3: the inconvenient version offered by the DJ is given away for free, while the user must pay for the convenient CD version.

The desire for repetition is common among children. There is something very comforting to a child in reading the same story, or hearing the same song, or seeing the same video over and over and over again. This means that giving away a single view of the product is often an attractive marketing strategy for information goods targeted at the children's market.

Take, for example, our old purple friend Barney the Dinosaur. Barney's saccharine personality makes him a controversial character, at least in some circles. He made it to the Internet early on, in the form of a Usenet newsgroup called alt.barney.dinosaur.die.die.die, which was devoted to anti-Barney diatribes and explicit descriptions of how to dismember, torture, and mutilate the lovable purple thereopod. There are also numerous Web pages devoted to Barney, including one that purports to prove that Barney is Satan.

But Barney has a following: The Barney Web site claims that he has sold more than 35 million kid vids and has a fan club with more than a million members in the United States alone. *Barney & Friends* is the most watched show on TV by children under the age of six.

Barney wasn't the creation of a media conglomerate; it was truly a grass-roots effort. Sheryl Leach, a former teacher, created Barney in the late 1980s. She found it relatively easy to make the shows, produce the tapes, and even get the tapes into the stores on consignment. The hard part was getting people to buy them. Then she had an inspiration: if the customers wouldn't buy Barney, she would give him away. Ms. Leach started sending free videos to day care centers and preschools near the retail outlets that carried Barney tapes. In each video case was a note telling parents where they could buy copies of tapes for their children. Ms. Leach's strategy is an example of the "multiplayer" strategy of bribing one party to lock in another party, which we discuss in Chapter 6: she offered Barney for free to the true decision makers, the kids, thus effectively locking in their agents, who (supposedly) control the money, the parents.

Leach's strategy was phenomenally successful: Barney has become a cultural icon. Recently Microsoft and PBS announced that they are collaborating on a new Barney series that will include an encoded signal that operates a Barney robot.

The Barney marketing strategy should be contrasted with the behavior of another purveyor of children's media, the Walt Disney Company. According to John J. Tormey, a Disney attorney based in New York, "We pursue all known infringements of our rights." In their view, there's no such thing as a Mickey Mouse lawsuit—or, more properly, a Mickey Mouse™ lawsuit. Disney has taken several day care centers to court for showing Disney videos without a proper license, and in the early 1990s the company threatened to sue three day care centers in Florida that had painted Disney characters on their walls.

Disney is perfectly within its legal rights to engage in such actions; indeed, it must actively defend its trademarks or risk losing them. It's not the *propriety* of Disney's actions that we question—it's their profitability. And Disney is not alone. The American Society of Composers, Authors, and Publishers (ASCAP), which licenses rights for music performances, threatened to sue Girl Scout camps for singing songs written and published by ASCAP composers and publishers. This is despite the limited revenue potential from Girl Scout camps, the obvious negative public relations implications, and the prospect that singing an artist's songs would spur demand for that artist's CDs. The instinct to seek out and charge all those who use copyrighted material runs deep and can easily cause otherwise sensible executives to defend their rights past the point of economic return.

In our view, it would make a lot of sense for Disney to at least experiment with some marketing campaigns directed at the day care centers and preschools along the same lines that the Barney promoters used. For example, it could provide a special package of Disney videos, with a license allowing them to be exhibited for a limited period of time, as long as the day care center distributed coupons to the parents offering deals on purchasing their own copies of the videos from local retailers or direct from Disney. The videos shown at the preschool would be very effective at advertising themselves, creating a demand for home viewing.

There is also considerable demand for repeat viewing of videos among adults, sometimes for surprising reasons. Recall *Good Morning Vietnam*, discussed in Chapter 2, for which the demand for repeat viewing came from the fact that the audience did not catch all the jokes the first time through. Video rentals have been flat for the past seven years; all the industry growth has come on the video purchase side, reflecting, in part, the strong desire for repeat viewing of many kinds of videos.

Similar, but Not Identical, Products

A closely related strategy has to do with giving away samples to sell similar, but not identical, products. The images we see in various media—magazines, television, on-line—are a good example: customers don't want repeat viewing of the *same* images, they want some variation—but not too much. *Playboy* magazine is a natural example: the audience would soon tire of seeing *exactly* the same images over and over again. They want variation, but variation on the same basic theme.

Like other content producers, the Playboy organization is worried about piracy of its "intellectual property" and is now adding "digital watermarks" to the centerfold pictures it posts on the Web. This is a technology that modifies brightness characteristics of the pixels that make up the image so as to encode copyright information. Other suppliers of non-erotic on-line images, such as Corbis, use similar technology.

DigiMarc, which provides the service that Playboy is using, adds a new twist. It also sells a software product called the MarcSpider that searches the Web for images marked with the DigiMarc watermarks. Not only does this allow DigiMarc to track the use of its own technology, it also provides customers with a valuable service by alerting them to unauthorized use of their images.

Although digital watermarks are a neat idea from a technological point of view, we think their most profitable use may be a bit different from that envisioned in the popular press. For example, just as with Barney, it is certainly in Playboy's interest to give away some of its content to create demand for other items it sells. Indeed, the organization posts a "free" image of the Playmate of the Month without making much of a fuss about copyright. And why should it? Playboy certainly makes a profit on the photo by charging more than $10,000 per month for a banner ad on its Web site. But to charge the advertisers this kind of money, Playboy has to give them some idea of how many people will see their ads and, demographically, who these people are. Playboy can count the hits on its Web site, but can't see who is making copies of the images posted. The MarcSpider gives Playboy a way to follow the image through the Web to find out "who's doing what, where, and when to our stuff," to use the words of a Playboy spokesperson.

Such market research can be very valuable. Remember the basic maxim of marketing: know thy customer? Technologies like MarcSpider will help you do this. It makes sense for Playboy to give away its Play-mate of the Month picture, *as long as people associate it with the Playboy brand.* Logos, text, and embedded hyperlinks can be used to tell the viewers where the image comes from. And if the viewers know where the image comes from, they know where to go to get more. Playboy, in turn, realizes revenue from these viewers on their visits to Playboy's site via advertising, subscription, and/or pay-per-view.

> **Make sure that free samples direct customers back to you.**

The strategy of giving away a sample isn't limited to images. McAfee Associates sells computer security tools; its flagship product is Virus-Scan, a program that detects and deletes computer viruses. The company was started by engineer John McAfee, who handled virus problems for Lockheed. In 1989 he posted a virus fix on a computer bulletin board and asked those who downloaded it to send him whatever they thought it was worth. He made $5 million in his first year.

McAfee went public in 1992 and had a $3.2 billion market value by 1997, shipping more than half of the world's antivirus software that year. The company continues to offer many of its products for free via the Web, making its revenues on upgrades and customer service. Companies purchase site licenses, and individuals pay $53 to $160 per year for additional services. In December 1997 McAfee merged with Network General, creating Network Associates, the largest independent network security company and the tenth largest independent software company. The new company's pending merger with Trusted Information Systems will push it still higher on the list. Not bad for a company that "gives away" its products!

Ultimately, we believe that digital technology and the Internet offer great opportunities for the creative use of informational free samples, whether the content consists of images, news articles, databases, or stock quotes. Free samples of information are effective for two reasons: (1) consumers need samples to see what it is you are selling (the experience good effect) and (2) it costs you almost nothing to provide these extra bits (the zero marginal cost effect). But how, you ask, can you convince freeloaders to become revenue generators, if you offer extensive free samples? The answer is versioning: your low-end version is free, but limited in scope, convenience, quality, and/or quantity.

Complementary Products

The next strategy we examine is selling complementary products. This has been around as long as razors and blades, but takes a variety of new twists on the Internet.

One attractive idea is to give away an index or table of contents and to sell access to the main material. This exploits the obvious complementarity between the contents and the content. The scientific publishing house Elsevier now puts the table of contents for each of its journals on the Web and also provides a push service, Contents Alert, which sends out e-mail notifications of the contents of new issues. The *Wall Street Journal* and the *Economist* allow free full-text searching of their back issues archives and then charge a couple of dollars to download the retrieved articles. Each of these examples takes the same form: you offer the index or search service for free to increase demand for priced content.

Sometimes it's the other way around: the content is free and the organization is what is valuable. Farcast is one of several companies that sell "current awareness" services. Farcast describes its service, Inquisit, as a "business intelligence service." You can use "droids" to search a variety of information sources, which then report back to you with what they've found. Some (but not all) of the information sources the droids look at are already available for free on-line. The value that Farcast adds is not in providing the content itself but rather in providing a service that both searches for and organizes the content. Farcast sells this service for about $13 a month and (of course!) it offers a two-week subscription as a free trial.

Illicit Copying

All these tactics are very clever, you may say, but what about the product that you *don't* give away for free? What about the stuff that you want to sell? If people can take your content without compensation, where do the revenues come from? "Bitlegging" can't be ignored: there's no doubt that it can be a significant drag on profits. Luckily, there are some compensating factors.

First, information that is timely, or that people tire of quickly, is less susceptible to illicit copying. Sports scores, financial information, and gossip—all three widely available on the Internet—are most valuable when fresh. How many illicit copies of last month's sports scores have you seen?

Dated copies of this sort of material can serve as illustrations of the quality of the fresh material that you provide. However, there is a danger in providing too much of the "old" content. Giving away a few free samples from the archive is a fine idea; giving away unlimited access, including search capabilities, is quite another matter. This is why the *Wall Street Journal* gives away a couple of weeks of its archive but makes you pay for older material. Such an archive or library can be immensely valuable.

Second, bitleggers have the same problem that any other sellers of contraband material have: they have to let potential customers know how to find them. But if they advertise their location to potential customers, they also advertise their location to law enforcement authorities. In the contraband business it pays to advertise . . . but not too much.

This puts a natural limit on the size of for-profit, illegal activities: the bigger they get, the more likely they are to get caught. Products such as MarcSpider can automate the search for contraband. Digital piracy can't be eliminated, any more than any other kind of illegal activity, but it *can* be kept under control. All that is required is the political will to enforce intellectual property rights.

MAKING LOWER REPRODUCTION COSTS WORK FOR YOU

Let us turn now to the other significant cost factor charged by digital technology: reproduction. Digital copies are *perfect* copies of the original. For digital content, production *is* reproduction. Illicit CDs can be stamped out for well under a dollar apiece, and they're all perfect copies of the master. These illicit perfect copies are perfect substitutes for the original. And if a perfect copy is available at a bargain basement price, who would want to buy the original?

> *For digital content, production* **is** *reproduction.*

It is easy to overstate this case. "Perfection" really isn't as important as is sometimes thought. An analog copy of a heavy metal CD is just about as good as the original digital version— maybe even better. In one test, professional record producers could distinguish a second-generation analog copy from a twentieth-generation analog copy only 63 percent of the time—that is, only 13 percent better than they would have done by chance alone. And sometimes the experts preferred the twentieth generation!

The fact that a *perfect* digital copy can be made isn't that much scarier than the fact that a *very good* analog copy can be made. We've learned to live with analog copies of documents, music, and video—we can learn to live with digital copies as well.

HISTORICAL EXAMPLES

It is important to recognize that the introduction of cheap production and distribution mechanisms isn't really that new. In the Middle Ages, professors used a primitive form of intellectual property protection: they lectured in darkened rooms so that the students couldn't take notes.

Today, middle-aged professors still lecture in darkened rooms, but now it's so the students can see the PowerPoint presentation.

History may not repeat itself, but it rhymes. Printing presses, xerography, and the Internet have made text reproduction progressively cheaper, and express mail and fax machines have reduced the costs of text distribution immensely. With each new reduction in cost, the *amount* of information being distributed has increased dramatically. There is more being published today, and more money being made in publishing, than ever before.

The photocopying machine was supposed to be the death knell for the publishing business. But, in fact, cheap photocopying has probably *increased* the demand for printed content. For example, the fact that photocopying is widely available allows producers of library materials (such as academic journals) to charge more for the content they produce. The fact that library materials can be copied easily makes them more valuable to their users.

The Rise of the Library

Libraries themselves are a wonderful example of an innovation that first appeared to threaten the publishing industry but ended up vastly expanding it.

In the eighteenth century only the wealthy could afford to buy books. A single book cost the equivalent of an average worker's weekly wage. And *because* books were expensive, there was little reason to invest in becoming literate. At the start of the nineteenth century, there were only 80,000 frequent readers in all of England.

The big breakthrough came in 1741 with the publication of *Pamela*. Instead of the usual dull theological treatise, the public was offered a racy and entertaining tale of a young girl's life. *Pamela*'s success spawned many imitators, and a whole new genre, the English novel, was born. *Pamela* begat *Moll Flanders* and *Moll* begat *Tom Jones* and so it went. These classic novels were denounced by the literati such as Samuel Coleridge: "As to the devotees of these [novels], I dare not compliment their *pass-time* or rather *kill-time* with the name of *reading*. Call it rather a sort of beggarly day-dreaming, during which the mind of the dreamer furnishes for itself nothing but laziness and a little mawkish sensibility."[2] Sounds almost as bad as television, doesn't it?

But the public paid little attention to the critics. People couldn't get enough of these lurid tales. English bookstores were unable to keep up with the demand for novels and romances, so they started renting them out. These circulating libraries, as they were called, were denounced by the literate classes as "slop shops of literature." What's more, they were also denounced by the publishers and booksellers for an entirely different reason: the publishers and booksellers were afraid that the circulating libraries would cut into their business: "[W]hen circulating libraries were first opened, the booksellers were much alarmed; and their rapid increase added to their fears, and led them to think that the sale of books would be much diminished by such libraries."[3]

In the long-run, however, there is no doubt that the circulating libraries were much to the benefit of the publishing industry. The availability of low-cost entertainment motivated many to learn to read. According to Charles Knight, author of *The Old Printer and the Modern Press,* the 80,000 frequent readers in 1800 grew to over 5 million by 1850. The publishers who served the new mass market for books thrived, while those who sold only to the elite disappeared.

As the market grew, people started to buy rather than rent their books. The passage cited above continues: "But experience has proved that the sale of books, so far from being diminished by them, has been greatly promoted; as from these repositories many thousand families have been cheaply supplied with books, by which the taste of reading has become more general, and thousand of books are purchased each year by such as have first borrowed them at those libraries, and after reading, approving of them, have become purchasers."[4]

Note carefully the causality: it was the presence of the circulating libraries that killed the old publishing model, but at the same time it created a new business model of mass-market books. The for-profit circulating libraries continued to survive well into the 1950s. What killed them off was not a lack of interest in reading but rather the paperback book—an even cheaper way of providing literature to the masses.

The Rise of the Video

The same industry dynamics occurred in the market for prerecorded videos in the 1980s. In the early 1980s VCRs cost more than a thousand dollars and videotapes sold for $90. Videos were a medium for the rich—just as books had been in 1800.

Video rental stores changed all that. Like the circulating libraries

300 years earlier, they brought this new form of entertainment to the masses. The stores made it possible for an ordinary family to rent both the video machine and the cartridge. The additional revenue flowing to VCR manufacturers allowed them to exploit economies of scale. By the mid-1980s, the average middle-class family could afford a VCR and video rental stores were thriving.

Hollywood didn't like the rental business. Studios tried to control the stores through various licensing arrangements, but the owners of these mom-and-pop stores wouldn't cooperate. In the end, of course, despite its objections to video rentals, Hollywood made a lot of money off them. The availability of inexpensive content meant that people watched many more movies. By the late 1980s, video machines were selling for less than $200 and 85 percent of American families owned one. Video rental was a blockbuster business. (Or should we say a Blockbuster business?)

During the early 1980s there was little change in the sales price of videos; they continued to sell for about $90 retail and $60 to video stores, which rented them out for $2 or $3. But then Disney realized that people—ordinary people—would actually *buy* a video if the price was right. Its first video targeted for home purchase, *Lady and the Tramp,* sold 3.2 million copies at $29.95.

Pretty soon the market was flooded with cut-rate videos selling for $19.95, $14.95, even $9.95—and for movies that were just a few months old. Since 1990, the video rental market has been flat, and all the action has been in the sales market. In the last fifteen years, video purchase prices have dropped by more than 90 percent. And Hollywood is making money like never before.

The spread of the video machine is a beautiful example of positive feedback (which we mentioned in Chapter 1 and examine in depth in Chapter 7). The more VCRs there were, the greater the demand for prerecorded videos. And the more prerecorded videos there were, the greater the demand for VCRs. Home video, time shifting, and rental of VCRs got the market to critical mass. Once it was there, positive feedback took over.

Far from being Hollywood's death knell, prerecorded video tapes have been its savior. Just as in the case of books, the rental market for videos created a huge new opportunity for both renting *and* buying the product. The companies that recognized the implications of the new technology succeeded beyond their wildest dreams, while those which stuck with the old model were consigned to the dustbins of history.

Growing the Market

Producers of digital content are in much the same position now that the producers of books were in 1800 or producers of film were in 1975. It's easy to see the threats inherent in the new media; it's hard to see the promise. The key issue is how to exploit economies of scale: a thousand consumers paying a dollar a piece to download a piece of software that costs pennies to produce and distribute is a lot more profitable than 100 consumers paying $10 a piece for software that costs $5 to produce and distribute.

The book producers in 1800 and the video producers in 1980 didn't appreciate how dramatically the market could grow. Publishers used to dealing with a wealthy elite didn't foresee that literacy would dramatically increase if there was something interesting to read. Hollywood producers didn't recognize that VCRs would become a mass-market item if popular content was available for them. The publishers and movie producers understood their *own* industries, but they didn't understand their *complementors'* industries.

> *Vastly cheaper distribution may feel like a threat, but it offers great opportunity.*

We think that the natural tendency is for producers to worry *too* much about *protecting* their intellectual property. The important thing is to *maximize the value* of your intellectual property, not to protect it for the sake of protection. If you lose a little of your property when you sell it or rent it, that's just a cost of doing business, along with depreciation, inventory losses, and obsolescence.

CHOOSING TERMS AND CONDITIONS

But enough of the past; what about the present? Let us suppose that you are the owner of some intellectual property and have the legal right to market it as you will. How should you think about the terms and conditions under which you will make your product available?

The first thing to do is to recognize the fundamental trade-off between control and customer value. The more liberal you make the terms under which customers can have access to your product, the more valuable it is to them. A product that can be shared with friends, loaned out, rented, repeatedly accessed, or sold in a resale market is obviously more valuable to a potential user than one that can be accessed only once, under controlled conditions, by only a single party.

The fact that liberal terms and conditions increase the value of the product has two effects. First, you can charge a higher price, and second, more consumers will want to buy it. But there is a mitigating factor. More liberal terms and conditions also create competition for your product: rental markets and resale markets cut into the sales of the originals, which reduces revenues. And consumers are willing to pay less for your product if there are close substitutes available, such as used copies.

The challenge of intellectual property management lies in trading off these two effects: in choosing the terms and conditions that maximize the value of your property. The more generous the terms on which you offer your intellectual property, the more you can charge, but the less you sell.

The Analytics of Rights Management

We can examine this trade-off using a staple from the economist's toolkit: the demand curve. Since unit costs are very low for most information goods, and negligible for purely digital goods, we will ignore production costs in what follows.

Your goal is to set a price that maximizes your revenue. The demand curve in Figure 4.1 illustrates the standard trade-off: a high price leads to low volume. With the help of a good marketing study, you should be able to choose the price that maximizes revenues, which are represented by the area of the revenue box, as shown in panel A, the baseline case.

But what about the terms and conditions under which the product is offered? Offering more liberal terms and conditions increases the value of the product to the consumers, which shifts the demand curve up. However, the more liberal the terms and conditions, the more copying and sharing, and the less the producer sells. In Figure 4.1, the demand curve in panel B is twice as steep as it is in panel A. This means that every consumer is willing to pay twice as much for the intellectual property offered under more liberal terms and conditions. But owing to

Figure 4.1. *Balancing Terms and Conditions of Sale with Amount Sold*

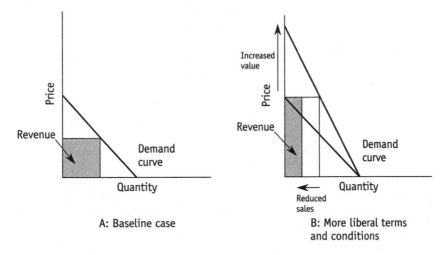

A: Baseline case

B: More liberal terms
and conditions

the more liberal terms, the producer sells less; in this diagram, we've assumed that sales fall by 50 percent. This means that the new revenue box has twice the height and half the width, leaving revenue unchanged.

Granting consumers expanded rights increases price but reduces sales.

If more liberal terms and conditions reduced sales by *more* than 50 percent, this change would *reduce* producer revenue; if they reduced sales by *less* than 50 percent, this change would *increase* producer revenue. Making terms more liberal increases profit if the increased value to the consumers, which can be captured by the producer through higher prices, is larger than the decrease in sales.

This observation helps you understand the terms and conditions trade-off in practical ways. Consider, for example, Blockbuster's recent experimentation with terms and conditions for its video rental. Our local store now has 1-day, 3-day, and 5-day rentals, along with free popcorn and discounts for early return. In choosing which titles fall under these various categories, Blockbuster thinks about how the terms will affect both consumer value *and* rentals. If consumers will pay twice as much for a 5-day rental as they will for a 1-day rental, but would rent only half as many videos, Blockbuster would make the same revenue from each rental period. If consumers find the longer period twice as valuable, but they rent only 40 percent of the videos they otherwise would have rented, Blockbuster would want to choose the shorter period.

Transaction Costs

As we saw in Chapter 2, one important influence on consumer value is transaction costs. These are the costs that the consumer or the producer pays to make the transaction happen. For example, to rent the latest video you must go to the store; if the video is very popular you may have to go many times. When you finally get the video, you have to take it home and view it, then return it the next day. The cost of travel and delay can be significant. For many consumers, buying a video at $12.95 is preferable to renting at $3 because they avoid the hassle of returning the video.

A new technology known as Digital Video Express, or Divx, offers pay-per-view DVDs. You purchase a movie on disk for $5, and when you're done you can simply throw away the disk. By selling Divx disks at $5 the producers are guessing that consumers are willing to pay at least $2 to avoid the hassle of returning a video that rents for $3. Both sides of the transaction are potentially better off: the producers get the extra $2, and the users avoid a late night trip to the video store.

Another good example of the importance of transaction costs are site licenses for software. Site licenses are often priced at a low multiple of the software's unit purchase price. Table 4.1 depicts the site license per seat for three different office suites.

It is attractive to sell these products via site license since transaction costs are reduced for both the buyer and the seller. It is much cheaper to load a program from a file server than it is to create, warehouse, and distribute a copy for each purchaser in the organization. This is especially true if user support costs are handled by the organization rather than the producer.

Table 4.1. Site Licenses for Software Office Suites

Suite	1,000 Sites	5,000 Sites	10,000 Sites
Lotus SmartSuite	$133 per seat	$125 per seat	$125 per seat
Corel WordPerfect	69	64	64
Microsoft Office	158	171	167

Source: InfoWorld, October 28, 1996, p. 14.

Site licenses are also an attractive strategy for pricing and selling information content. Members of a large investment bank, for example, would find it much more attractive to have an electronic site license to, say, the *Wall Street Journal* than to each manage his or her own purchase. With the site license they could redistribute articles within the organization with no liability; without it, there could well be heavy transaction costs in verifying and complying with terms and conditions. (See our earlier discussion of group pricing in Chapter 2 for more on the marketing advantages of this form of pricing.)

As an owner of an information good, you should ask yourself: "Is it cheaper for me to distribute my product directly to the end-user, or is it cheaper for the organization to distribute my product to the end-user?" If the distribution cost advantage lies with the organization, then you should be able to reach a bargain where both you and the organization share the gains from the more efficient distribution system.

In addition, organizations often realize significant savings by choosing particular products as standards, and, once they commit to a product, they may be very reluctant to switch. This loyal installed base can give you a steady stream of revenue from upgrades that can be well worth initial discounts you must extend to make the sale. In the next chapter we will discuss in detail strategies for dealing with switching costs.

LESSONS

- **Digital technology poses two challenges for rights management.** First, it reduces the cost of making copies. Second, it allows the copies to be distributed quickly, easily, and cheaply. These challenges also offer opportunities.

- **Reduced distribution costs help to advertise your product by making it cheap to give away samples.** This is useful when there is significant demand for repeated views or for closely related content. Giving away samples helps to sell more content.

- **Reduced distribution costs are beneficial to those who sell illicit copies as well, but their need to advertise helps keep**

"bitlegging" under control. A bitlegger that gets too big and attracts too much attention will soon be caught.

- **Copy protection schemes impose costs on users and are highly vulnerable to competitive forces.** Trusted systems, cryptographic envelopes, and other copy protection schemes have their place but are unlikely to play a significant role in mass-market information goods because of standardization problems and competitive pressures.

- **When choosing terms and conditions, recognize the basic trade-off: more liberal terms and conditions will tend to raise the value of your product to consumers but may reduce the number of units sold.** The trick is to pick the terms and conditions to maximize the value of your intellectual property, not to maximize the protection.

- **Site licenses and other group-pricing schemes are a valuable tool for managing terms and conditions.** They economize on transaction costs for both the buyer and seller.

5 | Recognizing Lock-In

Visionaries tell us that the Internet will soon deliver us into that most glorious form of capitalism, the "friction-free" economy. How ironic, then, is the event that will usher in the next millennium: the dreaded Year 2000 Problem, a testament to the enormous rigidities that plague the information economy.

We agree that the Internet will make shopping easier than ever, but much of the talk about friction is fiction. You don't have to drive to the store to order a new computer, but your choices for the future will still be hemmed in by the selections you made in the past. Like it or not, in the information age, buyers typically must bear costs when they switch from one information system to another. Understanding these costs of switching technologies, or even brands, is fundamental to success in today's economy.

Compare cars and computers. When the time comes to replace the Ford you've been driving for several years, there is no compelling reason to pick another Ford over a GM or a Toyota. Your garage will hold a Chevy just as well as a Ford, it won't take long to learn the controls of a Toyota, and you can haul the same trailer with either vehicle. In short, you can easily transfer your investments in "automotive infrastructure" to another brand of car. In contrast, when the time comes to upgrade the Macintosh computer you've been using for years, you are going to need a mighty good reason to pick a PC or a Unix machine instead of another Mac. You own a bunch of Mac software, you are familiar with how to use the Mac, your Mac printer may have years of good service left in it, and you probably trade files with other Mac users. You are facing significant costs if you decide to switch from one information technology to another.

With the Mac you have made significant *durable investments in complementary assets* that are specific to that brand of machine. These investments have differing economic lifetimes, so there's no easy time to start using a new, incompatible system. As a result, you face *switching costs,* which can effectively lock you into your current system or brand.

When the costs of switching from one brand of technology to another are substantial, users face *lock-in.* Switching costs and lock-in are ubiquitous in information systems, and managing these costs is very tricky for both buyers and sellers. Simple rules, such as "Don't get locked in" or "Evaluate costs on a life-cycle basis," don't help much. In using or selling information systems, fully anticipating future switching costs, both yours and those of your customers, is critical. Lock-in can be a source of enormous headaches, or substantial profits, depending on whether you are the one stuck in the locked room or the one in possession of the key to the door. The way to win in markets with switching costs is neither to avoid lock-in nor to embrace it. You need to think strategically: look ahead and reason back.

> **To understand lock-in, look ahead and reason back.**

This advice probably seems a bit cryptic, but its implications will become clear in this chapter and the next. Here we describe the common patterns that give rise to switching costs so as to help you properly measure switching costs and recognize situations involving lock-in. In the next chapter we'll show you how to use lock-in to your advantage, or at least to neutralize others who try to use it against you.

But before classifying switching costs and analyzing business strategy in the presence of lock-in, let's look at a few examples of the problems it can cause.

EXAMPLES OF LOCK-IN

The best way to understand the phenomenon of lock-in is to examine lock-in in action. The examples here show how large companies (Bell Atlantic) and individuals (with assigned telephone numbers) alike can fall prey to lock-in.

Bell Atlantic

In the mid- to late-1980s, Bell Atlantic invested $3 billion in AT&T's 5ESS digital switches to run its telephone network. These are large, complex devices that sell for millions of dollars each—essentially, specialized mainframe computers linked to transmission and other equipment. In effect, Bell Atlantic selected AT&T over Northern Telecom and Siemens to bring its telephone system into the digital age. No doubt AT&T's switches were impressive at the time, but did Bell Atlantic look ahead to the mid-1990s and take steps to protect itself from the ensuing lock-in?

The problem? The 5ESS switches employ a proprietary operating system controlled by AT&T. So, every time Bell Atlantic wanted to add a new capability, or connect these switches to a new piece of peripheral hardware, Bell Atlantic found itself reliant on AT&T to provide the necessary upgrades for the operating system and to develop the required interfaces. Since it was extremely expensive for Bell Atlantic to replace the AT&T equipment, Bell Atlantic was locked into the AT&T switches.

This left AT&T in the driver's seat. AT&T was in the powerful position of having monopoly control over a wide range of enhancements and upgrades to its switches. For example, when Bell Atlantic wanted its system to be able to recognize toll-free calls to telephone numbers beginning with "888," Bell Atlantic had to negotiate with AT&T, since AT&T had not provided Bell Atlantic with the computer code necessary for Bell Atlantic to develop this capability itself. Dealing from a position of strength, AT&T charged Bell Atlantic $8 million for the software that recognized 888 numbers. Similarly, when Bell Atlantic wanted to offer "voice dialing," so that customers could speak a name rather than dial a telephone number, Bell Atlantic again had to turn to AT&T, which charged $10 million for the software. In both of these cases, Bell Atlantic believed that it could have obtained the software on better terms had it been able to shop around for the necessary improvements.

From AT&T's position, its installed base of 5ESS switches was an extremely valuable asset, expected to generate a nice stream of revenues. According to Bell Atlantic, AT&T's aftermarket software upgrades account for between 30 percent and 40 percent of its switch-related revenues. Annual upgrades to the operating system from Bell Atlantic alone (one of a number of large switch buyers) were around $100 million per year. In addition, AT&T stood to make lucrative sales of peripheral equipment to Bell Atlantic. AT&T had incentives to provide improvements and upgrades to the switches and the ability to charge dearly for them. AT&T also stood to gain, at least in the short run, by using its control over proprietary interfaces to prevent others from offering compatible equipment that might compete with AT&T's own offerings.

Bell Atlantic was none too happy about AT&T's strong position in the aftermarket for upgrades and plug-ins to AT&T 5ESS switches. In fact, in 1995, Bell Atlantic sued AT&T for monopolization.

Why did Bell Atlantic put up with all this? Because Bell Atlantic would bear substantial costs if it tried to replace the AT&T switches with those of another switch supplier. These switches have a useful lifetime of fifteen years or more, and they are costly to remove and reinstall. Furthermore, the switches Bell Atlantic had paid for and used were worth much less on the used market than they were new, in part because any buyer would also have to deal with AT&T for enhancements and upgrades.

This is a fine example of lock-in. Once Bell Atlantic purchased and installed the AT&T switches, it was locked in to AT&T—that is, dependent on AT&T to use the switches effectively. To put this differently, Bell Atlantic would bear significant switching costs in replacing the AT&T gear with another brand of equipment.

Computer Associates

Another nice example of lock-in is illustrated by the plight of companies that have massive databases on large IBM mainframe computers running highly specialized software. These companies are heavily locked into these computers and their operating systems, making the business of supplying the necessary software quite lucrative, especially for software supplied by only a small number of vendors.

A major beneficiary of this particular lock-in to IBM mainframe computers is Computer Associates. Computer Associates is the leading supplier of a variety of systems management software that works with IBM's MVS (Multiple Virtual Storage) and VSE/ESA (Virtual Storage Extended/Enterprise Systems Architecture) operating systems. Computer Associates' products include tape management software, disk management software, job scheduling software, and security software for the VSE operating environment, and tape management software and job scheduling software for the MVS operating environment.

Computer Associates earned $3.5 billion in revenues in its fiscal year ending March 1996, making it the third largest independent software company, behind Microsoft and Oracle. Computer Associates enjoyed revenues of $432,000 per employee, versus Microsoft's $422,000 and Oracle's $180,000.

Lock-in occurs in this market on two separate levels: the system level and the vendor level. Customers are certainly loathe to switch computers or operating systems; they are locked into an IBM system. But they are also wary of switching vendors for their systems management software; they are locked into their software suppliers, too. Since this software is mission critical, the risks in using a new vendor, especially an unproven one, are substantial. Switching costs for customers include the risk of a substantial disruption in operations. And for critical pieces of information technology, the danger of disruption can dwarf out-of-pocket switching costs. The fact that Computer Associates software is known to work allows it to command a hefty premium for its software.

Of course, a customer strongly locked into an IBM VSE or MVS operating system is not as firmly locked into Computer Associates for its systems management software. Much of this software is available from alternative sources. However, in 1995 Computer Associates moved to reduce those choices and gain greater control of these customers by acquiring Legent Corporation, the second largest independent supplier of software for IBM-compatible mainframe computer systems, for $1.8 billion. Recognizing that this acquisition would restrict the choices of these locked-in consumers, the U.S. Department of Justice required

Computer Associates to spin off certain software products as a condition of completing the acquisition of Legent.

In this situation, locked-in customers were partially protected from exploitation by the oversight of the Justice Department's Antitrust Division. You can ill afford to be passive if you seek this protection, however. If a proposed merger or acquisition narrows your choices materially, you can improve your chances of blocking the deal, or extracting concessions from the merging parties, by alerting the Federal Trade Commission (FTC) and the Justice Department of your concerns. These agencies have strong powers to prevent deals that are adverse to the interests of consumers. But beware: to really help yourself, you must be ready to testify to your own vulnerability in open court.

Mass Market Lock-In

Our examples so far have involved huge switching costs, like those to Bell Atlantic of replacing switches worth billions of dollars. Do not be misled: even when switching costs appear low, they can be critical for strategy. A million customers, each of whom has switching costs of $100, are just as valuable, collectively, as a single customer whose switching costs are $100 million. The point is that you must compare any switching costs to revenues on a *per-customer basis* and add up these costs across your entire installed base to value that base. These principles apply equally to customers who are businesses or households.

Compare switching costs to revenue on a per-customer basis.

To illustrate how "small" switching costs can have a profound impact on strategies and market outcomes, one need only follow the current contentious debate in telecommunications regarding "number portability," namely, your ability to keep your local telephone number when (and if) you choose a new local telephone company. The issue: do you have the right to keep your telephone number when you select MCI as your local carrier, or does your local Bell company have the right to hang onto your phone number, forcing you to change numbers if you want to use MCI? AT&T, MCI, and Sprint are pushing for number portability; the local Bell companies are dragging their feet. Everyone recognizes that number portability is critical if local telephone competition is to become a reality. The cost per person of changing phone numbers may not be huge, but when you add up these costs across millions of telephone subscribers, the stakes grow large.

Regulatory obligations are forcing the incumbent local telephone companies to offer number portability as soon as possible. Debate is currently raging over whether these local monopolists are in fact complying with those duties by offering "interim number portability," which typically involves remote call forwarding. Would-be competitive local exchange carriers are pushing hard for incumbent carriers to develop "true" number portability. This is reminiscent of the debate over "equal access" long-distance dialing in the mid-1980s. Back then, MCI and Sprint were handicapped in the long-distance telephone market when customers had to dial extra digits to use their services. The lesson is that small consumer switching costs can constitute large barriers to entry, especially for mass-market products.

The market for on-line services provides another example of how "small" switching costs can have a large market impact. Changing from America Online to another Internet service provider (ISP) requires changing one's e-mail address. In comparison with buying a new mainframe computer, it is cheap to switch e-mail addresses. However, in comparison with the monthly fees for on-line services, the cost of changing e-mail addresses is not negligible. Furthermore, the incumbent Internet service provider may raise these switching costs by refusing to forward mail sent to an old address. For example, e-mail sent to AOL users who have discontinued their service is bounced back to the sender.

One Internet business that has exploited this e-mail address lock-in is Hotmail. Hotmail offers *free* e-mail service via a Web browser that can be used from any Internet service provider. So how does Hotmail make money? Hotmail places ads on the border surrounding the e-mail workspace. Hotmail also asks each new user to fill out a form indicating his or her interests, and the ads are then targeted to each user's special interests. This is an example of the kind of personalized advertising we discussed earlier in the book. Hotmail's 9.5 million subscribers made its Web site the fourteenth most visited site on the Web and caught the attention of both Microsoft and Netscape. Microsoft recently acquired

Hotmail for an estimated $300 million–$400 million: not bad for a company that has yet to turn a profit.

Some professional organizations, such as the Association for Computing Machinery, offer e-mail forwarding as a way to avoid address lock-in. CalTech and other universities offer this service to alumni, which, not incidentally, helps them keep in touch with potential donors.

Address lock-in may be a "small" problem for individual users, but it is a major headache for large organizations. One of the reasons that the recent debates about how to manage Internet domain names have been so heated is the potential lock-in problems. Imagine starting a Web site, building a customer following, and then being told that your Web address was being taken away from you by the central authority, or that your annual fees for using "your" Web address were being raised sharply. Fears such as these have prompted intense interest in the management of the Domain Name System and other aspects of Internet governance.

A final example of why small lock-in matters involves user behavior on the Web. Several user studies have documented that people don't read Web content the way they read paper content. Web readers are very fickle; if you lose their interest, you quickly lose their presence. Web years move seven times as rapidly as ordinary years, but Web attention spans are seven times shorter as well.

Part of the explanation for this behavior is ergonomic—it's just unpleasant reading text on a computer monitor. But part of the explanation is switching costs. When you pick up a magazine or a book and sit in your favorite chair, you have to exert effort, however small, to switch to a different magazine or book. When you are looking at one Web page, other pages are just a mouseclick away.

This means that writing for the Web is different from writing for paper. You have to get your message across quickly and concisely. Requiring readers to change the screen, by either scrolling or clicking, gives them a good excuse to go to a different site. A Web surfer in motion tends to stay in motion—and a Web reader standing still has probably just gone for a snack.

Switching Costs Are Ubiquitous

Switching costs are the norm, not the exception, in the information economy. As you consider your own business, we suspect that you, too, will recognize lock-in and switching costs as factors that you must deal with on a regular basis. Perhaps your customers will become locked into your products and services; certainly you are susceptible to lock-in yourself in your own use of information systems.

You compete at your own peril if you do not recognize lock-in, protect yourself from its adverse effects, and use it to your advantage when possible. In many markets involving the storage, manipulation, or transmission of information, hard-core, tangible lock-in is substantial, and fortunes can be made or lost by anticipating or neglecting its role. If you are a supplier seeking new customers, you have to overcome customer inertia and lock-in to rivals. If you are a locked-in customer, you may find yourself in a weak bargaining position that could have been avoided by negotiating protections for yourself at the outset. Alternatively, you might seek an initial "sweetener" to compensate you for anticipated lock-in, if you can see it coming.

This chapter will help you learn to recognize switching costs and lock-in and to assess their significance. Remember, lock-in is a two-edged coin; you may loathe it as a customer yet embrace it as a supplier. Either way, you must understand switching costs and be able to anticipate and measure them. In the next chapter, we'll see how to craft strategy based on that understanding.

VALUING AN INSTALLED BASE OF CUSTOMERS

To understand lock-in and deal with it effectively, the first step is to recognize what constitutes true switching costs. Switching costs measure the extent of a customer's lock-in to a given supplier. When America Online (AOL) decides how aggressively to seek new customers, and how to price to its existing customers, it must be able to measure customers' switching costs. Put differently, AOL must value what is perhaps its most important asset, namely, its installed base of customers. Like credit-card companies, long-distance telephone companies, and cable-television companies, Internet service providers need to estimate their revenue stream from a new customer to figure out how much to spend to acquire that customer. A similar exercise is necessary when buying customers wholesale, as when banks buy credit-card portfolios or when IBM acquired Lotus. This is harder than you might think.

We've emphasized the customer's switching costs so far, but the supplier also bears some costs when it acquires a new customer. These may be small, such as creating a new entry in a database, or they may be quite large, such as assembling a team of support personnel. Both the customer's and the supplier's costs are important. Adding them up gives the *total switching costs* associated with a single customer; these costs are the key to valuing an installed base.

The total cost of switching = costs the customer bears + costs the new supplier bears.

The total cost associated with Customer C switching from Supplier A to Supplier B is the cost that must be borne collectively by Customer C *and by Supplier B* to place the customer in a position with Supplier B that is comparable to the one that Customer C currently has with Supplier A.

Look at how this concept plays out in the long-distance telephone business. When you switch your long-distance service from AT&T to MCI, the total switching costs include your time and trouble in making the move, plus the marketing and setup costs incurred by MCI. There's not a lot that MCI can do to reduce these costs. If MCI offers you $25 to change carriers, this tactic has no impact on total switching costs: the switching costs borne by you fall by $25, and those borne by MCI rise by $25. What if MCI offers you 100 free minutes of calling as a sweetener? If you value these minutes at 15 cents per minute, or $15 in total, they reduce your switching costs by $15. If the cost to MCI of offering these minutes is 5 cents per minute (for access charges, say), or $5 in total, the costs borne by MCI rise by only $5. The free-minutes offer has reduced total switching costs by $10. Whenever the seller enjoys a nice margin (price minus marginal cost) on its products or services, there is scope for in-kind sweeteners of this sort to lower total switching costs.

You might find it odd to look at extra costs borne not just by the customer but also by the new supplier, but this is essential for a sound analysis of whether it is worthwhile to acquire a new customer. Whether you or MCI spends the time or bears the cost of shifting your long-distance account from AT&T does not alter the fact that the time and money spent is a cost of switching brands. Indeed, very often new suppliers will help subsidize customers who are switching brands; for example, the Apollo computerized reservation system compensated travel agents for payments owed by the travel agent to the rival Sabre system if the agent stopped using Sabre. Nowadays, long-distance telephone companies are offering signing bonuses in the form of free minutes to attract customers from rival carriers.

How much should you spend to attract a new customer? The answer depends on the costs that you and your new customer both bear. Suppose, for example, that you are an ISP trying to build your customer base. Imagine that switching Internet providers involves $50 worth of hassle for the customer, and it costs you $25 to set up a new account, so the total switching costs are $75. You should encourage a customer to switch only if you expect the discounted flow of profit from this customer to be greater than $75. If you anticipate a discounted flow of profit of $100, you can afford to offer the consumer a couple of free months of service (valued at $25 per month) to overcome the $50 switching costs, pay the $25 account setup costs, and still be left with $25 of profit. Alternatively, you could invest $50 in advertising (rather than the free months) to convince the customer that switching to your service from his or her current ISP is worth the hassle. But if you anticipate a present value of only $70 of profit from the new customer, it just isn't worth trying to attract him, since the total switching costs of $75 exceed the benefits of $70.

In many cases, the disruption in service associated with changing suppliers is a major consideration, as we saw in the Computer Associates case. For mission-critical information and communications, these disruption costs can make up the bulk of the switching costs. Worse yet for customers, these costs are potentially subject to strategic manipulation by the vendor. For example, would-be competitors in local telephone service are finding in trials that customers tend to lose telephone service for a period of time when switching service to them from the incumbent local exchange carriers. Needless to say, this disruption is a huge barrier to switching local telephone companies, especially for business customers, and the subject of repeated complaints to regulators.

Measuring customer switching costs is a big piece of valuing an installed base of customers. As a rule of thumb, the profits a supplier can expect to earn from a customer are equal to the total switching costs, as just defined, *plus* the value of other competitive advantages the supplier enjoys by virtue of having a superior product or lower costs than its rivals. Customer perceptions are paramount: a brand premium based on superior reputation or advertising is just as valuable as an equal pre-mium based on truly superior quality. As a general principle, if your rivals have cost and quality similar to yours, so that your market is highly competitive, the profits that you can earn from a customer—on a going-forward, present-value basis—*exactly equal the total switching costs.*

> ***Profit from current customer = total switching costs + quality/cost advantage.***

Life is more complicated if you cannot easily measure these switching costs, es-pecially if customers differ widely in their switching costs, but the same prin-ciple still applies.

To illustrate this principle, consider the value of your patronage to your local telephone company. Under current FCC rules, local phone companies are required to make their facilities available at cost to would-be com-petitors seeking to provide basic telephone service. Under these condi-tions, the local phone company can expect to earn a profit on basic service only if it can command a premium based on its brand name, or if consumers bear switching costs in using other carriers. Take a customer for whom the hassle of switching phone numbers has a monetary cost of $100. Our valuation principle says that the incumbent telephone com-pany can earn precisely $100 in extra profits from this customer, in present-value terms. This might come in the form of a $1 per month premium over the rates charged by competitors (since $1 per month in perpetuity has a present value of roughly $100 at conventional interest rates).

The day the regulators mandate full number portability, and ensure that switching phone companies is easy and involves no disruption in service, consumer switching costs will tumble close to zero—essentially, to the transaction costs of changing carriers. When that day comes, the value of the incumbent phone company's installed base will decline. The prospect of that day arriving reduces the per-customer value of the incumbent carrier's installed base from a perpetuity to a shorter and shorter annuity. You can see why incumbent carriers are resisting the move to full number portability. Likewise, entrants are fighting hard to force the Bell companies to reconfigure their operational support sys-tems to enable customers to switch smoothly to their services. Once full number portability is in place, the Bell companies will lose one (of several) advantages that they currently enjoy based on their incumbency position in local telephone markets. Anticipating the arrival of competition, local companies are seeking to enter long-distance markets, to become ISPs, and generally to bolster their customer relationships and customer loyalty to withstand the eventual reduction in customer switching costs.

This same valuation principle applies when switching costs are based on the ownership of durable capital equipment or long-term contractual commitments. For example, Ticketmaster enters into multi-year contracts to provide stadiums and other venues with ticketing services. A would-be competitor of Ticketmaster (there are a few, encouraged by Pearl Jam's very public dispute with Ticketmaster) must either wait for these contracts to expire (by which time the contract-based switching costs will be absent) or buy the venue out of its contract. If the venue purchases a ticketing system dedicated to Ticketmaster, trains its employees to use the Ticketmaster system, or publicizes that its customers can obtain tickets at Ticketmaster outlets, the switching costs will outlive the contract, however. As we'll see, one of the distinctive features of information-based lock-in is that it tends to be so durable: equipment wears out, reducing switching costs, but specialized databases live on and grow, enhancing lock-in over time.

Our valuation principle can be used for several purposes:

- First, by anticipating the value of tomorrow's installed base of customers, you can determine how much to invest today—in the form of price discounting, advertising, or R&D, for example—to attract more customers and build that installed base.

- Second, you can use these methods to evaluate a target company whose installed-base of customers constitutes a major asset. Rather than figure out the revenue and cost streams associated with the target company's customers, you may be able to take a shortcut and calculate these customers' switching costs.

- Third, valuation information will help inform decisions affecting your customers' switching costs—for example, your product design and compatibility decisions.

CLASSIFICATION OF LOCK-IN

So far we've said the following about lock-in:

- Customer lock-in is the norm in the information economy, because information is stored, manipulated, and communicated using a "system" consisting of multiple pieces of hardware and software and because specialized training is required to use specific systems.

- Switching costs must be evaluated relative to revenues on a per-customer basis. Even "small" switching costs can be critical in mass markets such as the telephone industry or consumer electronics.

- Total switching costs include those borne by the consumer to switch suppliers and those borne by the new supplier to serve the new consumer.

- As a rule of thumb, the present discounted value to a supplier of a locked-in customer is equal to that customer's total switching costs, plus the value of all other advantages enjoyed by the incumbent supplier based on lower costs or superior product quality, real or perceived.

We are now ready to look more closely at the underlying *sources* of switching costs, with an eye to their strategic implications. There are a handful of types of switching costs that arise in one industry after another. Table 5.1 summarizes our classification of lock-in. Knowing these patterns will help you identify and anticipate lock-in, estimate your switching costs or those of your customers, and plan accordingly. We will examine each entry of the table in detail.

Contractual Commitments

Our first category of lock-in is the most explicit: a contractual commitment to buy from a specific supplier. Common sense dictates that you should not commit yourself to a single supplier unless the price is specified. Nonetheless, many contracts give the seller the discretion to make annual adjustments in rates, subject to certain limits, or even to

Table 5.1. Types of Lock-In and Associated Switching Costs

Type of Lock-In	Switching Costs
Contractual commitments	Compensatory or liquidated damages
Durable purchases	Replacement of equipment; tends to decline as the durable ages
Brand-specific training	Learning a new system, both direct costs and lost productivity; tends to rise over time
Information and databases	Converting data to new format; tends to rise over time as collection grows
Specialized suppliers	Funding of new supplier; may rise over time if capabilities are hard to find/maintain
Search costs	Combined buyer and seller search costs; includes learning about quality of alternatives
Loyalty programs	Any lost benefits from incumbent supplier, plus possible need to rebuild cumulative use

charge so-called "reasonable" rates. Beware of these vague protections when you are buying. Even with ironclad price protection, there is inevitably some room for the vendor to control nonprice variables, such as the quality of service provided. Buyers are well advised to consider such "noncontractible" aspects of the product or service in advance.

> **Beware of contracts that guarantee price but not quality.**

Indeed, price commitments sought by customers from vendors can be positively harmful if they merely induce the vendor to exploit lock-in by reducing quality and other nonprice dimensions of service.

The extent of lock-in depends on the nature of the contract. One contractual form, a *requirements contract,* commits the buyer to purchase all of its requirements exclusively from a specific seller for an extended period of time. In another form, a *minimum order-size commitment,* the buyer promises to make a certain quantity of purchases, potentially leaving open the option of turning elsewhere for additional supplies as needed if the original vendor is not performing well.

With explicit contractual commitments, the damages for breach of the contract can loom large and may constitute the bulk of the switching costs. Of course, a new supplier may be willing to buy you out of your current contract (probably to lock you in anew). Alternatively, you can compensate your existing supplier under your contract and still come out ahead if your new supplier offers a sufficient discount. If the liquidated damages in your existing contract are large enough, you really will be locked in. Also, be careful about *evergreen contracts,* which automatically renew sixty or ninety days before the initial ending date.

When negotiating such contracts, think beyond the terms, conditions, and duration of the contract itself. Anticipate your switching costs and options *after* the contract terminates. For example, if you purchase a specialized piece of equipment with a ten-year lifetime, and if you arrange for a three-year service contract at the time of purchase, consider what your service options will be for the remaining seven years after the initial contract expires. If you enter into a five-year contract with a vendor to manage your customer databases, think carefully about the switching costs you will face in five years time if you seek to change vendors. Design the contract to minimize those costs, perhaps by reserving for yourself nonexclusive rights to some of the computer code developed to manage or exploit your data.

Durable Purchases

In looking at Bell Atlantic and Computer Associates, we examined examples of lock-in involving the purchase of expensive, durable equipment (telephone switches and mainframe computers and operating systems, respectively) at one point in time, followed by purchases of complementary products at a later time (transmission equipment or voice messaging equipment, and systems management software, respectively). This is one of the most common and important patterns of lock-in: after the initial purchase is made, the customer must buy follow-on products that work with the durable equipment. As a result, many suppliers of durable equipment—be it medical equipment sold by Siemens to hospitals, large copiers sold by Xerox to corporations, or Zip drives sold by Iomega to individuals and businesses—derive the bulk of their profits, if not their revenues, from "aftermarket" sales.

In these situations, the economic lifetime of the durable equipment is critical. If the equipment quickly depreciates in economic value, perhaps because of rapid technological progress, then expenditures on that equipment do not lock customers in for very long, or very strongly. If there is a market for used equipment, so the customer can recover some of the initial outlay for the equipment upon replacing it, switching costs are again reduced. Indeed, rival vendors seeking to make their own new-equipment sales often reduce customers' switching costs by accepting used equipment for trade-in at above-market prices. Active used-equipment markets facilitate this tactic.

With durable hardware, switching costs tend to fall over time as the hardware depreciates. Thus, lock-in tends to be self-limiting. The switching costs, which here are the cost of replacing the existing hardware with equally capable hardware (or the cost of replacing the existing hardware with superior, state-of-the-art hardware, less the extra benefits of that hardware) fall as the user's machine ages. Rapid technological advance reduces hardware lock-in.

With durable equipment, switching costs fall over time because of depreciation.

There is an exception to the principle that hardware lock-in declines with time: when a customer has multiple pieces of similar equipment and enjoys efficiencies from having all or most of its equipment come from the same vendor. In this case, even when one machine is fully depreciated, the customer still bears large switching costs because of the other complementary equipment. The customer is least attached to the incumbent supplier when most of its equipment is nearing the end of its useful lifetime. The supplier is most vulnerable to being replaced at just such a point of *minimal* lock-in, just as the weakest link governs the strength of a chain. Recognizing this, the supplier may aim for its customers to have staggered equipment vintages or may offer inducements to replace older equipment before the end of its lifetime to maximize the minimal lock-in.

One effective way for customers to reduce or eliminate switching costs based on durable equipment is to rent or lease the equipment rather than buying it. By pushing more transactions into the "foremarket" and out of the "aftermarket," the buyer takes advantage of the flexibility to be enjoyed prior to becoming locked-in. For example, if you contract for complements such as repair parts and maintenance service when you initially rent or lease a copier, you need not worry that service prices will rise during the lifetime of the lease. Extended warranties serve the same function. In contrast, if you buy the copier, even with an initial service contract, you may still be subject to a steep price increase to renew when the original service contract expires.

Another key issue with this type of lock-in is the extent of choice available to the locked-in consumer: *technology lock-in is not the same as vendor lock-in.* Customer lock-in is far less important if there remain many alternative suppliers of the complementary products purchased later. Bell Atlantic is not reliant on AT&T if there are alternative suppliers of transmission equipment (or other software and hardware) that attaches to the AT&T switch. In other words, the aftermarket choices are an important part of understanding the entire pattern of equipment purchase and lock-in, an observation that will be important in our discussion of interfaces and compatibility in Chapter 7.

The fact is, most durable equipment requires follow-on purchases, making this pattern of lock-in extremely common. Obviously, a great deal of equipment is durable. Beyond that, however, there are all manner of complementary products that customers need in the future. Upgrades and product improvements are common, both for durable equipment and for other durable investments including computer software. Very often only the original vendor offers these upgrades, perhaps owing to patent or copyright protection that the vendor enjoys. Aftermarket service and spare parts are a necessity for most equipment, and they may also be supplied exclusively or largely by the equipment manufacturer. Notable examples include computer hardware, high-speed printers and copiers, telecommunications equipment, aircraft, weapons systems, and medical equipment. In fact, aftermarket policies constitute a key strategic choice for manufacturers of high-tech, durable equipment.

The limits of these strategies are now being tested in the courts. Indeed, a whole cottage industry has sprung up in which customers are suing manufacturers under the antitrust laws via class actions, alleging that the manufacturers have impeded their ability to obtain aftermarket service from independent service organizations (ISOs). These ISOs also are suing manufacturers directly, emboldened by a key 1992 Supreme Court decision (*Image Technical Services v. Eastman Kodak*) ruling that manufacturers may be found to have monopoly power in their own brand-specific aftermarkets and are not immune from antitrust challenges by competition with other equipment manufacturers.

Brand-Specific Training

A pattern of lock-in similar to that associated with the purchase of durable products results when personnel are trained to use them. This training is often brand-specific, in that considerable additional time and effort would be required to learn to work with a new brand of product with equal proficiency. In this case, the complementary products are the durable product itself and the training that is specific to it. General training (as opposed to brand-specific training) does not give rise to lock-in. As we will discuss in Chapter 8 in regard to strategic standard setting, a key question for buyers and sellers is whether training can be effectively transferred to other brands of software, perhaps through the use of standardized user interfaces or protocols.

With brand-specific training, switching costs tend to *rise* with time, as personnel become more and more familiar with the existing system. The opposite is true for durable hardware, which becomes less costly to replace as it ages and as new models with superior performance are introduced.

The obvious example for many of us is computer software. We all know how time consuming it can be to learn to use a new piece of software, much less to become adept at it. And the training

> **With brand-specific training, switching costs rise over time.**

costs associated with replicating one's proficiency with a familiar piece of software tend to grow the more experience one has with the familiar program. Moreover, the software vendor can maintain high switching costs by introducing a series of upgrades that offer enhanced capabilities in return for the investment of additional time learning the new features.

Of course, a new brand can emerge that is easy to learn, thus reducing switching costs. Indeed, one strategy for breaking into a market with significant brand-specific customer training is to imitate existing brands or otherwise develop a product that is easy to learn. Borland tried this with Quattro Pro, aimed at Lotus 1-2-3 users, and Microsoft Word has built-in, specially designed help for (former!) WordPerfect users.

With brand-specific training, lock-in can easily outlive an individual piece of equipment. This is most evident when customers desire to standardize all of their equipment by using a single vendor. For example, commercial airlines now place great value on "fleet commonality"— that is, on having most if not all of the aircraft in their fleet come from a single airframe manufacturer, and even with a similar cockpit configuration. Airlines have found that a uniform fleet can result in substantial savings on maintenance and training costs and can improve flight safety. This is one of the reasons why American, Delta, and Continental recently agreed to buy all of their new aircraft from Boeing over the next twenty years. Indeed, the demand for fleet commonality hastened the demise of McDonnell-Douglas: lacking a full family of aircraft, and lacking loyal customers with an all-Douglas fleet, McDonnell-Douglas threw in the towel in 1996, concluding that it could no longer survive in the commercial aircraft industry, and agreed to be acquired by Boeing.

Information and Databases

In our third type of switching cost, the complementary products giving rise to lock-in are the hardware and software used to store and manage information, on the one hand, and the information or database itself, on the other. Users with massive information encoded in a specialized format are vulnerable if and when they require new hardware or improved software to work with the data. In these situations, a key question is whether the information can easily be ported over to another system. You must ask yourself what are the costs of transferring the information and what aspects of the information would be lost in a transfer.

Many of the examples in this book fit into this category. For example, consumers purchase a CD player and then build up a library of CDs. When the CD player starts skipping (a seemingly inevitable event), or when new and better audio technologies appear on the scene, the consumer is locked into the CD format. In this case, the information cannot be transferred, making it important for anyone selling equipment that reads new formats, such as DVD, to make that equipment backward-compatible—that is, capable of reading CDs as well. Videotape players, laser disks, DVDs, and phonographs in an earlier day all conform to this pattern of hardware/software switching costs.

Computer software programs and data files are another critical category of format-specific information. In these cases, like the library of CDs, the library of information grows over time, causing lock-in to grow stronger with time. Any system in which information is collected over time in special formats raises these issues. Tax preparation software that incorporates tax information from prior years, accountant software that relies on historical data, and graphics software that uses designs developed over time are all examples of this type of lock-in. For years, Ashton-Tate's dBase language was enormously valuable because so many users had written programs in the dBase language. It's typically far easier to transfer raw data from one format to another than to port over code. In all of these cases, vendors' strategies revolve around methods designed to raise or lower consumers' switching costs and capitalize on the crucial distinction between proprietary and standardized formats.

Keep control of information and databases by using standardized formats and interfaces.

With information and databases, switching costs tend to rise with time as more and more information comes to reside in the historical database. One way for users to limit these switching costs is to insist on employing standardized formats and interfaces, if possible, or to insist that the vendor publish its interface specifications so as to permit competition from fully or largely compatible products. We discuss such "open" interfaces further in Chapter 8.

Specialized Suppliers

Another important pattern arises when buyers purchase specialized equipment gradually over time. As a buyer, remember that your choices today will dictate your needs tomorrow. By picking a single supplier of that equipment, you will become dependent on that source in the future. Your initial purchases of the equipment are complementary to later purchases because of the advantages of sticking with a single brand for all of your purchases.

Worse yet from the customer's point of view, comparable alternative suppliers may no longer exist after the initial bid is awarded to a single winner. Remember, with specialized equipment, the switching costs depend on the ability of new suppliers to offer comparable equipment when needed in the future. If the durable equipment or software is highly specialized, it will be relatively difficult to find alternative suppliers in the future, giving the incumbent vendor the advantage of substantial lock-in for the next round of purchases.

More and more companies in the information economy are facing lock-in to specialized suppliers. Yet this pattern is hardly unique to information industries. In fact, a large sector of our economy has been dealing with this problem for decades at least: the defense sector. The Department of Defense takes flack now and again for its procurement practices, but we believe that today's information sector can learn much from the Pentagon's methods of dealing with specialized suppliers, especially in the 1990s, during which time the defense contractor base has been sharply downsized.

Very often the Pentagon finds that the losers in the bidding to produce a complex weapons system cannot maintain the necessary specialized capabilities without ongoing business. Furthermore, the winner surely gains from its experience and comes to know the customer's needs better as part of fulfilling its contract. This problem plagues all buyers of state-of-the-art technology: now that NASA has picked Lockheed Martin's "Venturestar" design for its next-generation, single-stage-to-orbit space shuttle, it won't be easy for NASA to turn to others in the future should Lockheed's performance prove lacking. To a lesser extent, relationships between advertising firms, accounting firms, and law firms and their corporate clients also exhibit lock-in to specialized suppliers.

The upshot is that large buyers with specialized needs commonly find their options limited after they initially pick a supplier to serve them. The Pentagon often handles this by carefully structuring the competition for a single, huge, long-term procurement contract. For example, in 1996 the Pentagon "down-selected" from three to two the number of possible suppliers for the Joint Strike Fighter, funding additional development by Boeing and Lockheed Martin but dropping McDonnell Douglas. Over the next five years, Lockheed Martin and Boeing will develop prototypes for this new combat aircraft, with funding of some $2.2 billion by the Department of Defense. Then, around 2002, the Pentagon will pick a single supplier after a fly-off between the competing prototypes. The winner stands to earn revenues of some $200 billion over the lifetime of the Joint Strike Fighter program.

If the Pentagon could fully anticipate its needs and obtain contractual commitments from the winner as part of the process of selecting the ultimate winner, lock-in would not be an issue. But the world is not so simple. Even if the Pentagon obtains the option to buy a large number of planes at a specified cost, there will inevitably be issues down the line—such as the cost of making improvements to the plane in 2006 that were not envisioned in 2002—in which the winner will have some bargaining leverage by virtue of the Pentagon's lock-in. True, the Pentagon is a powerful buyer, with strong auditing rights to monitor costs and limit payments, and the contractor has a strong incentive not to be seen as exploiting its position as the sole supplier so as not to lose future competitions. Nevertheless, a significant degree of lock-in is inevitable.

We discuss procurement strategies below, but note here two important ones from the Pentagon's perspective: (1) get a variety of commitments and options as part of selecting the winner for a big contract and/or (2) keep alive an alternative source of supply, a strategy commonly known as *dual sourcing*. For example, in 1997 the Air Force decided to fund development of new low-cost rockets known as Evolved Expendable Launch Vehicles by both Lockheed Martin and Boeing rather than choosing just one of the companies. The Pentagon realized that two companies could be supported in part because of the growing commercial demand for rockets. Even when true dual sourcing is not possible because of specialized needs and large fixed costs, a large buyer can make efforts to nurture capabilities at more than one supplier to spur future rivalry. The Pentagon does this by providing its contractors with funds to maintain their capabilities to develop new designs and to bid on the next major contract.

Many high-tech firms are familiar with dual sourcing from the now-famous story of IBM and Intel. IBM attempted to keep its options open via dual sourcing when it selected a supplier of the microprocessors for its personal computers back in the early 1980s. In choosing Intel, IBM insisted on having a second source as an alternative to Intel. This created an opening for Advanced Micro Designs (AMD). To us, the Intel story illustrates the limitations of dual sourcing from the buyer's (IBM's) point of view: disagreements between Intel and AMD over the scope and duration of AMD's rights under its dual-sourcing agreement led to protracted litigation between Intel and AMD, and Intel has captured a commanding share of the market during the 1990s. The lesson: dual sourcing is most likely to be successful in the long run with two strong sources rather than one strong and one weak source. In rapidly moving markets, the buyer is best protected if each source has the independent ability to develop and improve its own technology over time.

Dual sourcing is clearly in the interest of purchasers who want to keep their options open. Less obvious is the fact that dual sourcing can also be in the interest of suppliers. If you are trying to get your technology established, the comfort of two or more sources can help convince potential customers to put their trust in you. We'll discuss this tactic further in Chapter 8 when we examine the logic of open systems and standards.

> *Dual sourcing is usually in the interest of buyers and sometimes in the interest of sellers.*

Search Costs

Our next category includes switching costs that are more mundane, but not to be ignored, especially in mass markets: the search costs incurred by buyers and sellers to find each other and establish a business relationship. These costs may seem small, but ask yourself how often you shop around for a new travel agent, insurance agent, or bank. Do you really know you are getting the best deal possible? Will your search behavior or loyalty change as more vendors become available on-line?

As we stressed above in defining switching costs, what matters in evaluating the extent of lock-in caused by search costs are the "two-sided" search costs, as borne by both customers and would-be suppliers. Search costs borne by consumers when switching brands include the psychological costs of changing ingrained habits, the time and effort involved in identifying a new supplier, and the risks associated with picking an unknown supplier. Search costs borne by would-be suppliers in reaching and acquiring new customers include promotional costs, the costs of actually closing the deal, the cost of setting up a new account, and the risks involved in dealing with an unknown customer, such as credit risk.

The credit card industry displays many of these search costs: customers tend not to move their credit card balances from one bank to another, and card-issuing banks spend considerable amounts on direct mail and other promotional activities in search of new customers. Likewise, banks find it costly to attract new accounts because of the danger of adverse selection—that is, ending up with customers who will ultimately default on their balances or, oddly enough, customers who will *not* incur finance charges at all and thus who are less profitable to the bank. Banks recoup these expenses in the form of high interest rates on consumer credit. Indeed, a bank portfolio with $100 million in credit card receivables would typically be worth around $120 million when sold to another issuer or when securitized. This is one nice example in which the market explicitly values a bank's installed base of "loyal" credit card customers.

Search costs depend on the time and expense involved in locating an attractive new supplier and the costs incurred by vendors in locating customers. If you are a customer who tends to be loyal, switching vendors only rarely, this can work to your advantage: if you can communicate this to potential suppliers, they will value your account all the more if your "churn" rate is likely to be low.

In the information economy, various search costs are likely to be reduced. This claim of the proponents of the "friction-free economy" is certainly correct. Distribution on the Internet is going to be far cheaper than it has ever been in the past, both for information products and for traditional items. Based on our principles for valuing an installed base of customers, reductions in search costs can represent a grave threat to the value of established mass-market companies lacking truly superior products. Advances in distribution will have an especially important effect on consumers who are currently the most costly to reach.

Even if search costs fall, however, there will always be some degree of pure consumer inertia and loyalty to incumbent vendors. This inertia and loyalty are due in part to our human limitations: no matter how inexpensive it becomes for suppliers to send messages to prospective customers, it will remain costly for customers (even with the help of their computer agents) to review and evaluate these proposals. So, even if banks can broadcast messages to prospective customers via the Internet, saving on direct mail costs, consumers will still need to take the time to sort through the proposals and run the risk of rejection, or loss of privacy, if they apply for a new credit card.

Loyalty Programs

Our next category of lock-in might be called "artificial lock-in" because it is entirely a construct of firms' strategies. We are referring to the increasingly popular programs in which customers are rewarded for their repeat purchases. These loyalty programs involve explicit inducements to customers to buy largely or exclusively from a single vendor.

The most popular and well-known of these are the airlines' frequent flier programs. Recently, hotels have followed suit with frequent guest programs. Even local retailers use this tactic, giving one unit for free after ten purchases. For example, our local film store will develop one roll of film for free after you have paid for ten rolls. The nearby Mexican restaurant does the same with burritos, if you remember to bring along your card and have it punched.

Loyalty programs create switching costs in two ways. First, you may forfeit certain credits if you stop buying from your regular supplier. If you have 15,000 miles in your airline account, and it takes 25,000 miles to get a free ticket, the 15,000 miles will be lost if you fail to fly another 10,000 miles before they expire. These switching costs can be minimized by changing carriers after cashing in the bulk of your credits. Second, and more important, are benefits based on cumulative usage, such as double miles or preferential service for members who fly more than 50,000 miles a year. These benefits become part of the total switching costs: either the customer loses them (a customer switching cost) or the new carrier matches them (a supplier switching cost). As on-line commerce explodes, more and more companies will adopt loyalty programs giving preferential treatment to customers based on their historical purchases precisely to create such switching costs.

Loyalty programs will become far easier to administer as companies keep more and more information about their customers' purchasing patterns, as we saw in the discussion of personalized pricing in Chapter 2. Already, many retailers collect detailed information on individual customers' buying patterns; with these databases at their disposal, these suppliers are well placed to target their promotional efforts based on customers' historical buying patterns or to offer discounts based on cumulative purchases. We predict an enormous informational tug-of-war: companies will increasingly use customer-specific information both to identify and contact attractive new prospects and to implement loyalty programs to retain existing customers.

In the information economy, the traditional sources of friction such as search costs and distribution costs will be eroded. But the same computational power that reduces these frictions allows for the creation of new "synthetic frictions" such as loyalty programs. Frictions don't disappear—they just mutate into new forms.

The variations on these discount programs are virtually endless. You can offer your customers a discount for buying exclusively from you or for committing to a certain minimum order size. You can offer discounts for customers who buy more than they did last year. You can utilize volume discounts to encourage customers to keep buying from you rather than sampling other suppliers. Or, to attract new customers, you can offer introductory discounts as a way of helping defray their costs of switching to you from a rival. Perhaps the ultimate weapon here is to base the offer you make to a prospective new customer on information about that customer's status in your rival's loyalty program.

Loyalty programs will proliferate.

We anticipate that more and more businesses will use loyalty programs as customer information becomes more detailed and more widely available. In addition, complementary suppliers will coordinate their programs, much as hotels and airlines now cooperate in their repeat-buyer programs. With on-line trading, the possibilities will explode. And keeping track of historical sales of different products will be a lot easier than licking Green Stamps or having your card punched every time you buy a burrito.

With loyalty-inducing programs, customers can with relative ease calculate the costs they bear when switching vendors, both in terms of lost awards and of reduced marginal returns to additional business. Some vendors will buy credits from their competitors, much like competitive upgrades in the software industry. For example, an airline will often offer "gold status" to someone who holds gold status on a competing airline in hopes of inducing them to switch carriers.

The on-line book store Amazon.com has a very nice twist on a loyalty program. In the "Associates Program," anyone who recommends a book on his or her Web site can add a link to Amazon that can be used by those who wish to purchase the book through Amazon. In exchange, the site that created the link to Amazon gets a "referral fee" of $5\frac{1}{8}$ percent of the purchase price of the book. As of March 1998, there were more than 35,000 Amazon associates.

This base of associates gives Amazon a potent weapon in its battle with Barnes & Noble. Barnes & Noble has struck back with its Affiliates Program, which offers on-line bookstores order processing, payment, and shipping services and up to 7 percent of the revenue from book sales. Amazon responded with a special deal for the top 500 Web sites, giving them a bonus 50 percent larger than the standard payment.

We think Amazon could make an even better response: they should base the royalty rate on *cumulative* referrals, giving a payoff only after the consumer passes certain milestones. If Amazon structures the rates correctly, their associates will want to stick with only one on-line book provider, who will most likely be Amazon. Just as it is costly to switch to another frequent flyer program, it will be costly for associates to switch to another on-line book service.

SUPPLIERS AND PARTNERS FACE LOCK-IN, TOO

We've spoken so far as if buyers are uniquely susceptible to switching costs. Not so. Although we will continue to focus on buyers' switching costs, suppliers are hardly immune to lock-in. The fact is, anyone who makes investments that are specific to a particular supplier, customer, or partner is subject to lock-in for the economic lifetime of those investments. The key point is that the investments will have to be written down if the customer or partner walks, balks, or simply fails.

In fact, it is not uncommon for suppliers and customers to be locked in to each other at the same time. Such bilateral, or two-sided, lock-in can lead to a certain balance of terror, not to mention some high-stakes negotiations. The classic case was that of a railroad that built a spur line to serve an individual customer, such as a coal mine or a coal-fired power plant. Once the line was built, it had little or no value apart from serving the one customer, so the railroad was locked into that customer. At the same time, the customer would find it very expensive to finance a new spur line, so the customer was locked into the railroad, leading to what economists call a bilateral monopoly. The same relationship exists in the information economy when a software vendor writes a specialized piece of software for an individual client.

Nor is lock-in restricted to customers and suppliers; partners are susceptible as well. For example, Pratt & Whitney, as the manufacturer of certain aircraft engines designed specifically for Douglas aircraft, was long locked into McDonnell Douglas, even though it had no intention of selling the engines directly to McDonnell Douglas.

We see seller lock-in, bilateral lock-in, and partner lock-in frequently in information industries. Software houses that initially specialized in writing software for Apple computers learned all too soon that they needed to retool and thus bear very real switching costs: they had to become adept at writing programs to run on DOS or Windows. Likewise for companies specializing in writing games for Sony's PlayStation or the Nintendo 64 platform.

The same economic principles that give rise to buyer lock-in also describe seller lock-in and partner lock-in. Even when you're not the buyer, you need to be alert when making investments that will leave you in a weak bargaining position in the future. If you're a supplier, you can protect your downside by getting your customer(s) to commit to buying enough from you to cover most, if not all, of your costs. One nice way to do this is to have a large customer defray some or all of the costs of designing a product tailored to that customer, while reserving the rights to make distinct versions of the product for other customers. If you're a partner, think like a customer: get commitments from your partner on rollout dates, product specs, and prices. There's no point in developing software for a machine that is late to market or so expensive that few end users buy one.

THE LOCK-IN CYCLE

Lock-in is inherently a dynamic concept, growing out of investments made, and needs realized, at different points in time. Switching costs can grow or shrink with time, but they do not stand still.

We have developed a diagram to help you think dynamically about lock-in. The diagram applies to all of the flavors of lock-in we have just discussed. We call this the lock-in cycle, as shown in Figure 5.1.

The easiest place to hop onto the lock-in cycle is at the *brand selection point*—that is, when the customer chooses a new brand. Brand choice could mean purchasing a new multimillion dollar switch, buying a videodisk player, purchasing a new software program, or signing up for a new frequent-flier program. The first time a specific customer picks a brand, that customer will have no preference for any one brand based

Figure 5.1. *The Lock-In Cycle*

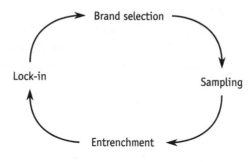

on lock-in. You are not born "locked in"; you only get locked in by virtue of choices you make. The next time around the cycle, the playing field will not be so level, however.

Brand selection is followed by the *sampling phase,* during which the customer actively uses the new brand and takes advantage of whatever inducements were made to give it a try. One of the dangers of offering powerful sweeteners to attract new customers is that they will take the free sample but never turn into revenue-paying customers. Some book clubs take this risk in offering eight books for a dollar; others require new members to buy a minimum number of books at regular prices. As we discussed in Chapter 2 on pricing, extending introductory offers to new customers is especially tempting for information providers because of the low marginal cost of information. This is all the more so with a CD that costs less than a dollar to produce, in comparison with printed material that could cost five dollars or more to produce.

Customers who do more than sample move into the *entrenchment phase.* This is when the consumer really gets used to the new brand, develops a preference for that brand over others, and perhaps becomes locked in to that brand by making complementary investments. Usually, the supplier tries to drag out this phase and delay active consideration of other brands, hoping that the customers' switching costs will go up. The entrenchment phase culminates in *lock-in* when the switching costs become prohibitively expensive.

We return to the brand selection point when the customer either switches brands or actively considers alternative brands without selecting them. Of course, circumstances will have changed in comparison with their last time around the cycle. Certainly the customer's switching costs are higher than the first time around. For specialized products, as in our Pentagon examples, some alternative suppliers may have dropped out in the interim or lost capabilities. On the other hand, new technologies can emerge.

The most basic principle in understanding and dealing with lock-in is to anticipate the entire cycle from the beginning. In fact, you need to go beyond any one trip around the circle and anticipate multiple cycles into the future in forming your strategy from the outset. Valuing your installed base is part of looking ahead: by figuring out how much customers will be worth to you in the future (next time around the cycle), you can decide how much to invest in them now (by inducing them to take the next step and enter the sample phase, for example). This is especially true if switching costs are rising over time (as with information storage and brand-specific training) rather than falling over time (as with durable equipment that depreciates and will be replaced by new and superior models).

The next chapter looks more closely at each point in this cycle, both from the perspective of buyers and suppliers, drawing out lessons and suggesting winning strategies.

LESSONS

- **Switching costs are the norm in information industries.** They can be huge—as when Bell Atlantic invested billions of dollars in telephone switches with a proprietary AT&T operating system—or small—as when consumers must obtain credit approval to get a new credit card. Either way, fortunes can be made or lost based on lock-in and switching costs. You just cannot compete effectively in the information economy unless you know how to identify, measure, and understand switching costs and map strategy accordingly.

- **As a customer, failure to understand switching costs will leave you vulnerable to opportunistic behavior by your suppliers.** Even if you cannot avoid some lock-in, you may miss out on the up-front sweetener that would help the bitter lock-in pill go down better.

- **As a supplier, switching costs are the key to valuing your installed base.** You will be unlikely to successfully build an installed base of customers—one of the most potent assets in the information economy—unless you can overcome the initial costs of switching customers from rival firms. To help defray these costs, you must anticipate customers' lock-in cycle, including the costs your would-be customers will incur if they ever leave *you*.

- **Fortunately, lock-in arises in one industry after another according to certain identifiable patterns.** All of these patterns conform to the lock-in cycle, from brand selection point, through the sampling and entrenchment phases, and back to the next brand selection point. To map strategy for one part of the lock-in cycle, you must understand and anticipate the entire cycle.

- **The essence of lock-in is that your choices in the future will be limited by your investments today. These linkages differ from one technology to another, but are predictable.** We have identified seven primary economic patterns leading to lock-in: contractual commitments, durable equipment and aftermarkets, brand-specific training, information and databases, specialized suppliers, search costs, and loyalty programs. By taking stock of your own expenditures over time in these areas, and those of your customers (and suppliers), you can systematically identify how lock-in affects your business.

In the next chapter, we build on these principles to help you shape your strategies to make lock-in work for you, not against you.

6 | Managing Lock-In

The great fortunes of the information age lie in the hands of companies that have successfully established proprietary architectures that are used by a large installed base of locked-in customers. And many of the biggest headaches of the information age are visited upon companies that are locked into information systems that are inferior, orphaned, or monopolistically supplied.

In the last chapter we saw how to identify, quantify, and classify the basic sources of switching costs and lock-in. Armed with an improved understanding of switching costs, we are now poised to explore strategies for managing lock-in.

The first portion of this chapter is directed at *buyers* of information technology, which includes virtually everyone in today's economy. We all experience some degree of lock-in, yet we all make mistakes dealing with it. To help prevent those mistakes, we provide you with a catalog of strategies to minimize lock-in and avoid monopoly exploitation. We'll see that you can even make your *own* switching costs work for you, if you get the timing right.

The remainder of the chapter delves more deeply into competitive strategies for companies that sell their products and services in markets where customers face significant switching costs. As a vendor, you might think that your customers' switching costs are their problem, not yours. Not so. If you're trying to break into the market with a new technology, you can ill afford to ignore the costs that your target customers must bear to switch to your products. By the same token, if you are an established player, the extent of the threat you face from upstarts is driven in large part by your customers' total costs of switching from you to your competitors. Understanding and valuing customer lock-in is a key component to competitive strategy in the network economy.

LOCK-IN STRATEGY FOR BUYERS

Every user of information technology faces switching costs. Before you can craft a strategy for dealing with your own switching costs, you need to know how to identify and measure them. We covered that ground in the previous chapter.

Suppose you are about to select a brand of software to build a mission-critical database. A major consideration in this decision should be how difficult it may be to convert your data to other formats in a few years. You would also be well advised to learn whether you will be dependent on a single vendor to make improvements to the database in the future. Properly measuring these switching costs before lock-in occurs could be worth millions of dollars to your organization down the road.

Once you recognize these future switching costs, what can you do about them? Basic strategy for buyers of information technology who are anticipating lock-in consists of two key elements:

- Bargain hard at the outset of the lock-in cycle for a sweetener or some form of long-term protection before you become locked in.

- Take steps to minimize your switching costs throughout the lock-in cycle.

We are not advocating using either of these tactics exclusively; they should be employed in concert. Let us examine them more closely.

Bargaining before You Become Locked In

As a buyer negotiating for the purchase of a new information system, the best time to bargain for all manner of goodies is *before* you get locked in.

Some sweeteners put money in your pocket right away: initial discounts on hardware, an extended warranty rather than a service contract, or support in switching from your previous information system. But don't think only in terms of today's savings. Think ahead to the entire lock-in cycle as you negotiate, and be creative in what you seek: service and support guarantees, free upgrades for some period of time, or most-favored customer treatment. Whatever concessions you seek, your bargaining position will be weaker once you make sunk, supplier-specific investments. An excellent and current example of a savvy buyer exerting his or her influence early in the lock-in cycle can be found in TCI's choice of suppliers of operating systems for digital set-top boxes for its cable subscribers. As the *Wall Street Journal* reported, "For eight months, the cable-television industry, led by Tele-Communications Inc., has approached negotiations with Microsoft Corp. for the next generation of television set-top boxes as if it were about to mate with a black widow spider."[1] Fearful of becoming locked-in to Microsoft, or anyone else, TCI has carefully kept its options open. While ordering millions of copies of Windows CE from Microsoft, TCI retained the right to use Sun's Java operating system as well.

To extract the best possible deal, you should emphasize the switching costs you will need to incur in selecting a new vendor, such as retraining costs and disruption costs. This tactic is especially effective if you can credibly threaten to continue using your existing system for a while and thereby avoid bearing any switching costs at all. If you can convince a would-be new supplier that your current system still works for you, or that your costs of switching to his new system are large, you stand to get a better deal. Pointing to companies like your own that are doing fine without investing in state-of-the-art technology will strengthen your hand. In relatively mature markets where most buyers already have incumbent suppliers, delay can be a very valuable negotiating ploy.

Another tactic to extract favorable terms up front is to convince your supplier that you are the type of customer most worthy of a very attractive initial package. Perhaps you can establish that you are likely to make substantial follow-on purchases. Honeywell will discount its factory automation system to establish a beachhead at one site of a multisite customer.

A third approach is to convince suppliers that you are capable of influencing the purchase decisions *other* customers will make. This is a wonderful tactic if you can pull it off: you are effectively getting a referral fee for these customers in the form of an up-front discount. You are in the best position to obtain favorable treatment as an "influential customer" if you can make the case that (1) you will generate a large number of additional unit sales to other customers, (2) these sales will be at a high gross margin, something especially likely with information goods and services, and (3) these effects will be long-lasting because of lock-in. We are regularly solicited by numerous business publications with offers of free subscriptions in exchange for signing up our students.

Bargain hard during initial negotiations, emphasizing your influence as a customer.

These publishers recognize well that today's MBA student subscriptions generate tomorrow's business readers.

Oddly enough, one very effective method you can use to negotiate attractive initial terms is to convince the seller that you will bear very high switching costs later in the lock-in cycle. The greater the vendor believes your switching costs will be, the more you are worth as a locked-in customer, and the more he will invest to get your business. For example, you can negotiate a more attractive up-front price for a specialized information management system if the vendor believes you will face high switching costs in the future when you need various proprietary add-ons.

Emphasizing your own future switching costs is a tricky business, however: you will want to sing a different tune later in the lock-in cycle, so don't reveal too much about your future vulnerabilities! The truly clever buyer initially leads her supplier to believe her switching costs will be large, thereby extracting a big sweetener. Later, she establishes that her switching costs are in fact much smaller, which helps her to avoid any monopolistic charges later in the lock-in cycle. This is a delicate game in which superior information is the key. Just as you seek to exaggerate your future switching costs, the supplier will try to downplay them. Who is better informed? You know more about your own operations, but the vendor knows more about the technology and the experience of other customers. Be wary.

You should certainly insist that your supplier sign a contract offering you protections throughout the lock-in cycle. You should be aware, however, that some "protections" are not worth the paper they are written on. Even if you can obtain a price commitment for the servicing of a machine you have bought, the seller will retain considerable control over the quality of that service, including response time, the training level of service technicians, and so on. Indeed, you may be worse off if you insist on such "partial" protections: they may merely induce your supplier to cut corners in other costly and annoying ways rather than simply raising price. Ultimately, your best protection will come from your initial discount and from keeping your options open, as we discuss in the next section.

Be wary of vague commitments offered by a supplier eager to lock you in. In the Bell Atlantic example described in Chapter 5, the company claimed it had a commitment to "openness" from AT&T in the design of its switches. But after the choice of switches was made, the two companies had a major dispute over whether AT&T had failed to honor any commitments it made.

Rockwell and Motorola wound up in a similar situation. Rockwell agreed on a specific technical standard for the 28.8 kbps generation of modems that incorporated technology covered by certain Motorola patents. To gain Rockwell's support for this particular standard, Motorola agreed to license its key patents on "fair, reasonable, and nondiscriminatory" terms. Motorola and Rockwell then had a major dispute over the interpretation of this phrase.

These disagreements are costly to both sides. Prolonged negotiations over the supplier's commitments absorb valuable management time. The resulting uncertainty makes it difficult to select technology for the future: as a buyer, should you make further investments that will leave you more dependent on the very supplier you no longer trust? Is the supplier truly committed to the relationship or simply milking the situation for a short-term gain? Finally, the sheer transaction costs can mount. As in a messy divorce, only the lawyers end up as winners.

Keeping Your Options Open

Whatever terms you have negotiated at the brand selection point, you'll want to keep your own switching costs under control. Equally important, you need to convince your supplier that you can easily switch, even if you can't! This is the best way to obtain favorable treatment once you are past the entrenchment phase.

The time to start managing your switching costs is before you even have any. In other words, from the outset you should structure your relationship to maximize your options later in the lock-in cycle. One such tactic we noted earlier is to establish a second source of supply to which you can easily switch. Your switching costs will then be the costs associated with shifting your business to the alternative source, not the far greater costs of moving to a whole new technology or architecture. A related approach is to pick an "open" system at the outset, so you will not become beholden to a single vendor. If this is your strategy, we urge you to be quite explicit about what "open" means.

Once you have reached the entrenchment phase of the lock-in cycle, or when you arrive at the next brand selection point, you will have a strong incentive to convince your incumbent supplier that your switching costs are low, thereby negotiating the best deal for yourself. One way to do this is to actually switch! Changing vendors can be expensive in the short run but may pay off in the long run if you are then recognized as a customer with low switching costs. This tactic makes the most sense if you, as a buyer, have superior information regarding your own costs of switching. For example, in some cases internal disruption costs make up a significant portion of the switching costs; you are likely to know a great deal more about these costs than would any supplier. You can credibly signal that your disruption costs are low by changing suppliers. You might send this signal to your current vendor by *partially* switching—for certain parts of your business, or for certain geographic areas—as a way of gaining leverage in negotiations about other parts of your business. This latter tactic is attractive only if the costs of managing a "mixed shop" are not prohibitive.

As a buyer you must be continually aware of the danger of creeping lock-in. Even if lock-in is modest during the sampling phase of the lock-in cycle, it can grow as more equipment is purchased, as more data are stored in certain formats, and as *your* customers in turn become accustomed to certain types of products or product features for which you are reliant on a particular supplier. As you make these additional investments, you should apply the same principles we have stressed at the brand selection phase: extract favorable terms from your supplier each and every time you become more entrenched as the result of another round of hardware or software purchases, brand-specific training, and so on. This may require coordination within your organization: if one part of your company effectively raises switching costs for the company as a whole, appropriate discounts for others should be negoti-ated in exchange. This is a major reason to centralize a number of information systems decisions.

In the information economy, buyers can go a long way toward pro-tecting themselves by insisting that they retain the rights to information on their relationship with the seller. It is a lot harder to switch doctors if you cannot have your personal medical files transferred to a new doctor. Like-wise, maintenance records on a piece of equipment may be very useful to a new service provider, and data about your measurements will be helpful in seeking a new cyber-clothier. Records on your telephone calling patterns can be very valuable in identifying the best carrier and service plan when you shop for a new provider of telecommunications services. The answer is either to keep records your-self or to retain the rights to transfer records from your supplier to a new one should you decide to switch or contemplate doing so.

> *Watch out for creeping lock-in.*

Buyer's Checklist

Here's a checklist of the items in our recommended strategy for buyers facing lock-in:

- Bargain for initial sweeteners, such as discounts or support for switching from your previous system.

- Don't be too anxious. Convey the impression that your benefits from switching are small and the costs large.

- Depict yourself as an attractive customer down the road, because of either your own future purchases or your ability to influence other purchasers.

- Seek protection from monopolistic exploitation down the road, but beware of vague promises offering such protection.

- Keep your options open via second sourcing. Partial switching is a way to gain leverage in negotiation.

- Watch out for creeping lock-in, and retain information about us-age records.

LOCK-IN STRATEGY FOR SELLERS

Let's shift perspective now and see how suppliers of information products and services can deal most effectively with the lock-in experienced by their customers. Of course, buyers' and sellers' strategies are closely related, and tensions are inevitable in any buyer-seller relationship. Looking over the lock-in cycle, there is a natural tug of war between buyers and sellers: sellers hope to profit from locked-in buyers, while buyers seek to strengthen their bargaining position by keeping their options open. As we will see, however, the lock-in cycle is not a zero-sum game. Both buyers and sellers benefit by structuring their relationship wisely at the outset of the cycle.

As a supplier of information systems, your basic strategy for dealing with lock-in should utilize these three key principles:

1. *Invest.* Be prepared to invest to build an installed base of customers. Companies unwilling or unable to offer concessions to gain locked-in customers cannot prevail in a competitive battle. Employ tactics to build your installed base at the least possible cost. Figure out how valuable different customers are to you, and tailor your offerings to match.

2. *Entrench.* Aim for customer entrenchment, not mere sampling. Design your products and promotions so that customers continue to invest in your product or system and become more and more committed to you over time. Incorporate proprietary improvements into your system to lengthen the lock-in cycle and convince customers to reaffirm their choice at the next brand selection point.

3. *Leverage.* Maximize the value of your installed base by selling complementary products to loyal customers and by selling access to these customers to other suppliers.

In the remainder of this chapter we develop these principles and show you how to put them into practice.

Investing in an Installed Base

Imagine you are about to launch a new information system, such as a new palmtop device or the latest in voice-recognition software. Perhaps you are blessed with a blockbuster technology that simply sells itself. If you are doubly blessed, buyers naturally become locked in, and you are suddenly the proud owner of an enormously valuable installed base of customers that generates income for years to come. If you are this charmed, your biggest problem is what to do for an encore; skip ahead to the section on leveraging your installed base.

Alas, we doubt that many readers can afford to skip this section. Rare indeed is the new technology obviously superior to all other alternatives and naturally giving rise to lock-in. In most cases, you will have to fight to build and retain a base of loyal customers.

Iomega is an illustrative example. In 1995 it launched its now-famous Zip drive, a removable storage device for personal computers with seventy times the storage capacity of traditional floppy drives (100 mB versus 1.44 mB). Iomega designed its Zip system so that Zip drives would accept only Zip-compatible disks manufactured by Iomega. The plan was to build an installed base of Zip-drive users and then earn profits from the sale of Zip disks to these locked-in users. To realize this strategy Iomega invested in building an installed base of Zip drives, using heavy promotional spending and offering deep discounts on the drives, setting the price below their break-even point.

Iomega realized these investments were necessary since there were numerous other competing storage devices, including tape backup systems and ever-bigger hard drives. Confident in its product, Iomega hoped that, based on favorable word-of-mouth advertising, initial sales of the drives would spur sales of more drives and that profits would eventually flow as owners of Zip drives purchased Zip disks on which Iomega earned a good margin. By 1998, Iomega had shipped 12 million drives, but its stock price was rapidly dropping in the face of stiff competition from Syquest, Imation, and others selling rival drive/disk systems.

Your product may be a technological breakthrough, or just one of many vying for consumers' dollars. Either way, you will need to know how much to invest to build up an installed base of customers and what is the most cost-effective way to make that investment.

LOOKING AHEAD AT THE WHOLE LOCK-IN CYCLE. First and foremost, you must look ahead to the entire lock-in cycle as you invest to build an installed base. It's all too easy to miss this basic point, which is why we have repeated it several times. At any point in time, you are likely to enjoy a steady stream of operating profits from your installed base, in the form of upgrades, maintenance contracts, sales of new equipment, sales of products complementary to your flagship product, etc. But snapshots like this are of limited value in managing the lock-in cycle. What you really need to do is evaluate the profitability of each type of prospective customer over the lock-in cycle.

The financial analysis of lock-in centers depends on present discounted value calculations, not on this quarter's income statement. You can value a customer in your installed base by estimating the profit margins on products you will sell to that customer over time. As we learned in Chapter 5, you can also estimate the value of a locked-in customer as the sum of two components: that customer's total switching costs plus the dollar value of your underlying competitive advantage based on product quality and cost. (This will be a "minus" if your product is regarded as inferior or your costs are higher.)

To guide your promotional investments in new customers as well as your pricing of different components of your information system, you must treat each locked-in customer as a valuable asset. Only in this fashion can you determine how much to invest in attracting new customers. For example, in using a competitive upgrade program to sell computer software, you need to quantify the likely follow-on sales to a customer you have captured from a rival to properly set the competitive upgrade price.

Recognize that your locked-in customers are valuable assets.

Traditional, static accounting data are likely to be of limited use in this exercise. Comparing your current promotional expenditures to margins on your software will simply not do the job. You need to look ahead throughout the lock-in cycle, and you need to break down the analysis by type of customer.

While you surely want to tout to the investment community the steady income stream you expect to earn from your installed base of loyal customers, looking at that stream may be of limited value in determining how aggressively to seek new customers. The reason is that old and new customers are likely to have different demographic and usage profiles. For example, as cellular telephone companies increased penetration of their products over the past decade, they typically found that average calling volumes declined with each influx of new customers. The reason is not hard to see: the early adopters were the heaviest users, those with long commutes, urgent business, and high incomes. Valuing new customers based on the calling patterns of these hard-core customers would have been a mistake. As a general rule, the stream of margins you earn from an established group of customers is primarily helpful in determining how hard to fight to keep those customers if a rival is trying to steal them away from you. Be careful using them as a guide to valuing a new group of customers.

FIGHTING FOR NEW CUSTOMERS. Some pundits would tell you that traditional economic principles, and especially the textbook model of "perfect competition," retain no value in the information economy. You know by now that we disagree. The logic of lock-in affords a good example. Under classical perfect competition, many small firms compete on price. This intense rivalry drives price to cost and excess profits to zero.

What happens when perfect competition meets lock-in? How can we reconcile vigorous competition, which eliminates excess profits, with lock-in, which makes an installed base a valuable asset? Think about the extreme (and unpleasant) case in which you face fierce competition from equally capable rivals to attract customers in the first place. Both you and your rivals know that each customer will be locked into whatever vendor he or she selects. The result is that competition indeed wrings excess profits out of the market, but only on a life-cycle basis. The inescapable conclusion: firms will lose money (invest) in attracting customers, and (just) recoup these investments from profitable sales to locked-in customers.

In the presence of lock-in, intense competition will force you to offer very attractive initial terms to customers, so that on an overall, life-cycle basis, you would earn no more than a normal rate of return on your investments. Once you have an installed base in place, it will look like you are earning substantial operating margins, but this is merely the normal return on your initial investment in attracting and building the installed base. Economists call the margins earned on sales to the installed base *quasi-profits:* they look like real (excess) profits at a particular point in time but are merely a normal rate of return on prior investments.

How can you earn more than a "normal" rate of return in a market with lock-in? By and large, the key to obtaining superior financial performance in "lock-in" markets is the same as in other markets: by product differentiation, offering something distinctly superior to what your rivals can offer, or by cost leadership, achieving superior efficiency. Ideally, you would seek both differentiation and cost advantages.

Revenue from your locked-in customers is the return on the investment you have made in them.

In the network economy, simply being first to market can generate both differentiation and cost advantages. The key is to convert a timing advantage into a more lasting edge by building an installed base of users. Like Amazon, you may have a first-mover advantage that allows you to build an installed base before full-fledged competition arrives. You may have a superior product as with Intuit and its Quicken software. Or, like the *Wall Street Journal Interactive,* you may have an informational advantage in reaching or identifying customers based on sales of other products or based on a distribution network or brand name.

Within the broad categories of product differentiation and cost leadership, some distinct tactics arise in the presence of lock-in; we'll discuss these directly below. Our point here is that you should not confuse quasi-profits with real profits. Unfortunately, in some cases the federal courts are doing just this, classifying firms as "monopolists," potentially subject to antitrust liability, merely because they have some locked-in customers. This happened to Kodak in the copier business.

Kodak's share of the high-volume copier market was some 20 percent and declining in 1995; it was earning such anemic returns that Kodak ultimately put its copier business on the block and sold off the copier servicing business to Danka. Despite this, Kodak was hit with a $70 million jury verdict (halved on appeal) in 1995 for "monopolizing" the market for servicing Kodak high-volume copiers. Kodak's supposed crime? Refusing to sell its own patented and proprietary parts to independent service organizations (often former Kodak service technicians) who wanted to compete with Kodak. Kodak's misfortune is especially relevant to high-tech firms, since the jury verdict was affirmed by the Ninth Circuit Court of Appeals, which has jurisdiction over the entire

Western United States. Ironically, Xerox, with a commanding 70 percent share in the very same market for high-volume copiers, was spared a similar result by a federal court in the Midwest, which ruled that Xerox had the legal right to refuse to sell its own patented parts to potential aftermarket competitors. Kodak's request for review by the U.S. Supreme Court was denied in 1998.

In our view, Kodak's revenues from the service business were simply economic returns on its deep discounts on initial sales in the highly competitive copier market. Just as industry participants should look at the entire lock-in cycle, so should the antitrust authorities and the courts.

STRUCTURING THE LIFE-CYCLE DEAL. As in any complex negotiation, there are mutual gains to trade from structuring the life-cycle deal to best reflect both buyer's and seller's needs, tolerance for risk, time value of money, and beliefs about the future evolution of the market.

For example, buyers sometimes have separate budgets for capital expenditures as distinct from operating expenses. In selling durable equipment to a buyer with a tight capital budget, you should offer a discount on the equipment and capture a greater portion of your revenues in the form of a multiyear service contract. This approach will also be attractive to a buyer with an especially high cost of capital.

Vendors offering proprietary systems naturally shift customers' payments over the life cycle into the future, or the back end, from the front end. Buyers obtain a sweet deal at the brand selection point, knowing they will then face real switching costs throughout the remainder of the cycle.

If your customers are worried more about lock-in than obtaining the very best terms up front, you can take the opposite tack and assure them that they will not be in your power in the future. This approach underlies companies' promises that their products will have an "open" interface. Promising "openness" is a tricky business, however, because eventually you will want to get your customers more entrenched. We mentioned earlier that buyers should be wary of such promises. Well, the same holds true for vendors. Don't promise more openness than you really want to deliver. The risks to your reputation, not to mention legal risks, are very real.

Even with the best of intentions, the meaning of an "open" system will be subject to interpretation in the future. Microsoft has at times indicated that its operating system is "open" in the sense that independent software vendors (ISVs) will have full access to the Application Program Interfaces (APIs) necessary to make their applications work well with Windows. Yet Microsoft's own programmers remain in a preferred position in writing applications for the Windows platform since, inevitably, they are going to know first about changes in the operating system.

In contrast to Microsoft, Netscape has adopted an "open" strategy in the browser wars. Netscape's approach is much like that used by Adobe when it introduced its page description language PostScript (see Chapter 8): the intent was to convince potential adopters that the product is open enough that they would not be captive to Netscape (or Microsoft!) down the road. On the other side, both Microsoft and its customers know that the customers are already locked in to Microsoft's desktop applications. Microsoft now wants to convince the customers to extend this lock-in to the Internet by integrating Web applications with the desktop and local-area applications. Users face a clear choice: go with Netscape, open standards, and relatively low lock-in, or go with Microsoft, which offers a highly integrated system and high switching costs in the future.

Beyond this, "open" and "closed" aspects of an information system often coexist. A software publisher may have a nonproprietary, open interface with limited functionality and a proprietary interface that performs far better. For example, Cadence Design Systems, a leading supplier of electronic design automation software, has several industry standard interfaces that other software companies can use to move designs and/or data between its flagship product, Virtuoso, and other programs. However, Cadence also has a superior, proprietary interface for internal use. Another example of an "open" standard with limited functionality is Microsoft's Rich Text Format (RTF) for word processing files. This format lends itself to fairly easy conversion, but it is quite limited in its scope, and some of the formatting attached to the original document is inevitably lost in the conversion process.

> **Be explicit about commitments to openness you make to attract customers.**

HIGH MARKET SHARES DON'T IMPLY HIGH SWITCHING COSTS.
Certainly it makes sense to extend introductory offers to attract customers from whom you can expect to earn sizable profit margins in the future, after they become "loyal," or "locked-in," depending on your perspective. However, the quickest and surest way to take a bath in lock-in markets is to count on lock-in that does not materialize. If you give your product away, anticipating juicy follow-on sales based on consumer loyalty/switching costs, you are in for a rude surprise if those switching costs turn out to be modest. You have to form an accurate estimate of each customer's future switching costs to determine the revenues you can expect to earn from that customer and thus the maximal prudent investment you should make to acquire the customer in the first place.

One danger is the emergence of aftermarket rivals that can serve your customers without imposing significant switching costs on them. This was Borland's strategy in offering Quattro Pro: to attract Lotus 1-2-3 users and minimize their switching costs. Kodak and Xerox each faced a similar problem in the market for copiers: after competing aggressively to place new, high-volume copiers in anticipation of earning healthy gross margins for servicing those machines, they found third-party service providers attacking their installed bases. Hewlett-Packard has faced a similar threat from third-party refillers of cartridges for its printers.

It is all too easy for companies in the information business to downplay the likelihood that imitators will emerge and drive down prices and/or drain away their installed base. Part of the problem is that rivals often design their products to minimize switching costs. The battle of the browsers between Netscape Navigator and Microsoft's Internet Explorer has this character. To judge by Netscape's market capitalization, investors believed for some time that Netscape's installed base of Navigator users was an extremely valuable asset. We are skeptical, though, since we doubt that the costs of switching from Navigator to Explorer are very significant for most users. Consequently, Netscape's share in the browser market has been steadily evaporating with Microsoft improving Explorer, giving it away for free, and incorporating browser functions into the operating system.

Microsoft, of course, has a key strategic advantage in its dominance of the desktop operating environment. It wants to integrate its Internet browser with the file browser and other components of Windows 95 in a way that Netscape will find hard to imitate. Microsoft has said that Internet Explorer will "always be free," but what this means is that it will simply be bundled with the company's desktop environment, either through bundling or by some type of product integration.

A large market share need not indicate lock-in.

Another company with an impressive market share but little evident buyer lock-in is Cisco Systems, the supplier of some 80 percent of the routers that make up the basic plumbing of the Internet. Cisco enjoys a breathtaking market capitalization: some $67 billion as of this writing, based on roughly $8 billion in annual revenues. Cisco's value depends on its reputation for high quality, its full line of compatible offerings of networking hardware, and especially its ability to stay one step ahead of the competition in terms of product performance. Cisco's value by and large is *not* based on its ability to earn profits from a captive installed base of customers. Cisco's router designs generally employ open standards for the flow of traffic over the Internet. These open standards have done wonders to fuel the growth of the Internet, and they make Cisco's products attractive to customers. But this same openness makes Cisco vulnerable to competition. In an attempt to reduce this vulnerability, Cisco has now branded the software that runs its routers under the acronym IOS (Internetwork Operating System).

A key question for Cisco is whether it can continue to outpace its rivals using an open architecture, or successfully incorporate proprietary features into some of its products to give it a more lasting competitive advantage. So far, Cisco has thrived in the open Internet environment. It has wisely plowed a considerable fraction of its retained earnings into acquisitions of providers of products and technology that are complementary to its core router business, such as hubs (simpler devices that link together small groups of computers) and frame-relay devices and switches, which Cisco gained in its $4 billion acquisition of StrataCom in 1996. Indeed, Cisco is widely seen as having mastered the art of acquisition: it relies on acquisitions to help stay ahead of the competition *and* have access to new, proprietary technologies.

The fact that a company has a large share of the installed base, as does Cisco in routers, is no guarantee that it will also have a large share of current shipments. Indeed, a divergence between these two measures of market share should serve as an early warning system for any firm: if your share of new shipments exceeds your share of the installed base, you are gaining ground on your rivals. The higher the switching costs, the greater the inertia in the market, and the smaller will be divergences between historical shares, as reflected in shares of today's installed base, and current placements.

Indeed, recently Cisco has found itself under attack from rival router vendors such as 3Com. 3Com's strategy is to offer comparable technology at a much lower price; it is offering high-end routers at $15,000 to $20,000 that are directly competitive with Cisco's offerings at $65,000. We will soon see how locked in Cisco's customers really are!

Netscape is also finding itself in this position. Netscape's share of the installed base of browsers remains high, but its share of new "placements" is considerably lower. But this figure, too, must be interpreted with care since Microsoft is giving away Internet Explorer to so many users. Because lots of software just clutters up people's hard drives, monitoring *usage* of the software is critical; the "active" installed base is far more meaningful than cumulative historical placements. In the case of browsers, it is possible to measure usage by looking at the records kept by Web servers, which record access by each type of browser.

Just as a large market share does not automatically imply lock-in profits, a company with a small market share may still have a valuable franchise if its customers generate substantial ongoing revenues and are unlikely to switch vendors. Our discussion of Computer Associates in Chapter 5 illustrates this point. Despite the fact that the market for mainframe computers has been stagnant for years, Computer Associates has performed very well. It is not an especially popular company, but many of CA's customers would rather pay a premium price than bear the disruption costs and risks associated with going elsewhere for vital software.

Sure, having a large market share and customers with high switching costs is the best of both worlds. But you may never build a large share without giving customers choices. And a small, secure piece of the market can make for a very profitable operation. If you go with such a niche strategy, just make certain you really have a unique offering that will continue to appeal to a certain portion of the market. Be prepared to be at a cost disadvantage based on your small scale, and don't be surprised if your share gradually erodes over time, especially if your product, like computer software and content provision, is subject to strong economies of scale.

ATTRACTING BUYERS WITH HIGH SWITCHING COSTS. The higher a buyer's switching costs, the harder it is worth working to get the buyer in the first place. But there are two things to watch out for. First, any buyer who is expected to become locked into your products is likely to be locked into a rival's products already, making that buyer more difficult to attract in the first place. Second, as we noted above, the buyer has an incentive to inflate his switching costs up front precisely to obtain a hefty sweetener. Don't believe everything you are told!

Still, you can study the buyer's operations and needs to estimate switching costs. For example, if you make an initial sale of hardware or software, will the buyer have a strong preference to buy additional units in the future as new "seats" need to be filled, so as to maintain "single vendor simplicity"? If the buyer's lock-in is significant in magnitude and/or duration, you can expect more follow-on business, and you will be able to capture larger margins down the line.

Furthermore, you may need to fight hard to overcome the buyer's costs of switching to you. This means that you may need to subsidize the buyer's costs of switching. But watch out for customer churn: if you offer a deep discount to subsidize a customer's switching costs, and this particular customer turns out to have low switching costs, you may never recoup the subsidy, since any attempt to do so later in the lock-in cycle will induce this customer to switch again. Indeed, some individuals repeatedly switch long-distance telephone companies to exploit the introductory offers made by AT&T, MCI, and Sprint to attract new customers.

Buyers with growing needs, and thus growing switching costs, are especially attractive. If you are lucky, a small incentive now will generate healthy gross margins on a significant volume of "aftermarket" needs, including demand for various complementary products.

SELLING TO INFLUENTIAL CUSTOMERS. Marketing aggressively to influential buyers can be a very effective way of building up an installed base of customers. When deciding how much to invest in capturing an influential buyer, it is important to quantify the benefits that can result from such investment. The critical measure of a buyer's "influence" is not cash, income, or even visibility. It is much more specific. The appropriate measure of a buyer's influence is the *total gross margin on sales to other customers that results from convincing this buyer to purchase your product.*

Offer discounts to influential buyers.

If you sell into one part of a large company, will you have a better chance of making more sales within the rest of the company? Will this buyer stimulate other sales through word of mouth or referrals, or when its employees join other companies? Will other buyers be impressed that you sold to this buyer, perhaps because the buyer is sophisticated or is known to be good at evaluating products like yours? These are the kinds of questions you should ask yourself when trying to decide how much to invest in swaying the decisions of a potentially influential buyer.

By convincing Industrial Light & Magic to use its graphics computers to create the dinosaurs for *Jurassic Park,* Silicon Graphics hoped to showcase its workstations and spur future sales. The resulting benefit to Silicon Graphics was especially large, since programmers at Industrial Light & Magic created new object-oriented software tools for the project that complemented SGI's hardware and since *Jurassic Park* helped deepen the long-standing relationship between SGI and IL&M.

A large company may be influential because it dictates to others the format in which it insists on receiving information. If you can convince Intel to use your protocols and formats for its electronic design automation software, it is a good bet that other, smaller companies engaged in designing integrated circuits and printed circuit boards will do likewise. If you can convince a major motion picture studio to use your software for creating special effects, that may effectively lock in other, smaller customers to your formats as well. By discounting to Intel or Sony, you stand to capture valuable business from others who will pay a premium for your products. Of course, Intel and Sony know this full well.

A big buyer may also be influential because it helps establish or promote a product standard, as we discuss in Chapter 8. For example, in the modem industry Rockwell manufactures the majority of the chipsets that are the brains of the modem. Consequently, it is in a position to greatly influence the standards and protocols by which modems communicate with each other.

Even little buyers can be highly influential if compatibility is an issue. When modem speeds upgraded from 1,200 bps to 2,400 bps in the early 1980s, manufacturers offered special discounts to operators of bulletin board systems, since they realized that consumers would be more likely to upgrade if there were lots of bulletin board systems that consumers could access with their high-speed modems. For each modem given away at cost to the system operators, the manufacturers managed to land dozens of modem users who wanted to access that system. We will examine this sort of strategy further when we discuss the concept of "network externalities" in Chapter 7.

Buyers can gain influence because they are perceived as leaders, be they large or small. This has also been a driving force in the fashion industry. In high technology, demonstration effects are very important, as is the implied or explicit endorsement of respected users. Just as a highly respected hospital can lead the way in commercializing a new medical procedure, a leading-edge, high-tech information services company can induce others to adopt new information technology by using and endorsing it. A big part of Sun's marketing strategy for Java was bringing in big-name players to endorse the product. Eventually, Sun managed to land the biggest fish of all, Bill Gates, although rumor has it that he had his fingers crossed behind his back when he announced Microsoft's support for Java. Currently, Microsoft has banned Java from its Web site, has added Windows-specific enhancements, and is pushing Dynamic HTML and XML as alternatives, all of which are viewed as attempts to derail Sun's Java plans.

MULTIPLAYER STRATEGIES. Selling to influential buyers takes advantage of the fact that one customer can influence others. The pursuit of several related "multiplayer" strategies rests on this same idea, although it involves different combinations of players. None of these strategies is entirely new, but they all work best for products with high gross margins and thus are especially well suited for information products.

Airline frequent-flier miles are a good example. These loyalty programs often involve three players: the airline, the passenger, and the passenger's employer—that is, the one who is actually paying for the ticket. As you are no doubt aware, there is a temptation for the traveler to book with the airline giving him or her the greatest frequent-flier benefits, at least if the individual can personally appropriate the miles. In this way, the airline can effectively bribe the traveler, with a relatively small frequent-flier benefit, to fly its airline, despite what might be a steep price for airfare. The airline is using the frequent-flier program to drive a wedge between the interests of the payer (the employer) and the decision maker (the employee/traveler).

This pattern often arises when one customer participates at the outset of the lock-in cycle and others follow on later. For example, infant-formula manufacturers make very attractive offers to hospitals for their formula because they know new moms display a strong tendency to use the same brand at home after they leave the hospital. Likewise, automobile manufacturers have historically obtained very attractive terms from spark plug makers because many consumers displayed a tendency to replace the spark plugs in their car with the brand used by the original equipment manufacturer.

When several parties are involved in a purchase, look for opportunities to exploit divergent interests.

Focusing attention on one party that can lock in others also works when the decision maker and the payer are inside the same buying organization: a medical device manufacturer may try to enlist the support of a key physician to sell a hospital its brand of medical equipment, be it a catheter or a complex diagnostic machine. The manufacturer knows that the doctor will have considerable say in how the hospital spends its money and that the hospital is likely to become locked in once it starts using a particular brand or model of medical device. The attention lavished by the manufacturer on the physician can range from straightforward marketing—selling the medical professional on the virtues of the product—to an outright bribe in the form of a research grant or an invitation to a boondoggle conference in Hawaii.

Another group of multiplayer strategies includes sales to users of complementary goods. For example, when Alias Research, a high-end graphics software house acquired by Silicon Graphics in 1995, sells its animation software, these placements help promote sales of its complementary rendering software, since the two types of software work smoothly together in the production flow generating computer simulations.

One way to exploit these complementarities is to subsidize the customer who purchases first, and to recoup this investment from subsequent customers of related products who will then pay you a premium.

Of course, this strategy works only if matching the first customer's brand choice improves performance for the second customer. A variant on this theme is to subsidize the more far-sighted customer group, recouping this subsidy with revenues earned from groups less able or less willing to factor in future costs at the beginning of the lock-in cycle.

Netscape tried to employ a complements strategy, building an installed base by giving away its Web client, Netscape Navigator, in order to sell its Web server product. However, as we just discussed, this strategy is risky if buyer lock-in to the primary product—in this case, the browser—is shaky.

Encouraging Customer Entrenchment

Your work is not done once a customer joins your installed base. You merely move on to the next stage of the lock-in cycle: entrenchment. Your goal is to structure your relationship with customers to simultaneously offer them value and induce them to become more and more committed to your products, your technology, or your services.

ENTRENCHMENT BY DESIGN. You can influence the magnitude of your customers' switching costs. Just as buyers are reluctant to become more reliant on a single source, sellers have incentives to encourage customers to invest in the relationship, thereby raising their own switching costs.

During the lock-in cycle, the buyer and the seller will perform an intricate dance, causing the magnitude of lock-in—that is, the buyer's switching costs—to vary over time. As a seller you should attempt to incorporate new proprietary features into your products and services to raise switching costs. Buyers will try to resist this. For example, in high-end graphical software, many advertising agencies and other users purchased both Adobe's Illustrator program and Aldus's Freehand program, despite considerable duplication in features, to reduce reliance on either Adobe or Aldus. Alas, this strategy did them little good when Adobe and Aldus decided to merge.

Another wonderful way to get your customers entrenched is to offer them more and more value-added informational services. The pharmaceutical drug wholesaling business illustrates this point nicely. Traditionally, this business entailed ordering pharmaceutical drugs from manufacturers, warehousing them, and delivering them to customers such as drugstores and hospitals. The role of information systems and services in this industry has grown markedly in the last decade. The industry leaders, McKesson, Cardinal, Bergen Brunswig, and Amerisource, now distinguish themselves by offering sophisticated reporting services to large, national customers. To further entrench these customers, the large wholesalers have developed their own proprietary automated dispensing and reporting systems, along with consulting services to deepen their relationships with clients.

> *Offer value-added information services to deepen your relationship with your customers.*

LOYALTY PROGRAMS AND CUMULATIVE DISCOUNTS. Vendors explicitly control buyers' switching costs with the "artificial" loyalty programs discussed in Chapter 5. The key to such programs is that the reward to past loyalty must be available only to customers who *remain* loyal. Usually, this is done in two ways, each of which involves ongoing special treatment of customers who have cumulated substantial usage in the past. First, those customers may be given preferential treatment; this is the essence of United Airline's Mileage Plus Premier program, whereby very frequent fliers are given preferential seating, chances to upgrade to first or business class, a special telephone number for service, and so on. Second, historically heavy users are given bonus credits when they buy more goods or services; with United Airlines, this takes the form of double or triple miles for those who travel heavily on United.

In the end, all these methods are forms of volume discounts: favorable terms *for incremental purchases* to customers who are heavy users on a cumulative basis. Again, we emphasize that these methods require tracking individual customer purchases over time, establishing accounts for each customer that record purchases, and maintaining a balance of some credits associated with frequent buying. As information technology continues to advance, this information processing will become less expensive, and more and more companies, including smaller retailers, will find customer tracing to be cost-effective. In an earlier era, numerous retailers banded together to offer cumulative discounts: that was the essence of the Green Stamps system, whereby customers would accumulate stamps issued by many vendors and then trade in books of stamps to earn prizes. In today's economy, smaller vendors will again find it attractive to link arms with companies selling noncompeting products to offer cumulative discounts. We doubt your customers will be using stamps. They will likely do more clicking than licking, accessing on-line reports of their cumulative purchases from you and other companies with whom you are affiliated. Smaller and smaller businesses will find it worthwhile to set up their own loyalty programs, as the information necessary to operate these programs becomes more accurate and more easily available.

We believe that one common type of switching that arises especially in information industries—the cost of finding, evaluating, and learning to use a new brand—is likely to change markedly in the near future. These search costs are being dramatically lowered for some products by the advent of the World Wide Web and more generally by the advances in information technology that are making targeted marketing easier, better, and cheaper. The Amazon Associates Program, described in Chapter 5, is a wonderful example of a loyalty program that rewards frequent referrals. We expect this sort of program to be widely imitated in the future.

Loyalty programs will turn conventional markets into lock-in markets.

These artificial loyalty programs have the prospect of converting more and more conventional markets into lock-in markets, as consumers find themselves bearing significant switching costs in the form of foregone frequent-purchaser benefits when they change brands. For the same reasons, consumer "loyalty," as measured by the tendency of consumers to frequent one or a few suppliers rather than many, is likely to grow. Whether the industry is clothing retailing (traditional catalog or on-line), hotels, or long-distance telephone service, the companies that can structure their charges to attract and retain the lucrative heavy users will edge out their rivals, in much the same way that American Airlines gained an edge by introducing the first frequent-flier program back in 1982. Competition is likely to take the form of sophisticated information systems and targeted promotional activities as much as traditional product design and pricing. When successful, these customer loyalty programs will have the effect of reducing customers' price sensitivity, permitting the seller to successfully charge higher list prices in order to support the costs of the awards given when customers cash in their cumulative benefits. Rivals will soon imitate any successful program you introduce; the prospect of rapid imitation puts a premium on generating some consumer lock-in early, especially for the most lucrative, highest-volume customers.

Switching costs are a hurdle separating incumbent suppliers of information systems from would-be suppliers of rival systems. Thus, companies benefit from their own customers' switching costs, even as they must overcome the switching costs of customers they seek. When U.S. Robotics introduced Palm Pilot, it had to convince users not only to try a hand-held computer device but also to transfer data such as names and addresses from existing databases to Palm Pilot's format. Customer-switching costs were a hurdle to be overcome. Now that Palm Pilot has proven to be a big hit, 3Com (which acquired U.S. Robotics) benefits from the costs Palm Pilot users must bear to switch to another system. 3Com's big challenge is to continue to grow the installed base of Palm Pilot users and to leverage its installed base by selling upgrades and new products to these customers.

Leveraging Your Installed Base

Suppose you've successfully built up a base of customers with switching costs. The next step is to leverage your position by selling complementary products to your installed base and access to your base of customers into the future.

SELLING COMPLEMENTARY PRODUCTS. There is no getting around the need to evaluate the likely future profit stream associated with a potential new customer in determining how aggressively to seek out that customer. You must think broadly in evaluating this "future profit stream" and make every effort to maximize it to achieve competitive success. If a rival can figure out more ways to generate profitable revenue streams from a new customer, that rival will likely "outbid" you to attract that customer. The name of the game is to be creative in generating revenue streams but realistic in terms of the magnitude of customer switching costs. One of the most effective ways to win in lock-in markets is to change the game by expanding the set of complementary products beyond those offered by your rivals. In this way, you can afford to fight harder to get new customers because you will capture more business from them later on.

We noted earlier that a customer may be locked into the purchase of various "ancillary" goods or services when buying the primary product. The example of maintenance for durable equipment fits this pattern, as does the purchase of upgrades or extensions to a computer software program.

Firms compete in lock-in markets by attempting to expand the *scope* of these complementary products subject to lock-in. Visa and MasterCard beat American Express in the market for payment services in this way for years. Banks that were members of Visa and MasterCard could afford to give away the "primary" product, payment services, in the form of lower charges to merchants and even rewards to cardholders based on charge volume, because Visa and MasterCard were also selling a lucrative complementary product: credit card loans at very high rates of interest. American Express was slow to recognize the need to offer credit cards rather than charge cards. In part, this was because American Express was not especially skilled at evaluating the risks associated with these consumer loans, as reflected by the significant problems faced by American Express when it first offered its Optima credit card. Visa and MasterCard and their member banks were thus able to grab a large "share of wallet" by linking payment services to something they were especially good at: consumer credit.

What is the general lesson of the battle between Visa, MasterCard, and American Express? The bank associations gained huge chunks of market share from American Express because they competed very aggressively to lock customers into the primary product—payment services—in order to make sales of a highly lucrative complementary product—consumer credit. This strategy worked especially well since consumers consistently underestimate the finance charges they will incur using their credit cards; this perceptual bias drives banks to compete in the form of low monthly fees and rebates for charge volume, but less so on interest rates. Hence the high and sticky rates charged for credit card debt.

The strategy of selling complementary products or services to your installed base has the very attractive feature that it can be executed profitably and successfully while enhancing, rather than jeopardizing, the buyer relationship, and while encouraging customer entrenchment.

Microsoft has done this very effectively in selling applications software to run on Windows. For information products, with their large price/marginal cost margins, all that is needed to gain significant profits is to capture a reasonable share of the business for such complementary products at market prices. Profits are not necessarily dependent on charging any sort of "monopoly" premium for these products. Nor is this strategy dependent on any lock-in with regard to these complementary products (although Microsoft also enjoys some of that with its applications products owing to the switching costs of learning new programs).

In medical imaging equipment, for example, the companies likely to win are those that can obtain follow-on revenues not only from servicing and spare parts but also from the sale of the medium itself (such as film) and from sales

Sell products that are complementary to your installed product base.

of other imaging equipment. As a specific instance of this, Boston Scientific seeks to sell sophisticated imaging catheters along with the hardware and software necessary to interpret these images; Boston Scientific would have trouble placing equipment if it could not rely on catheter margins to offer discounts on the equipment. The same has been true in the field of laser eye surgery, where Summit and VisX have competed to place sophisticated equipment, knowing that they will enjoy an after-market revenue stream from per-procedure charges collected when the equipment is used. They are effectively selling the information contained in their patents at least as much as they are selling pieces of medical equipment. In each of these examples, doctors with the highest volume of use can expect to receive the deepest discounts on their equipment.

Intuit has done well with a similar strategy for individual Quicken users. It sells not only supplies (checks and envelopes) but complementary products (tax preparation software), on-line services (shopping for insurance and mortgages on Quicken.com), and more powerful business products (QuickBooks).

Netscape is hoping to overcome the weak lock-in of its browser customers, and to extract the most value from its installed base, by selling an integrated package of complementary products, Communicator. Communicator consists of the browser, an e-mail tool, a collaboration tool, a calendar and scheduling tool, and several other components that all work together reasonably well. All are based on open standards, but Netscape has added more functionality to these applications in one way or another. Collabra, for example, is based on the tried-and-true Usenet news protocol, NNTP, but Netscape's version displays embedded HTML as rich text, with graphics and hotlinks.

The company that can successfully offer and sell the largest collection of attractive complementary products will enjoy a tremendous advantage in the primary lock-in market, because it will be able to set more attractive terms for the primary product. In effect, the company shares some of its profit margin on related products with the customer. The happy result is that the buyer-seller relationship is no longer a zero-sum game: the buyer is happy to buy the applications software from the same company selling the hardware and/or the operating system, so long as the applications are comparable to those offered by independent firms. Indeed, the customer may well value one-stop shopping and find highly integrated products easier to purchase and use. For example, a supplier of a computer operating system may indeed enjoy economies of scope and scale, allowing for cheaper or better integration of different pieces of software than other firms can achieve.

The prospect of employing this type of "complements" strategy will intensify competition in the primary product, since it increases the value of having an installed base. However, expanding the scope of the game by offering such complements can be an unalloyed plus for a firm that already has a secure installed base. For such a firm, adding complements to its product line is a wonderful way of maximizing the value of its installed base, bringing added value to customers at the same time.

SELLING ACCESS TO YOUR INSTALLED BASE. An installed base is a terrible thing to waste. Even if you don't have complementary products of your own that you can sell to your current customers, you can sell *access* to your customers to others.

America Online is doing a great job of this. In addition to developing its own content, it is selling access to its installed base to merchants and other content developers. As of August 1997, AOL had relationships with more than seventy on-line merchants. Rent for eyeball space on the AOL homepage starts at $125,000 per year, with commissions of 5 percent to 60 percent. As we mentioned in Chapter 2, the billing information AOL obtains from its customers automatically yields valuable

ZIP code information, from which it can deduce customer demographics, which is very valuable data for on-line marketing.

Microsoft is making deals left and right with content developers, in some cases encouraging them to build sites with special features accessible only via Internet Explorer software. Star Trek is a case in point: several convenient features can be used only by those with the Internet Explorer browser, although the last time we looked there was an announcement saying "expanded functionality for Netscape and Macintosh users coming soon."

This sort of cross-marketing is hardly limited to on-line services. Supermarkets have been doing it for years, offering banking and other services to give additional value to their own installed base of customers. However, it must be remembered that it is often the additional communications and record-keeping capabilities offered by information technology that have made such partnerships feasible.

SETTING DIFFERENTIAL PRICES TO ACHIEVE LOCK-IN. Suppose you are successfully building a readership for your new on-line magazine. So far, most of your money has come through advertising revenues. But you know that sooner or later you'll have to bite the bullet and start charging for subscriptions. You've done some surveys of readers and looked at competitors to help you set your monthly subscription fee. You know from Chapter 2 that you want to set different prices for different types of readers. But you're really stumped by one basic question: Who should get the better deal on a subscription, your loyal readers or the new customers you are trying to attract?

As discussed in Chapter 2, one of the great benefits of keeping track of customer information is the enhanced ability this gives you to tailor packages of products and prices to individual customers. Tracking customers' historical purchase patterns and tailoring your offerings to these histories very much fits into this pattern. But how should your offerings vary with customers' purchase histories?

Approach this problem in two steps. First, figure out the prices and versions you would *like* to offer to customers based on their historical usage patterns. Next, see how close you can get to these target offerings in light of three factors that limit what you can achieve: (1) commitments you have already made to your installed base, (2) the amount of information you have about actual and potential customers' past purchases, and (3) customers' ability to engage in arbitrage.

A good starting point is to divide customers into two groups: those who are currently using your product and those who are not. If you have an obvious group of close rivals, you should further divide the latter group into those who are currently using your rivals' products and those who are not currently using any product in this category. As an example, in the cellular telephone industry, for years there were just two cellular providers in each area, one of which was owned by the local telephone company. Each carrier could divide customers into three groups: its customers, its rival's customers, and those without cellular telephones. We'll refer to these three groups as (a) your installed base, (b) your rival's installed base, and (c) new customers.

How should you price to these three groups? In most cases, you'll be tempted to charge the highest price to your own installed base, because these customers have invested in your product and because they have revealed in prior purchases the fact that they value your product highly. If users bear costs of switching from one brand to another, you should discount to your rival's installed base to help customers overcome these switching costs. But don't be surprised if such efforts to "poach" your rivals' customers trigger similar attacks on your own installed base. New customers have revealed a low willingness to pay, and they should be extended discounts. These pricing rules obey the general principles for pricing that we developed in Chapter 2.

Subscriptions to information services illustrate these points nicely. Many magazines and newspapers offer special introductory rates (for the first 90 days or the first six months, for instance) to new subscribers. After all, those subscribers may be unfamiliar with the publication, and they have not demonstrated any special taste for it. To the contrary, unless they are simply uninformed about how much they would value your information service, they are likely to be marginal customers at best. Under these circumstances, special introductory offers make a great deal of sense, including deals that are better than any you would offer to regular subscribers. Discounting also makes sense to attract customers who are subscribing to rival information services: they are used to getting similar information in another format, and they may have some time to run on their subscription with the rival information service. In this case, there is no particular reason to reward loyalty: longtime subscribers have demonstrated a taste for your publication and are likely to have a high willingness to pay for it.

Beware the "burden of locked-in customers." If you have a large base of locked-in customers, you will be tempted to set higher prices. This, of course, is the reason why you worked so hard to attract those customers in the first place. However, if you cannot find a way to offer a selective discount to customers who are new to the market, your pricing will place you at a *disadvantage* in attracting those customers and thus in sustaining your market share. Price discrimination in the form of selective discounts for new customers (aided by tracking customers and their purchases) is the solution to this problem.

Prices aimed at locked-in customers may not appeal to new buyers. Differential pricing is the solution.

Be sure not to neglect the customer-relations aspects of any selective discounts to new customers. Such discounts can be offered without alienating your long-standing customers, if you are careful. One approach is to remind any regular customers who complain that they are not getting the best rates that they, too, obtained special terms when they first came aboard. An "introductory offer" sounds so much nicer than a "premium price" for long-standing customers! Another approach is to rely on versioning by offering long-standing customers enhanced services or functionality. Extra information makes a great gift: it is cheap to offer, and long-standing customers are likely to place a relatively high value on enhancements. As we learned in Chapter 3, versions should be designed to accentuate the differences between groups in their tastes. Software vendors are wise to offer an easy-to-use version for new customers along with a feature-rich version for the installed base (which also encourages entrenchment by existing users).

Whenever you contemplate special offers to groups other than your own installed base, you must consider the impact on your reputation for fair dealing. Future sales are at risk if you develop a reputation for exploiting your loyal customers. This is tricky, because the line between recouping your initial investments in your installed base and "exploitation" is not sharp. But remember that any adverse reputation could have a devastating impact on future sales to new customers, especially if you face significant competition to make such sales. Thus, an important lesson is to structure—and to communicate your prices—in a manner not perceived as unfair or opportunistic by your customers.

As we noted above, three factors apart from reputation are likely to limit your ability to extract premium prices from your own installed base. First, you must honor any commitments you previously made to attract your installed base in the first place. If you established loyalty programs rewarding existing customers with discounts, you can't very well charge them more than new customers. If you promised current customers most-favored customer treatment, you'll have to lower prices for them if you discount to attract new business. You may well be able to avoid triggering such most-favored customer clauses by offering distinct versions to new customers, however.

Second, the tactics available to you depend on the quality of the information you have about customers' historical purchasing behavior. This is a good reason to keep careful records of your customers' purchases. A customer who has responded to discounts in the past has revealed price sensitivity and warrants more discounts. In contrast, there is less reason to discount to a customer who regularly buys regardless of price. Information about customers you have *not* yet served is also very valuable. For example, you can use customers' prior purchase history to distinguish customers who have been using a rival brand from those who are new to the category. In the future, it should become easier for customers to prove that they have been using a rival information service or software product and, thus, to qualify for special discounts. Alternatively, we expect that such information will become cheaper to acquire from third parties, as more transactional information is tracked, to support targeted marketing efforts.

Third, you need to anticipate and block arbitrage—efforts by locked-in customers to pose as new customers (or to buy through intermediaries) to obtain any special rates extended to other groups. As discussed in Chapter 3, a good way to handle the arbitrage problem is to offer a special version of the product to new customers. Usually, this will be a stripped-down version, both because many new customers are less likely to need the full set of functions you have developed to serve your regular, long-standing customers and because the stripped-down version will be easier to learn, reducing switching costs. Once these customers are comfortable with your product and are past the sampling portion of the lock-in cycle, you can upgrade them to a version that is richer in features and easier to use, if not easier to learn. Photoshop, Adobe's image editing tool, is a good example. As we saw in Chapter 3, a stripped-down version comes bundled with many scanners and digital cameras. This is adequate for new users, but more serious users eventually decide to upgrade to the full-featured version.

A whole new set of issues arises when selling durable products, such as computer software. If you are selling a durable product, as opposed to an information service, your customers can just keep using what you have already sold to them. In this case, you can no longer assume that your own customers have the highest willingness to pay for your product. To the contrary, they may have the lowest willingness to pay, since they own an older version.

For computer software, which does not depreciate, you are necessarily selling the *improvements* to the older version. Improvements are likely to be worth considerably less than the basic functionality. So, even though the customer is locked in to using your program, making it unlikely that he or she will shift to an entirely different program, you still must price the upgrade according to its *incremental* value to the customer. You need to give customers a good reason to upgrade, and then make the upgrade path as painless as possible.

For replacement hardware, as for software upgrades, making a new sale does serve to further entrench the buyer and lengthen the lock-in cycle, giving you a better chance to make yet further sales or to place complementary products with this customer. This is especially true if the upgrade, or the new piece of hardware, incorporates additional proprietary features that were not present in earlier versions.

ATTEMPTS TO RAISE SEARCH COSTS. As we pointed out earlier in the chapter, the Web has generally tended to reduce search costs. You should certainly take advantage of this medium to make it easy for customers to find you and to learn about your products. By the same token, you may be tempted to make it difficult for your customers to seek out alternatives and compare your offerings with those of your rivals. This is worth trying, but we think it will be hard to do on the Web.

Make yourself easy to find and your rivals hard to find.

Remember Bargain Finder from Chapter 3? Three of the eight CD stores that Bargain Finder originally searched refused to allow it access to their sites so as to make it difficult to comparison shop. This sort of strategy will not be successful in the long run. Rather than banning searches, the CD stores should focus on reducing their costs and on providing differentiated products, as in the MusicMaker example also in Chapter 3. You don't have to worry about consumers searching for competitive products if the product you are selling is truly unique.

EXPLOITING FIRST-MOVER ADVANTAGE. First-mover advantages can be powerful and long lasting in lock-in markets, especially those in information industries where scale economies are substantial. If you can establish an installed base before the competition arrives on the scene, you may make it difficult for later entrants to achieve the scale economies necessary to compete. This is especially true in the common circumstance in which an entrant would be able to attract customers away from your installed base only gradually. This implies that your rival will be smaller than you for some time, and very likely less efficient if economies of scale are substantial.

One way to push this strategy, especially in markets with a relatively small number of key customers, is to control the length of the lock-in cycle by entering into multiyear contracts with large customers. For example, Ticketmaster has multiyear contracts with major stadiums and other venues to handle their ticketing needs, making it harder for up-start ticketing services to break into the market in any locale. Entry is made more difficult by the need to have a network of outlets in any given area where concert goers can purchase tickets. As this crude, historical method of selling tickets is displaced by new technologies, such as on-line ticket sales and e-tickets for concerts, Ticketmaster's grip will loosen. Selling tickets electronically to young rock concert fans who lack credit cards will be the hardest hurdle for electronic ticketing services.

One way to make the most of your first-mover advantage is to consciously stagger the termination dates on contracts with different customers. By this device, any entrant would have to operate well below efficient scale for some period of time, even while

Stagger termination dates on different customer contracts to keep rivals from achieving scale economies.

fighting to attract key customers away from you. In other words, "lock-in can lead to lock-out" when customer switching costs make rival entry unattractive. In the animal world, insects such as cicadas emerge to procreate at intervals of seven, thirteen, and seventeen years, all prime numbers, making it harder for predators to enjoy "scale economies" by emerging on the same cycle. It's a jungle out there!

Another way to control cycle length is through the frequency and timing of new versions or upgrades. Like the weakest link in a chain, you want to prevent aggregate customer lock-in at any point in time from getting too low, as that would be the optimal time for another company to enter and attack your installed base.

You may feel the presence of competition even before it arrives on the scene. If customers expect a rival of yours to introduce a new product in six-month's time, they will be less inclined to become locked into your current product. Similarly, a competitor may well seek customer commitments before actually launching its product. You can lock up certain customers before your rivals' plans have solidified enough for them to credibly approach your customers. This may involve making some concessions but could yield a large payoff if your rival's product plans prove successful. However, this type of information game is double-edged: your customers will be keen to point to new choices they see emerging in negotiating a better deal from you, and they have every incentive to be informed about those choices and to play them up. Plus, dominant hardware and software suppliers, including both Microsoft and IBM, have even been accused of "predatory product preannouncements" when announcing products ("vaporware") before they are available. (We'll discuss vaporware as a strategy for expectations management in Chapter 9.)

CONTROLLING CYCLE LENGTH. You can influence the duration of the lock-in cycle. Cycle length depends on such factors as the duration of contractual commitments, the lifetime of durable equipment, the presence of complementary products with different economic lifetimes that work together, the aggressiveness of outside suppliers and their tactics in approaching locked-in customers, the information outsiders have about the extent and timing of lock-in by various customers, and the frequency with which customers choose to bear the costs of putting their business up to bid.

You might think that your customers will try to keep the cycle short, while you will be pushing for a long cycle. This is not always so. American Airlines was content to sign a long-term contract with Boeing both because of American's desire to simplify fleet maintenance and because of the price protections it obtained in the contract. Indeed, if lock-in is long-lived, the customer may well insist on contractual protections of similar duration. Indeed, as a seller you might be happy with a relatively short-term contract, if buyers are locked in for a long period of time.

Get your customers to extend their contracts before those contracts expire.

This pattern will leave you in a strong position when the contract expires.

Consider employing the popular tactic of truncating the lock-in cycle by getting customers to sign a new, multi-year contract well before their current contracts expire. Likewise, consider selling new equipment or an upgrade to customers before their existing equipment wears out or the upgrade is really needed. Premature renewals are certainly common in real estate transactions, in part because both landlord and tenant need to know in advance if the tenant is moving. But even when planning needs are not nearly so significant, getting the jump on contract renewal or system replacement can work well for you as a seller of information or information systems. By preempting contract termination, you can negotiate with a customer who is still attached for some time, making it less likely that a rival will be knocking at the door and engaging in serious discussions. For these very same reasons, savvy buyers will be wary of renewing a contract without going through the exercise of getting a competitive bid.

LESSONS

Consumer lock-in to specific technologies, and even to specific brands, is an ever-present feature of the information economy. Both buyers and sellers have much to gain from evaluating the consequences of their actions over the entire lock-in cycle. Short-sightedness can be extremely costly when switching costs are involved.

We have three basic lessons for *purchasers* of information systems and technology:

- **Bargain hard before you are locked in for concessions in exchange for putting yourself in a vulnerable position.** If you can't avoid lock-in, at least get paid a sweetener up front to compensate you for becoming locked in.

- **Pursue strategies like second sourcing and open systems to minimize the extent of your lock-in.** Even if you must make investments in a particular technology, you can still plan ahead to avoid becoming beholden to a single supplier.

- **Look ahead to the next time you'll be picking a vendor, and take steps at the outset to improve your bargaining position at that time.** Retain information on your relationship with the seller, such as maintenance records, and use patterns that could reduce costs if you have to switch to a new supplier. These will be valuable assets if you decide to break off your relationship.

We also explored a number of strategies for *sellers* whose customers will experience lock-in. Our key points are these:

- **Be prepared to invest to build an installed base through promotions and by offering up-front discounts.** You can't succeed in competitive lock-in markets without making these investments.

- **Cultivate influential buyers and buyers with high switching costs.** These are your most profitable customers.

- **Design your products and your pricing to get your customers to invest in your technology, thereby raising their own switching costs.** Employ a loyalty program to make your product attractive to your customers at their next brand selection point. This requires keeping records of customers' cumulative purchases.

- **Maximize the value of your installed base by selling your customers complementary products and by selling access to your installed base.** An installed base is a wonderful springboard for marketing new products, especially because of your access to information about customers' historical purchases that you have gathered over time.

7 | Networks and Positive Feedback

The industrial economy was populated with oligopolies: industries in which a few large firms dominated their markets. This was a comfortable world, in which market shares rose and fell only gradually. This stability in the marketplace was mirrored by lifetime employment of managers. In the United States, the automobile industry, the steel industry, the aluminum industry, the petroleum industry, various chemicals markets, and many others followed this pattern through much of the twentieth century.

In contrast, the information economy is populated by temporary monopolies. Hardware and software firms vie for dominance, knowing that today's leading technology or architecture will, more likely than not, be toppled in short order by an upstart with superior technology.

What has changed? There is a central difference between the old and new economies: the old industrial economy was driven by *economies of scale;* the new information economy is driven by the *economics of networks.* In this chapter we describe in detail the basic principles of network economics and map out their implications for market dynamics and competitive strategy. The key concept is *positive feedback.*

The familiar if sad tale of Apple Computer illustrates this crucial concept. Apple has suffered of late because positive feedback has fueled the competing system offered by Microsoft and Intel. As Wintel's share of the personal computer market grew, users found the Wintel system more and more attractive. Success begat more success, which is the essence of positive feedback. With Apple's share continuing to decline, many computer users now worry that the Apple Macintosh will shortly become the Sony Beta of computers, orphaned and doomed to a slow death as support from software producers gradually fades away. This worry is cutting into Apple's sales, making it a potentially self-fulfilling forecast. Failure breeds failure: this, too, is the essence of positive feedback.

Positive feedback makes the strong grow stronger . . . and the weak grow weaker.

Why is positive feedback so important in high-technology industries? Our answer to this question is organized around the concept of a *network*. We are all familiar with physical networks such as telephone networks, railroad networks, and airline networks. Some high-tech networks are much like these "real" networks: networks of compatible fax machines, networks of compatible modems, networks of e-mail users, networks of ATM machines, and the Internet itself. But many other high-tech products reside in "virtual" networks: the network of Macintosh users, the network of CD machines, or the network of Nintendo 64 users.

In "real" networks, the linkages between nodes are physical connections, such as railroad tracks or telephone wires. In virtual networks, the linkages between the nodes are invisible, but no less critical for market dynamics and competitive strategy. We are in the same computer network if we can use the same software and share the same files. Just as a spur railroad is in peril if it cannot connect to the main line, woe to those whose hardware or software is incompatible with the majority of other users. In the case of Apple, there is effectively a network of Macintosh users, which is in danger of falling below critical mass.

Whether real or virtual, networks have a fundamental economic characteristic: the value of connecting to a network depends on the number of *other* people already connected to it.

This fundamental value proposition goes under many names: network effects, network externalities, and demand-side economies of scale. They all refer to essentially the same point: other things being equal, it's better to be connected to a bigger network than a smaller one. As we will see below, it is this "bigger is better" aspect of networks that gives rise to the positive feedback observed so commonly in today's economy.

Throughout this book we have stressed the idea that many aspects of the new economy can be found in the old economy if you look in the right places. Positive feedback and network externalities are not a creation of the 1990s. To the contrary, network externalities have long been recognized as critical in the transportation and communications industries, where companies compete by expanding the reach of their networks and where one network can dramatically increase its value by interconnecting with other networks. Anyone trying to navigate the network economy has much to learn from the history of the postal service, railroads, airlines, and telephones.

In this chapter we introduce and illustrate the key economic concepts that underlie market dynamics and competitive strategy in both real and virtual networks. Based on these concepts, we identify four generic strategies that are effective in network markets. We then show how these concepts and strategies work in practice through a series of historical case studies.

In the two chapters that follow this one, we build on the economic framework developed here, constructing a step-by-step strategic guide to the key issues facing so many players in markets for information technology. In Chapter 8 we discuss how to work with allies to successfully establish a new technology—that is, to launch a new network. As you might expect, negotiations over interconnection and standardization are critical. In Chapter 9, we examine what happens if these negotiations break down: how to fight a standards war, how to get positive feedback working in favor of your technology in a battle against an incompatible rival technology.

POSITIVE FEEDBACK

The notion of *positive feedback* is crucial to understanding the economics of information technology. Positive feedback makes the strong get stronger and the weak get weaker, leading to extreme outcomes. If you have ever experienced feedback talking into a microphone, where a loud noise becomes deafening through repeated amplification, you have witnessed positive feedback in action. Just as an audio signal can feed on itself until the limits of the system (or the human ear) are reached, positive feedback in the marketplace leads to extremes: dominance of the market by a single firm or technology.

The backward cousin of positive feedback is *negative feedback*. In a negative-feedback system, the strong get weaker and the weak get stronger, pushing both toward a happy medium. The industrial oligopolies listed in the beginning of this chapter exhibited negative feedback, at least in their mature phase. Attempts by the industry leader to capture share from smaller players would often trigger vigorous responses as smaller players sought to keep capacity utilization from falling. Such competitive responses prevent the leading firm from obtaining a dominant position. Furthermore, past a certain size, companies found growth difficult owing to the sheer complexity of managing a large enterprise. And as the larger firms became burdened with high costs, smaller, more nimble firms found profitable niches. All of these ebbs and flows represent negative feedback in action: the market found a balanced equilibrium rather than heading toward the extreme of a single winner. Sometimes sales fell below a critical mass, and companies like Studebaker went out of business or were acquired by more efficient rivals. But by and large, dramatic changes in market share were uncommon and oligopoly rather than monopoly was the norm.

Positive feedback should not be confused with growth as such. Yes, if a technology is on a roll, as is the Internet today, positive feedback translates into rapid growth: success feeds on itself. This is a *virtuous cycle*. But there is a dark side of this force. If your product is seen as failing, those very perceptions can spell doom. The Apple Macintosh is now in this danger zone, where "positive" feedback does not feel very positive. The virtuous cycle of growth can easily change to a *vicious cycle* of collapse. A death spiral represents positive feedback in action; "the weak get weaker" is the inevitable flip side of "the strong get stronger."

When two or more firms compete for a market where there is strong positive feedback, only one may emerge as the winner. Economists say that such a market is *tippy*, meaning that it can tip in favor of one player or another. It is unlikely that all will survive. It was clear to all parties in the battle over 56Kbps modem standards that multiple, incompatible modems could not coexist for long; the only question was which protocol would triumph or if a single, compromise standard could be negotiated.

Other examples of tippy markets were the video recorder market in the 1980s (VHS v. Beta) and the personal computer operating systems market of the 1990s (Wintel v. Apple). In its most extreme form, positive feedback can lead to a *winner-take-all market* in which a single firm or technology vanquishes all others, as has happened in several of these cases.

Positive feedback is a more potent force in the network economy than ever before.

Figure 7.1 shows how a winner-take-all market evolves over time. The technology starting with an initial lead, perhaps 60 percent of the market, grows to near 100 percent, while the technology starting with 40 percent of the market declines to 10 percent. These dynamics are driven by the strong desire of users to select the technology that ultimately will prevail—that is, to choose the network that has (or will have) the most users. As a result, the strong get stronger and the weak get weaker; both effects represent the positive feedback so common in markets for information infrastructure.

The biggest winners in the information economy, apart from consumers generally, are companies that have launched technologies that have been propelled forward by positive feedback. This requires patience and foresight, not to mention a healthy dose of luck. Successful strategies in a positive-feedback industry are inherently dynamic. Our primary goal in this part of the book is to identify the elements of winning strategies in network industries and to help you craft the strategy most likely to succeed in your setting.

Figure 7.1. *Positive Feedback*

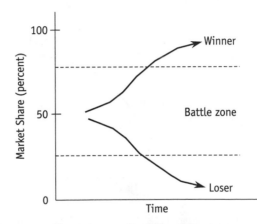

Nintendo is a fine example of a company that created enormous value by harnessing positive feedback. When Nintendo entered the U.S. market for home video games in 1985, the market was considered saturated, and Atari, the dominant firm in the previous generation, had shown little interest in rejuvenating the market. Yet by Christmas 1986, the Nintendo Entertainment System (NES) was the hottest toy on the market. The very popularity of the NES fueled more demand and enticed more game developers to write games to the Nintendo system, making the system yet more attractive. Nintendo managed that most difficult of high-tech tricks: to hop on the positive-feedback curve while retaining strong control over its technology. Every independent game developer paid royalties to Nintendo. They even promised not to make their games available on rival systems for two years following their release!

Our focus in this chapter is on markets with significant positive feedback resulting from demand-side or supply-side economies of scale. These scale economies apply most directly to the market leaders in an industry. But smaller players, too, must understand these same principles, whether they are planning to offer their own smaller differentiated networks or to hook into a larger network sponsored by an industry leader.

Positive-feedback systems follow a predictable pattern. Again and again, we see adoption of new technologies following an S-shaped curve with three phases: (1) flat during launch, then (2) a steep rise during takeoff as positive feedback kicks in, followed by (3) leveling off as saturation is reached. The typical pattern is illustrated in Figure 7.2.

Figure 7.2. *Adoption Dynamics*

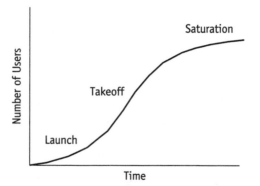

This S-shaped, or "logistic," pattern of growth is also common in the biological world; for example, the spread of viruses tends to follow this pattern. In the information technology arena, the S-shaped pattern can be seen in the adoption of the fax machine, the CD, color TV, video game machines, e-mail, and the Internet (we can assure you that current growth rates will slow down; it is just a matter of when).

DEMAND-SIDE ECONOMIES OF SCALE

Positive feedback is not entirely new; virtually every industry goes through a positive feedback phase early in its evolution. General Motors was more efficient than the smaller car companies in large part because of its scale. This efficiency fueled further growth by General Motors. This source of positive feedback is known as *economies of scale* in production: larger firms tend to have lower unit costs (at least up to a point). From today's perspective, we can refer to these traditional economies of scale as *supply-side economies of scale*.

Despite its supply-side economies of scale, General Motors never grew to take over the entire automobile market. Why was this market, like many industrial markets of the twentieth century, an oligopoly rather than a monopoly? Because traditional economies of scale based on manufacturing have generally been exhausted at scales well below total market dominance, at least in the large U.S. market. In other words, positive feedback based on supply-side economies of scale ran into natural limits, at which point negative feedback took over. These limits often arose out of the difficulties of managing enormous organizations. Owing to the managerial genius of Alfred Sloan, General Motors was able to push back these limits, but even Sloan could not eliminate negative feedback entirely.

In the information economy, positive feedback has appeared in a new, more virulent form based on the *demand* side of the market, not just the supply side. Consider Microsoft. As of May 1998, Microsoft had a market capitalization of about $210 billion. This enormous value is *not* based on the economies of scale in developing software. Oh, sure, there are scale economies, in designing software, as for any other information product. But there are several other available operating systems that offer comparable (or superior) performance to Windows 95 and

Windows NT, and the cost of developing rival operating systems is tiny in comparison with Microsoft's market capitalization. The same is true of Microsoft's key application software. No, Microsoft's dominance is based on *demand-side economies of scale.* Microsoft's customers value its operating systems *because* they are widely used, the de facto industry standard. Rival operating systems just don't have the critical mass to pose much of a threat. Unlike the supply-side economies of scale, demand-side economies of scale don't dissipate when the market gets large enough: if everybody else uses Microsoft Word, that's even more reason for you to use it too.

The positive relationship between popularity and value is illustrated in Figure 7.3. The arrow in the upper-right portion of the curve depicts a *virtuous cycle:* the popular product with many compatible users becomes more and more valuable to each user as it attracts ever more users. The arrow in the lower-left portion of the curve represents a *vicious cycle:* a death spiral in which the product loses value as it is abandoned by users, eventually stranding those diehards who hang on the longest, because of their unique preference for the product or their high switching costs.

Lotus 1-2-3 took great advantage of demand-side scale economies during the 1980s. Based on superior performance, Lotus 1-2-3 enjoyed the largest installed base of users among spreadsheet programs by the early 1980s. As personal computers became faster and more companies appreciated the power of spreadsheets, new users voted overwhelmingly for Lotus 1-2-3, in part so they could share files with other users and in

Figure 7.3. *Popularity Adds Value in a Network Industry*

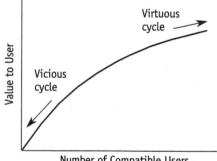

part because many users were skilled in preparing sophisticated Lotus macros. This process fed on itself in a virtuous cycle. Lotus 1-2-3 had the most users, and so attracted yet more devotees. The result was an explosion in the size of the spreadsheet market. At the same time, VisiCalc, the pioneer spreadsheet program for personal computers, was stuck in a vicious cycle of decline, suffering from the dark side of positive feedback. Unable to respond quickly by introducing a superior product, VisiCalc quickly succumbed.

Suppose your product is poised in the middle of the curve in Figure 7.3. Which way will it evolve? If consumers expect your product to become popular, a bandwagon will form, the virtuous cycle will begin, and consumers' expectations will prove correct. But if consumers expect your product to flop, your product will lack momentum, the vicious cycle will take over, and again consumers' expectations will prove correct. The beautiful if frightening implication: success and failure are driven as much by consumer expectations and luck as by the underlying value of the product. A nudge in the right direction, at the right time, can make all the difference. Marketing strategy designed to influence consumer expectations is critical in network markets. The aura of inevitability is a powerful weapon when demand-side economies of scale are strong.

The aura of inevitability is a powerful weapon when demand-side economies of scale are strong.

Demand-side economies of scale are the norm in information industries. In consumer electronics, buyers are wary of products that are not yet popular, fearing they will pick a loser and be left stranded with marginally valuable equipment. Edsel buyers at least had a car they could drive, but PicturePhone customers found little use for their equipment when this technology flopped in the 1970s. As a result, many information technologies and formats get off to a slow start, then either reach critical mass and take off or fail to do so and simply flop.

We do not mean to suggest that positive feedback works so quickly, or so predictably, that winners emerge instantly and losers give up before trying. Far from it. There is no shortage of examples in which two (or more) technologies have gone head-to-head, with the outcome very much in the balance for years. Winner-take-all does not mean give-up-if-you-are-behind. Being first to market usually helps, but there are dozens of examples showing that a head start isn't necessarily decisive: think of WordStar, VisiCalc, and DR-DOS.

Nor are demand-side economies of scale so strong that the loser necessarily departs from the field of battle: WordPerfect lost the lion's share of the word processor market to Microsoft Word, but is still a player. More so than in the past, however, in the information economy the lion's share of the *rewards* will go to the winner, not the number two player who just manages to survive.

Positive feedback based on demand-side economies of scale, while far more important now than in the past, is not entirely novel. Any communications network has this feature: the more people using the network, the more valuable it is to each one of them. The early history of telephones in the United States, which we discuss in detail later in the chapter, shows how strong demand-side scale economies, along with some clever maneuvering, can lead to dominance by a single firm. In the case of telephony, AT&T emerged as the dominant telephone network in the United States during the early years of this century, fending off significant competition and establishing a monopoly over long-distance service.

Transportation networks share similar properties: the more destinations it can reach, the more valuable a network becomes. Hence, the more developed network tends to grow at the expense of smaller networks, especially if the smaller networks are not able to exchange traffic with the larger network, a practice generally known as *interlining* in the railroad and airline industries.

Supply-side and demand-side economies of scale combine to make positive feedback in the network economy especially strong.

Both demand-side economies of scale and supply-side economies of scale have been around for a long time. But the combination of the two that has arisen in many information technology industries is new. The result is a "double whammy" in which growth on the demand side both reduces cost on the supply side and makes the product more attractive to other users—accelerating the growth in demand even more. The result is especially strong positive feedback, causing entire industries to be created or destroyed far more rapidly than during the industrial age.

NETWORK EXTERNALITIES

We said earlier that large networks are more attractive to users than small ones. The term that economists use to describe this effect, *network externalities,* usefully highlights two aspects of information systems that are crucial for competitive strategy.

First, focus on the word *network.* As we have suggested, it is enlightening to view information technologies in terms of *virtual networks,* which share many properties with *real networks* such as communications and transportation networks. We think of all users of Macintosh users as belonging to the "Mac network." Apple is the *sponsor* of this network. The sponsor of a network creates and manages that network, hoping to profit by building its size. Apple established the Mac network in the first place by introducing the Macintosh. Apple controls the interfaces that govern access to the network—for example, through its pricing of the Mac, by setting the licensing terms on which clones can be built, and by bringing infringement actions against unauthorized hardware vendors. And Apple is primarily responsible for making architectural improvements to the Mac.

Apple also exerts a powerful influence on the supply of products that are complementary to the Mac machine, notably software and peripheral devices, through its control over interfaces. Computer buyers are picking a network, not simply a product, when they buy a Mac, and Apple must design its strategy accordingly. Building a network involves more than just building a product: finding partners, building strategic alliances, and knowing how to get the bandwagon rolling can be every bit as important as engineering design skills.

Second, focus on one of economists' favorite words: *externalities.* Externalities arise when one market participant affects others without compensation being paid. Like feedback, externalities come in two flavors: negative and positive. The classic example of a negative externality is pollution: my sewage ruins your swimming or drinking water. Happily, *network externalities* are normally positive, not negative: when I join your network, the network is bigger and better, to your benefit.

Positive network externalities give rise to positive feedback: when I buy a fax machine, the value of your fax machine is enhanced since you can now send faxes to me and receive faxes from me. Even if you don't have a fax machine yet, you are more tempted to get one yourself since you can now use it to communicate with me.

Network externalities are what lie behind *Metcalfe's law*, named after Bob Metcalfe, the inventor of Ethernet. (Metcalfe tells us it was George Gilder who attributed this law

Metcalfe's law: The value of a network goes up as the square of the number of users.

to him, but he's willing to take credit for it.)

Metcalfe's law is more a rule of thumb than a law, but it does arise in a relatively natural way. If there are n people in a network, and the value of the network to each of them is proportional to the number of *other* users, then the total value of the network (to all the users) is proportional to $n \times (n - 1) = n^2 - n$. If the value of a network to a single user is $1 for each other user on the network, then a network of size 10 has a total value of roughly $100. In contrast, a network of size 100 has a total value of roughly $10,000. A tenfold increase in the size of the network leads to a hundredfold increase in its value.

COLLECTIVE SWITCHING COSTS

Network externalities make it virtually impossible for a small network to thrive. But every new network has to start from scratch. The challenge to companies seeking to introduce new but incompatible technology into the market is to build network size by overcoming the *collective switching costs*—that is, the combined switching costs of all users.

As we emphasized in Chapter 5, switching costs often stem from durable complementary assets, such as LPs and phonographs, hardware and software, or information systems and the training to use them. With network effects, one person's investment in a network is complementary to another person's similar investments, vastly expanding the number of complementary assets. When I invest by learning to write programs for the Access database language, then Access software, and investments in that language, become more valuable for you.

In many information industries, collective switching costs are the biggest single force working in favor of incumbents. Worse yet for would-be entrants and innovators, switching costs work in a nonlinear way: convincing ten people connected in a network to switch to your incompatible network is *more* than ten times as hard as getting one customer to switch. But you need all ten, or most of them: no one will want to be the first to give up the network externalities and risk being stranded. Precisely because various users find it so difficult to *coordinate* to switch to an incompatible technology, control over a large installed base of users can be the greatest asset you can have.

The layout of the typewriter keyboard offers a fascinating example of collective switching costs and the difficulties of coordinating a move to superior technology. The now-standard keyboard configuration is known as the QWERTY keyboard, since the top row starts with letters QWERTY. According to many reports, early promoters of the Type Writer brand of machine in the 1870s intentionally picked this awkward configuration to *slow down* typists and thus reduce the incidence of jamming, to which their machines were prone. This was a sensible solution to the commercial problem faced by these pioneers: to develop a machine that would reliably be faster than a copyist could write. QWERTY also allowed salesmen to impress customers by typing their brand name, Type Writer, rapidly, using keys only from the top row.

Very soon after QWERTY was introduced, however, the problem of jamming was greatly reduced through advances in typewriter design. Certainly, today, the jamming of computer keyboards is rare indeed! And sure enough, alternative keyboards developed early in the twentieth century were reputed to be superior. The Dvorak layout, patented in 1932 with a home row of AOEUIDHTNS that includes all five vowels, has long been used by speed typists. All this would suggest that QWERTY should by now have given way to more efficient keyboard layouts.

Why, then, are we all still using QWERTY keyboards? One answer is straightforward: the costs we all would bear to learn a new keyboard are simply too high to make the transition worthwhile. Some scholars assert that there is nothing more than this to the QWERTY story. Under this story, Dvorak is just not good enough to overcome the individual switching costs of learning it. Other scholars claim, however, that we would *collectively* be better off switching to the Dvorak layout (this calculation should include our children, who have yet to be trained on QWERTY), but no one is willing to lead the move to Dvorak. Under this interpretation, the collective switching costs are far higher than all of our individual switching costs, because coordination is so difficult.

Coordination costs were indeed significant in the age of the typewriter. Ask yourself this question: in buying a typewriter for your office, why pick the leading layout, QWERTY, if other layouts are more efficient? Two reasons stand out. Both are based on the fact that the typewriter keyboard *system* has two elements: the keyboard layout and the *human* component of the system, namely, the typist. First, trained typists you plan to hire already know QWERTY. Second, untrained typists you plan to hire will prefer to train on a QWERTY keyboard so as to acquire marketable skills. Human capital (training) is specific to the keyboard layout, giving rise to network effects. In a flat market consisting mostly of replacement sales, buyers will have a strong preference to replace old QWERTY typewriters with new ones. And in a growing market, new sales will be tilted toward the layout with the larger installed base. Either way, positive feedback rules. We find these coordination costs less compelling now, however. Typists who develop proficiency on the Dvorak layout can use those skills in a new job simply by reprogramming their computer keyboard. Thus, we find the ongoing persistence of the QWERTY keyboard in today's computer society at odds with the strongest claims of superiority of the Dvorak layout.

IS YOUR INDUSTRY SUBJECT TO POSITIVE FEEDBACK?

We do not want to leave the impression that *all* information infrastructure markets are dominated by the forces of positive feedback. Many companies can compete by adhering to widely accepted standards. For example, many companies compete to sell telephone handsets and PBXs; they need only interconnect properly with the public switched telephone network. Likewise, while there are strong network effects in the personal computer industry, there are no significant demand-side economies of scale *within* the market for IBM-compatible personal computers. If one person has a Dell and his coworker has a Compaq, they can still exchange files, e-mail, and advice. The customer-level equipment in telephony and PC hardware has been effectively standardized, so that interoperability and its accompanying network effects are no longer the problem they once were.

Another example of a high-tech industry that currently does not experience large network effects is that of Internet service providers. At one time, America Online, CompuServe, and Delphi attempted to provide proprietary systems of menus, e-mail, and discussion groups. It was clumsy, if not impossible, to send e-mail from one provider to another. In those days there were network externalities, and consumers gravitated toward those networks that offered the best connections to other consumers.

The commercialization of the Internet changed all that. The availability of standardized protocols for menus/browsers, e-mail, and chat removed the advantage of being a larger ISP and led to the creation of thousands of smaller providers. If you are on AOL, you can still exchange e-mail with your sister in Boston who is an IBM network customer.

This situation may well change in the future as new Internet technology allows providers to offer differential quality of service for applications such as video conferencing. A large ISP may gain an advantage based on the technological fact that it is easier to control quality of service for traffic that stays on a single network. Video conferencing with your sister in Boston could be a lot easier if you are both on the same network—creating a significant network externality that could well alter the structure of the ISP industry and lead to greater consolidation and concentration. A number of observers have expressed concern that the proposed acquisition of MCI by Worldcom will permit Worldcom to gain dominance by providing superior service to customers whose traffic stays entirely on Worldcom's network.

Our point is that you need to think carefully about the magnitude and significance of network externalities in your industry. Ford used to offer costly rebates and sell thousands of Tauruses to Hertz (which it owns) to gain the title of best-selling car. But was

> *Not every market tips.*

it really worth it? Who buys a car just because other people buy it? Don't let the idea of positive feedback carry you away: not every market tips.

Will *your* market tip toward a single dominant technology or vendor? This is a critical question to ask before forging ahead with any of the basic strategies we have just described. If your market is a true winner-take-all market subject to such tipping, standardization may be critical for the market to take off at all. Plus, these same positive feedback conditions make it very risky to compete because of the dark side

Table 7.1. Likelihood of Market Tipping to a Single Technology

	Low Economies of Scale	High Economies of Scale
Low demand for variety	Unlikely	High
High demand for variety	Low	Depends

of positive feedback: a necessary implication of "winner-take-all" is "loser-gets-nothing." On the other hand, if there is room for several players in your industry, competition takes on a different tone than if there will be only one survivor in a standards war.

Whether a market tips or not depends on the balance between two fundamental forces: economies of scale and variety. See Table 7.1 for a classification.

Strong scale economies, on either the demand or the supply side of the market, will make a market tippy. But standardization typically entails a loss of variety, even if the leading technology can be implemented with a broad product line. If different users have highly distinct needs, the market is less likely to tip. In high-definition television (HDTV), different countries use different systems, both because of the legacy of earlier incompatible systems and because of the tendency to favor domestic firms over foreign ones. As a result, the worldwide market has not tipped, although each individual country has. The fact is, most network externalities in television do not cross national or regional borders: not very many people want to take a TV from the United States to Japan, so little is lost when different regions use incompatible transmission standards.

We've emphasized demand-side scale economies, but tippiness depends on the sum total of all scale economies. True, the strongest positive feedback in information industries comes on the demand side, but you should not ignore the supply side in assessing tipping. Traditional economies of scale that are specific to each technology will amplify demand-side economies of scale. So, too, will dynamic scale economies that arise based on learning-by-doing and the experience curve.

Even though we started this section by saying that there are no significant demand-side economies of scale for IBM-compatible personal computers, it doesn't follow that this market is immune from positive feedback since there may well be significant economies of scale on the *production* side of the market. Four companies, Compaq, Dell,

HP, and IBM, now control 24 percent of the market for personal computers, and some analysts expect this fraction to grow, claiming that these companies can produce desktop boxes at a smaller unit cost than their smaller competitors. This may be so, but it is important to recognize that this is just old-fashioned supply-side economies of scale; these different brands of personal computers interoperate well enough that demand-side economies of scale are not particularly important.

Information goods and information infrastructure often exhibit *both* demand-side and supply-side economies of scale. One reason Digital Equipment Corporation has had difficulty making its Alpha chip fly as an alternative to Intel chips, despite its impressive performance, is that Digital lacks the scale to drive manufacturing costs down. Digital is now hoping to overcome that obstacle by sourcing its chips from Intel and Samsung, which can operate chip fabrication facilities at far greater scale than Digital has achieved. Still, whether Digital can attract enough partners to generate positive feedback for the Alpha chip remains to be seen. The United States and Europe are currently competing to convince countries around the world to adopt their HDTV formats. Tipping may occur for HDTV not based on network effects but because of good old-fashioned economies of scale in making television sets.

We have emphasized the network nature of information technology, with many of our examples coming from the hardware side. The same effects occur on the software side. It is hard for a new virtual reality product to gain market share without people having access to a viewer for that product . . . but no one wants to buy a viewer if there is no content to view.

However, the Internet has made this chicken-and-egg problem a lot more manageable. Now you can download the viewer prior to, or even concurrently with, downloading the content. Want to read a PDF file? No problem—click over to Adobe's site and download the latest version of Acrobat. New technologies like Marimba even allow your system to upgrade its viewers over the Internet automatically. If your viewer is written in Java, you can download the viewer *along with* the content. It's like using your computer to download the fax machine along with the fax!

The Internet distribution of new applications and standards is very convenient and reduces *some* of the network externalities for software by reducing switching costs. Variety can be supported more easily if an entire system can be offered on demand. But the Internet certainly doesn't *eliminate* network externalities in software. Interoperability is still a big issue on the production side: even if users can download the appropriate virtual reality viewer, producers won't want to produce to half-a-dozen different standards. In fact, it's because of this producer resistance that Microsoft and Netscape agreed on a Virtual Reality Markup Language standard, as we discuss in Chapter 8.

IGNITING POSITIVE FEEDBACK: PERFORMANCE VERSUS COMPATIBILITY

What does it take for a new technology to succeed in the market? How can a new technology get into a virtuous cycle rather than a vicious one? Philips and Sony certainly managed it when they introduced compact disks in the early 1980s. Fifteen years later, phonographs and long-playing records (LPs) are scarce indeed; our children hardly know what they are.

How can you make network externalities work for you to launch a new product or technology? How can you overcome collective switching costs and build a new network of users? Let there be no doubt: building your own base of users for a new technology in the face of an established network can be daunting. There are plenty of failures in consumer electronics alone, not to mention more arcane areas. Indeed, Sony and Philips have had more than a little trouble duplicating their CD feat. They teamed up to introduce digital audio tape (DAT) in 1987, which offered the sound quality of CD along with the ability to record music. But DAT bombed, in part because of the delays based on concerns about copy protection.

Philips tried on its own with the digital compact cassette (DCC) in 1992. These cassettes had the advantage that DCC machines (unlike DAT machines) could play conventional cassettes, making the new technology *backward compatible.* But the sound quality of the DCC offered no big improvement over conventional CDs. Without a compelling reason to switch, consumers refused to adopt the new technology. Sony, too, had its own offering around this time, the minidisk. While minidisks are still around (especially in Japan), this product never really got on the positive feedback curve, either.

There are two basic approaches for dealing with the problem of consumer inertia: the *evolution* strategy of compatibility and the *revolu-*

Figure 7.4. *Performance versus Compatibility*

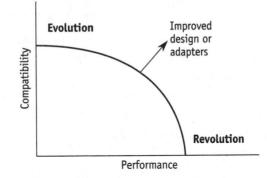

tion strategy of compelling performance. Combinations are possible, but the key is to understand these two fundamental approaches. These strategies reflect an underlying tension when the forces of innovation meet up with network externalities: is it better to wipe the slate clean and come up with the best product possible (revolution) or to give up some performance to ensure compatibility and thus ease consumer adoption (evolution)?

> *The evolution strategy offers consumers a smooth migration path. The revolution strategy offers compelling performance.*

Figure 7.4 illustrates the trade-off. You can improve performance at the cost of increasing customer switching costs, or vice-versa. An outcome of high compatibility with limited performance improvement, in the upper-left corner of the figure, characterizes the evolution approach. An outcome of little or no compatibility but sharply superior performance, in the lower-right corner of the figure, characterizes the revolution approach. Ideally, you would like to have an improved product that is also compatible with the installed base, but technology is usually not so forgiving, and adapters and emulators are notoriously buggy. You will inevitably face the trade-off in Figure 7.4.

EVOLUTION: OFFER A MIGRATION PATH

The history of color television in the United States, discussed later in the chapter, teaches us that compatibility with the installed base of equipment is often critical to the launch of a new generation of technology. The CBS color system, incompatible with existing black-and-white sets, failed despite FCC endorsement as the official standard. When compatibility is critical, consumers must be offered a smooth migration path to a new information technology. Taking little baby steps toward a new technology is a lot easier than making a gigantic leap of faith.

The evolution strategy, which offers consumers an easy migration path, centers on reducing switching costs so that consumers can gradually try your new technology. This is what Borland tried to do in copying certain commands from Lotus 1-2-3. This is what Microsoft did by including in Word extensive, specialized help for WordPerfect users, as well as making it easy to convert WordPerfect files into Word format. Offering a migration path is evolutionary in nature. This strategy can be employed on a modest scale, even by a relatively small player in the industry.

In virtual networks, the evolution strategy of offering consumers a migration path requires an ability to achieve compatibility with existing products. In real networks, the evolution strategy requires physical interconnection to existing networks. In either case, interfaces are critical. The key to the evolution strategy is to build a new network by linking it first to the old one.

One of the risks of following the evolution approach is that one of your competitors may try a revolution strategy for its product. Compromising performance to ensure backward compatibility may leave an opening for a competitor to come in with a technologically superior market. This is precisely what happened to the dBase program in 1990 when it was challenged by Paradox, FoxPro, and Access in the market for relational database software.

Intel is facing this dilemma with its Merced chip. The 32-bit architecture of Intel's recent chips has been hugely successful for Intel, but to move to a 64-bit architecture the company will have to introduce some incompatibilities—or will it? Intel claims that its forthcoming Merced chip will offer the best of both worlds, running both 32-bit and 64-bit applications. There is a lot of speculation about the Merced architecture, but Intel is keeping quiet about strategy, since it recognizes that it will be especially vulnerable during this transition.

Can you offer your customers an attractive migration path to a new technology? To lure customers, the migration path must be smooth, and it must lead somewhere. You will need to overcome two obstacles to execute this strategy: technical and legal.

Technical Obstacles

The technical obstacles you'll face have to do with the need to develop a technology that is at the same time compatible with, and yet superior to, existing products. Only in this way can you keep customers' switching costs low, by offering backward compatibility, and still offer improved performance. We'll see in our example of high-definition television how this strategy can go awry: to avoid stranding existing TV sets in the early 1990s, the Europeans promoted a standard for the transmission of high-definition signals that conventional TV sets could decipher. But they paid a high price: the signal was not as sharp as true HDTV, and the technology bombed despite strong government pressure on the satellite industry to adopt it.

Technical obstacles to the thorny compatibility/performance trade-off are not unique to upstart firms trying to supplant market leaders. Those same market leaders face these obstacles as well. Microsoft held back the performance of Windows 95 so that users could run old DOS applications. Microsoft has clearly stated that Windows 95 is a transition operating system and that its eventual goal is to move everyone to Windows NT.

One way to deal with the compatibility/performance trade-off is to offer *one-way* compatibility. When Microsoft offered Office 97 as an upgrade to Office 95, it designed the file formats used by Office 97 to be incompatible with the Office 95 formats. Word 97 could read files from Word 95, but not the other way around. With this tactic, Microsoft could introduce product improvements while making it easy for Word 97 users to import the files they had created using older versions.

This one-way compatibility created an interesting dynamic: influential early adopters had a hard time sharing files with their slower-to-adopt colleagues. Something had to give. Microsoft surely was hoping that organizations would shift *everyone* over to Office 97 to ensure full interoperability. However, Microsoft may have gone too far. When this problem became widely recognized, and potential users saw the costs of a heterogeneous environment, they began to delay deployment of Office 97. Microsoft's response was to release two free applications:

Word Viewer, for viewing Word 97 files and Word Converter, for converting Word 97 to Word 95.

Remember, your strategy with respect to selling upgrades should be to give the users a reason to upgrade and then to make the process of upgrading as easy as possible. The reason to upgrade can be a "pull" (such as desirable new features) or a "push" (such as a desire to be compatible with others). The difficulty with the push strategy is that users may decide not to upgrade at all, which is why Microsoft eventually softened its "incompatibility" strategy.

In some cases, the desire to maintain compatibility with previous generations has been the undoing of market leaders. The dBase programming language was hobbled because each new version of dBase had to be able to run programs written for all earlier versions. Over time, layers of dBase programming code accumulated on top of each other. Ashton-Tate, the maker of dBase, recognized that this resulted in awkward "bloatware," which degraded the performance of dBase. Unable to improve dBase in a timely fashion, and facing competition from Borland's more elegant, object-oriented, relational database program, Paradox, dBase's fortunes fell sharply. Ashton-Tate was slain by the dark side of positive feedback. Ultimately, Borland acquired Ashton-Tate with the idea of migrating the dBase installed base to Paradox.

We offer three strategies for helping to smooth user migration paths to new technologies:

Use creative design. Good engineering and product design can greatly ease the compatibility/performance trade-off. As shown in Figure 7.4, improved designs shift the entire trade-off between compatibility and performance favorably. Intensive effort in the early 1950s by engineers at NBC enabled them to offer a method of transmitting color television signals so that black-and-white sets could successfully receive these same signals. The breakthrough was the use of complex electronic methods that converted the three color signals (red, green, and blue) into two signals (luminance and color).

Think in terms of the system. Remember, you may be making only one component, but the user cares about the whole system. To ease the transition to digital television, the FCC is loaning broadcasters extra spectrum space so they can broadcast both conventional and HDTV digital signals, which will ease the burden of switching costs.

Consider converters and bridge technologies. HDTV is again a good example: once broadcasters cease transmitting conventional TV signals, anyone with an analog television will have to buy a converter to receive digital over-the-air broadcasts. This isn't ideal, but it still offers a migration path to the installed base of analog TV viewers.

Legal Obstacles

The second kind of obstacle you'll find as you build a migration path is legal and contractual: you need to have or obtain the legal right to sell products that are compatible with the established installed base of products. Sometimes this is not an issue: there are no legal barriers to building TV sets that can receive today's broadcast television signals. But sometimes this kind of barrier can be insurmountable. Incumbents with intellectual property rights over an older generation of technology may have the ability to unilaterally blockade a migration path. Whether they use this ability to stop rivals in their tracks, or simply to extract licensing revenues, is a basic strategy choice for these rights holders. For example, no one can sell an audio machine in the United States that will play CDs without a license from Philips and Sony, at least until their patents expire. Sony and Philips used their power over CD technology in negotiating with Time Warner, Toshiba, and others over the DVD standard. As a result, the new DVD machines will be able to read regular audio CDs; they will also incorporate technology from Sony and Philips.

REVOLUTION: OFFER COMPELLING PERFORMANCE

The revolution strategy involves brute force: offer a product so much better than what people are using that enough users will bear the pain of switching to it. Usually, this strategy works by first attracting customers who care the most about performance and working down from there to the mass market. Sony and Philips appealed first to the audiophiles, who then brought in the more casual music listeners when prices of machines and disks fell. Fax machines first made inroads in the United

States for exchanging documents with Japan, where the time and language differences made faxes especially attractive; from this base, the fax population exploded. HDTV set manufacturers are hoping to first sell to the so-called vidiots, those who simply must have the very best quality video and the largest TV sets available. The trick is to offer compelling performance to first attract pioneering and influential users, then to use this base to start up a bandwagon propelled by self-fulfilling consumer beliefs in the inevitable success of your product.

How big a performance advance must you offer to succeed? Andy Grove speaks of the "10X" rule of thumb: you need to offer performance "ten times better" than the established technology to start a revolution. We like the idea, and certainly agree that substantial improvements in performance are necessary to make the revolution strategy work. But in most applications performance cannot easily be reduced to a single measure, as implied by the 10X rule. Also, as economists, we must point out that the magnitude of switching costs enters into the calculation, too. Sega's ability to make inroads against Nintendo in the video game business in the early 1990s was aided by the presence of lots of customers with low switching costs: there is a new crop of ten-year-old boys every year who are skilled at convincing Mom and Dad that they just *have* to get the system with the coolest new games or graphics.

Likewise, a growing market offers more opportunities to establish a beachhead against an established player. New customers alone can provide critical mass. More generally, a rapidly growing market tends to enhance the attractiveness of the revolution strategy. If the market is growing rapidly, or if consumer lock-in is relatively mild, performance looms larger relative to backward compatibility.

The revolution strategy is inherently risky. It cannot work on a small scale and usually requires powerful allies. Worse yet, it is devilishly difficult to tell early on whether your technology will take off or crash and burn. Even the successful technologies start off slowly and accelerate from there, following the logistic, or S-shaped, growth pattern we noted earlier.

IGNITING POSITIVE FEEDBACK: OPENNESS VERSUS CONTROL

Anyone launching a new technology must also face a second fundamental trade-off, in addition to the performance/compatibility trade-off. Do you choose an "open" approach by offering to make the necessary interfaces and specifications available to others, or do you attempt to maintain control by keeping your system proprietary? This trade-off is closely related to our discussion of lock-in in Chapters 5 and 6.

Proprietary control will be exceedingly valuable if your product or system takes off. As we discussed in Chapter 6, an installed base is more valuable if you do not face rivals who can offer products to locked-in customers. Likewise, your network is far more valuable if you can control the ability of others to interconnect with you. Intel's market capitalization today would be far less if Intel had previously agreed to license all the intellectual property embodied in its Pentium chips to many rival chip makers.

However, failure to open up a technology can spell its demise, if consumers fear lock-in or if you face a strong rival whose system offers comparable performance but is nonproprietary. Sony faced precisely this problem with its Beta video cassette recorder system and lost out to the more open VHS system, which is now the standard. Openness will bolster your chances of success by attracting allies and assuring would-be customers that they will be able to turn to multiple suppliers down the road.

Which route is best, openness or control? The answer depends on whether you are strong enough to ignite positive feedback on your own. Strength in network markets is measured along three primary dimensions: existing market position, technical capabilities, and control of intellectual property such as patents and copyrights. In Chapter 9 we will explore more fully the key assets that determine companies' strengths in network markets.

Existing market position, technical capabilities, and control of intellectual property are critical strengths.

Of course, there is no one right choice between control and openness. Indeed, a single company might well choose control for some products and openness for others. Intel has maintained considerable control over the MMX multimedia specification for its Pentium chips. At the same time, Intel recently promoted new, open interface specifications for graphics controllers, its accelerated graphics port (AGP), so as to hasten improvements in visual computing and thus fuel demand for Intel's microprocessors. Intel picked control over MMX, but openness for AGP.

In choosing between openness and control, remember that your ultimate goal is to maximize the *value* of your technology, not your *control* over it. This is the same point we discussed in the case of intellectual property rights in Chapter 4. Ultimately, your profits will flow from the competitive advantages you can retain while assembling enough support to get your technology off the ground.

Think of your reward using this formula:

> Your reward = Total value added to industry
> × your share of industry value

The total value added to the industry depends first on the inherent value of the technology—what improvement it offers over existing alternatives. But when network effects are strong, total value also depends on how widely the technology is adopted—that is, the network size. Your share of the value added depends on your ultimate market share, your profit margin, any royalty payments you make or receive, and the effects the new technology has on your sales of other products. Does it cannibalize or stimulate them?

Roughly speaking, strategies to achieve openness emphasize the first term in this formula, the *total value added to the industry.* Strategies to achieve control emphasize the second term, *your share of industry value.* We will focus on openness strategies in Chapter 8 and on control strategies in Chapter 9.

The fundamental trade-off between openness and control is shown in Figure 7.5: you can have a large share of a small market (the upper-left portion of the diagram), or a small share of a large market (the

Figure 7.5. *Openness versus Control*

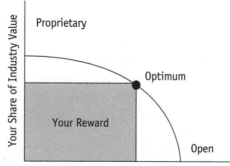

lower-right portion of the diagram). Unless you have made a real technical breakthrough or are extremely lucky, it is almost impossible to have it both ways. At the optimum, you choose the approach that maximizes your reward—that is, the total value you receive.

This trade-off is fundamental in network markets. To maximize the value of your new technology, you will likely need to share that value with other players in the industry. This comes back to the point we have made repeatedly: information technology is comprised of *systems,* and an increase in the value of one component necessarily spills over to other components. Capturing the value from improvements to one component typically requires the cooperation of those providing other components. Count on the best of those suppliers to insist on getting a share of the rewards as a condition for their cooperation.

Unless you are in a truly dominant position at the outset, trying to control the technology yourself can leave you a large share of a tiny pie. Opening up the technology freely can fuel positive feedback and maximize the total value added of the technology. But what share of the benefits will you be able to preserve for yourself? Sometimes even leading firms conclude that they would rather grow the market quickly, through openness, than maintain control. Adobe did this with its Post-Script language, and Sun followed its example with Java.

The boundary between openness and control is not sharp; intermediate approaches are frequently used. For example, a company pursuing an openness strategy can still retain exclusive control over *changes* to the technology, as Sun is attempting to do with Java. Likewise, a company pursuing a control strategy can still offer access to its network for a price, as Nintendo did by charging royalties to game developers who were writing games for its Nintendo Entertainment System.

Openness

The openness strategy is critical when no one firm is strong enough to dictate technology standards. Openness also arises naturally when multiple products must work together, making coordination in product design essential.

Openness is a more cautious strategy than control. The underlying idea is to forsake control over the technology to get the bandwagon rolling. If the new technology draws on contributions from several different companies, each agrees to cede control over its piece in order to create an attractive package: the whole is greater than the sum of the parts.

The term *openness* means many things to many people. The Unix X/Open consortium defines *open systems* as "systems and software environments based on standards which are vendor independent and commonly available."

As we emphasized in our discussion of lock-in, beware vague promises of openness. Openness may be in the eye of the beholder. Netscape insists that it is congenitally open, but some observers detect efforts by Netscape to keep control. Cisco is often lauded for using open Internet standards for its routers and switches, but, again, some see a deep proprietary streak there, too.

Openness involves more than technical specifications; timing is also important. Microsoft has been accused of keeping secret certain application programming interfaces (APIs), in violation of its earlier promises that Windows would be open. Even harder to assess, independent software vendors (ISVs) have at times been very concerned that Microsoft provides APIs for new versions of Windows to its in-house development team before giving them to the ISVs. To some extent this seems inevitable as part of improving the operating system and making sure it will work smoothly with new applications. On the other hand, ISVs are justifiably unhappy when placed at a competitive disadvantage relative to Microsoft's own programmers, especially since they already face the threat of having their program's functionality subsumed into the operating system itself.

Within the openness category, we can fruitfully distinguish between a *full openness* strategy and an *alliance* strategy for establishing new product standards. We study full openness and alliance strategies in Chapter 8 in the context of standards negotiations.

Under full openness, anybody has the right to make products complying with the standard, whether they contributed to its development or not. Under an alliance approach, each member of the alliance contributes something toward the standard, and, in exchange, each is allowed to make products complying with the standard. Nonmembers can be blocked from offering such products or charged for the right to do so. In other words, the alliance members all have guaranteed (usually free) access to the network they have created, but outsiders may be blocked from accessing it or required to pay a special fee for such access.

In some industries with strong network characteristics, full openness is the only feasible approach. For years, basic telecommunications standards have been hammered out by official standard-setting bodies, either domestically or internationally. The standard-setting process at the International Telecommunications Union (ITU), for example, has led to hundreds of standards, including those for fax machines and modems. The ITU, like other formal standard-setting bodies, insists, as a quid pro quo for endorsement of a standard, that no single firm or group of firms maintains proprietary control over the standard. We will discuss tactics in formal standard setting in detail in Chapter 8.

The full openness strategy is not confined to formal standard setting, however. Whatever the institutional setting, full openness is a natural way of overcoming a stalemate in which no single firm is in a position to drive home its preferred standard without widespread support.

One way to pursue a full openness strategy is to place the technology in the hands of a neutral third party. Even this approach can be plagued with difficulties, however. Is the third party really neutral, or just a cover operation for the company contributing the technology? Doubts have arisen, for example, over whether Microsoft has *really* ceded control of ActiveX. We'll address ActiveX more fully in the next chapter.

In the end, it's worth asking who really wants openness and how everyone's interests are likely to evolve as the installed base grows or competition shifts. Usually, the upstart wants openness to neutralize installed-base disadvantages or to help assemble allies. In the Internet arena, where Microsoft was a latecomer, it initially pushed for open standards. Open Internet standards, at least initially, shift competition to marketing, brand name, and distribution, where Microsoft is strong. In desktop applications, where Microsoft is the dominant player, the company has not pushed for open standards and, it is claimed, has actively resisted them.

Build alliances to ignite positive feedback in the network economy.

Alliances are increasingly commonplace in the information economy. We do not mean those so-called strategic alliances involving widespread cooperation between a pair of companies. Rather, we mean an alliance formed by a group of companies for the express purpose of promoting a specific technology or standard. Alliances typically involve extensive wheeling and dealing, as multiple players negotiate based on the three key assets: control of the existing installed base, technical superiority, and intellectual property rights.

The widely heralded convergence between the computer and telecommunications industry offers many opportunities for alliances. Recently, for example, Compaq, Intel, and Microsoft announced a consortium for setting standards for digital subscriber line (DSL) technology, which promises to offer high-speed access to the Internet over residential phone lines. These three superstars of the information industry have partnered with seven of the eight regional Bell operating companies to promote unified hardware and software interfaces

Alliances come in many forms, depending on the assets that the different players bring to the table. Some of them operate as "special interest groups" (SIGs) or "task forces," groups of independent companies that meet to coordinate product standards, interfaces, protocols, and specifications. Cross-licensing of critical patents is common in this context, as is sharing of confidential design information under nondisclosure agreements. Some players hope to achieve royalty income and negotiate royalty arrangements that will attract critical allies. Others hope to gain from manufacturing skills or time-to-market prowess, so long as they are not blocked by patents or excessive royalty payments.

Alliances span the distance between full openness and control. At one end of the spectrum is an alliance that makes the technology freely available to all participants, but not (necessarily) to outsiders. Automatic teller machine networks and credit card networks work this way. For example, Visa and MasterCard both require merchant banks to make payments to card-issuing banks in the form of "interchange fees" as a means of covering the costs and risks borne by card-issuing banks, but the Visa and MasterCard associations themselves impose only modest fees on transactions to cover their own costs. And membership in Visa and MasterCard is generally open to any bank, so long as that bank does not issue rival cards, such as the Discover card.

At the other end of the spectrum is an alliance built like a web around a sponsor, a central actor that collects royalties from others, preserves proprietary rights over a key component of the network, and/or maintains control over the evolution of the technology. We described how Apple is the sponsor of the Macintosh network. Likewise, Sun is the sponsor of Java. If the sponsor charges significant royalties or retains exclusive rights to control the evolution of the technology, we would classify that situation as one of control, not openness. Sun is walking a thin line, wanting to retain its partners in the battle with Microsoft but also wanting to generate revenues from its substantial investment in Java.

Control

Only those in the strongest position can hope to exert strong control over newly introduced information technologies. Usually these are market leaders: AT&T was a prime example in its day; Microsoft, Intel, TCI, and Visa are examples today. In rare cases, strength flows from sheer technical superiority: at one time or another, Apple, Nintendo, Sony, Philips, and Qualcomm have all been in this privileged position.

Companies strong enough to unilaterally control product standards and interfaces have power. Even if they are not being challenged for supremacy, however, they have much to lose by promoting poorly conceived standards. For example, Microsoft is not about to lose its leadership position in desktop operating systems, even if it slips up when designing new APIs between its operating system and applications or makes some design errors in its next release of Windows. But this is not to say that Microsoft can be reckless or careless in this design process: Microsoft still needs to attract independent software developers to its platform, it still has powerful incentives to improve Windows to drive upgrade sales and reach new users, and it wants the overall Windows "system" to improve to make further inroads against Unix-based workstations.

GENERIC STRATEGIES IN NETWORK MARKETS

We are now ready to introduce the four generic strategies for companies seeking to introduce new information technology into the marketplace. These four strategies for igniting positive feedback follow logically from the two basic trade-offs discussed in the previous sections: (1) the trade-off between performance and compatibility as reflected in the choice between revolution and evolution and (2) the trade-off between openness and control. The combination of each of these two trade-offs yields the four generic strategies shown in Table 7.2.

The first row in Table 7.2 represents the choice of compatibility, the

Table 7.2. Generic Network Strategies

	Control	Openness
Compatibility	Controlled migration	Open migration
Performance	Performance play	Discontinuity

evolution strategy. The second row represents the choice to accept incompatibility in order to maximize performance, the revolution strategy. Either of these approaches can be combined with openness or control. The left-hand column in Table 7.2 represents the decision to retain proprietary control, the right-hand column the decision to open up the technology to others.

The four generic network strategies that emerge from this analysis can be found in Table 7.2: performance play, controlled migration, open migration, and discontinuity. In the next few pages, we describe the four strategies, say a bit about their pros and cons, and give examples of companies that have pursued them. We offer a more in-depth discussion of how the generic strategies work and when to use them in Chapters 8 and 9.

These four generic strategies arise again and again. The players and the context change, but not these four strategies. Incumbents may find it easier to achieve backward compatibility, but entrants and incumbents alike must choose one of our generic strategies. In some markets, a single firm or coalition is pursuing one of the generic strategies. In other cases, two incompatible technologies are engaged in a battle to build their own new networks. In these standards wars, which we explore in Chapter 9, the very nature of the battle depends on the pair of generic strategies employed by the combatants.

Performance Play

Performance play is the boldest and riskiest of the four generic strategies. A performance play involves the introduction of a new, incompatible technology over which the vendor retains strong proprietary control. Nintendo followed this approach when it introduced its Nintendo Entertainment System in the mid-1980s. More recently, U.S. Robotics used the performance play with its Palm Pilot device. Iomega did likewise in launching its Zip drive.

Performance play makes the most sense if your advantage is primarily based on the development of a striking new technology that offers users substantial advantages over existing technology. Performance play is especially attractive to firms that are outsiders, with no installed base to worry about. Entrants and upstarts with compelling new technology can more easily afford to ignore backward compatibility and push for an entirely new technology than could an established player who would have to worry about cannibalizing sales of existing products or stranding loyal customers.

Even if you are a new entrant to the market with "way cool" technology, you may need to consider sacrificing some performance so as to design your system to reduce consumer switching costs; this is the controlled migration strategy. You also need to assess your strength and assemble allies as needed. For example, you might agree to license your key patents for small or nominal royalties to help ignite positive feedback. The more allies you need, the more open you make your system, the closer you are to the discontinuity strategy than the performance play.

Controlled Migration

In controlled migration, consumers are offered a new and improved technology that is compatible with their existing technology, but is proprietary. Windows 98 and the Intel Pentium II chip are examples of this strategy. Upgrades and updates of software programs, like the annual release of TurboTax by Intuit, tend to fit into this category as well. Such upgrades are offered by a single vendor, they can read data files and programming created for earlier versions, and they rely on many of the same skills that users developed for earlier versions.

If you have secure domination in your market, you can introduce the new technology as a premium version of the old technology, selling it first to those who find the improvements most valuable. Thus, controlled migration often is a dynamic form of the versioning strategy described in Chapter 3. Controlled migration has the further advantage of making it harder for an upstart to leapfrog ahead of you with a performance play.

Open Migration

Open migration is very friendly to consumers: the new product is supplied by many vendors and requires little by way of switching costs.
Multiple generations of modems and fax machines have followed the
open migration model. Each new generation conforms to an agreed-
upon standard and communicates smoothly with earlier generations of
machines.

Open migration makes the most sense if your advantage is primarily
based on manufacturing capabilities. In that case, you will benefit from a
larger total market and an agreed-upon set of specifications, which will
allow your manufacturing skills and scale economies to shine. Owing to
its fine engineering and skill in manufacturing, Hewlett-Packard has
commonly adopted this strategy.

Discontinuity

Discontinuity refers to the situation in which a new product or technology is incompatible with existing technology but is available from multiple suppliers. The introduction of the CD audio system and the 3½"
floppy disk are examples of discontinuity. Like open migration, discontinuity favors suppliers that are efficient manufacturers (in the case of
hardware) or that are best placed to provide value-added services or
software enhancements (in the case of software).

HISTORICAL EXAMPLES OF POSITIVE FEEDBACK

The best way to get a feel for these strategies is to see them in action. In
practice, the revolution versus evolution choice emerges in the design of
new product standards and negotiation over those standards. The openness versus control choice arises when industry leaders set the terms on
which their networks interconnect.

Fortunately, positive feedback and network externalities have been
around for a while, so history can be our guide. As we have stressed,
while information technology is hurtling forward at breathtaking speeds,
the underlying economic principles are not all that novel. Even in this
consummately high-tech area of standards, networks, interfaces, and
compatibility, there is much to learn from history.

The case studies that follow illustrate the generic strategies and foreshadow some of the key strategic points we will develop in the next two chapters. All of our examples illustrate positive feedback in action: the triumph of one technology over others, in some cases by virtue of a modest head start or a fleeting performance advantage. One of the great attractions of historical examples is that we can see what happened after the dust finally settles, giving us some needed perspective in analyzing current battles.

When you stop to think about it, compatibility and standards have been an issue for as long as human beings have used spoken language or, more to the point, multiple languages. The Tower of Babel reminds us that standardization is hard. You don't hear Esperanto spoken very much (though its promoters do have a site on the Web). English has done remarkably well as an international language for scientific and technical purposes and is being given an extra boost by the Internet, but language barriers have hardly been eliminated.

Turning from biblical to merely historical times, Eli Whitney amazed President John Adams in 1798 by disassembling a dozen muskets, scrambling the parts, and then reassembling them in working order. As a result, Whitney received a government contract for $134,000 to produce 10,000 army muskets using his "uniformity system." This standardization of parts allowed for mass production and ushered in the American industrial revolution.

A humorous standards battle of sorts was triggered by the invention of the telephone. The early telephone links involved a continuously open line between two parties. Since the phone did not ring, how was the calling party to get the attention of those on the other end of the line? Thomas Edison consciously invented a brand-new word designed to capture the attention of those on the other end: "Hello!" This was a variant of the English "Hallow!" but reengineered by Edison to make it more effective. Edison, who was hard of hearing, estimated that a spoken "Hello!" could be heard ten to twenty feet away.

Soon thereafter, when telephones were equipped with bells to announce incoming calls, the more pressing issue was how to *answer* the telephone. This was a touchy issue; in the 1870s it was considered impolite to speak to anyone else unless you had been introduced! In 1878, when Edison opened the first public telephone exchange (in New Haven, Connecticut, on January 28, 1878), his operating manuals promoted "Hello!" as the proper way to answer the phone. ("What is wanted?" was noted as a more cautious alternative.) At the same time, Alexander Graham Bell, the inventor of the telephone, proclaimed that "Ahoy!" was the correct way to answer the telephone. By 1880, "Hello" had won this standards battle. This is an early example of how control over distribution channels, which Edison had through his manuals, can lead to control over interface standards.

Railroad Gauges

A more instructive example of standards battles involves the history of railroad gauges in the United States during the nineteenth century.

As railroads began to be built in the early nineteenth century, tracks of varying widths (gauges) were employed. Somewhat arbitrary early choices had major, lasting impacts. One of the first railroads in the South, for example, the South Carolina, picked 5-foot gauge tracks. Over time, other railroads all over the South followed suit. In the North, by contrast, the "standard" gauge of 4'8½", popular in England for mining, was common. Evidently, this was about the width of cart track in Roman times, being the most efficient width of a loaded vehicle that could be pulled by a flesh-and-blood (not iron) horse. The persistence of the 4'8½" gauge, which now is standard in the United States, is a good reminder that inertia is a powerful and durable force when standards are involved and that seemingly insignificant historical events can lead to lasting technological lock-in.

By 1860, seven different gauges were in use in America. Just over half of the total mileage was of the 4'8½" standard. The next most popular was the 5-foot gauge concentrated in the South. As things turned out, having different gauges was advantageous to the South, since the North could not easily use railroads to move its troops to battle in southern territory during the Civil War. Noting this example, the Finns were careful to ensure that their railroads used a gauge different from the Russian railroads! The rest of Europe adopted a standard gauge, which made things easy for Hitler during World War II: a significant fraction of German troop movements in Europe were accomplished by rail.

Despite these examples, standards are generally socially beneficial, since they allow for easy "interconnection" and thus larger networks.

But private interests can diverge from social interests. Battles over which standard to set, or whether there should be a standard at all, are common. Such battles can be severe, if not bloody, when there are entrenched users on both sides with high switching costs, when it is difficult for the various users to coordinate, and when some industry participants have much to lose from standardization. Railroad gauge standardization faced three major obstacles: (1) it was costly to change the width of existing tracks, (2) each group wanted the others to make the move, and (3) workers whose livelihoods depended on the incompatibilities resisted the proposed changes. In 1853 in Erie, Pennsylvania, where three different widths of railroad track met, there were riots over plans to standardize: workers were fearful of losing their jobs associated with loading and unloading cargo and jacking up cars to change their wheels.

Nonetheless, standardization was gradually achieved between 1860 and 1890. How? The westward expansion provided part of the answer. The big eastern railroads wanted to move western grain to the East and pushed for new lines to the West to be at standard gauge. Since the majority of the eastbound traffic terminated on their lines, they got their way. The Civil War played a role, too. The Union had pressing needs for efficient east-west transportation, giving further impetus for new western lines to be built at standard gauge. The Civil War and westward expansion interacted as well. In 1862, Congress specified the standard gauge for the transcontinental railroads. By this date, the southern states had seceded, leaving no one to push for the 5-foot gauge. After the war, the southern railroads found themselves increasingly in the minority. For the next twenty years, they relied on various imperfect means of interconnection with the North and West: cars with a sliding wheel base, hoists to lift cars from one wheel base to another, and, most commonly, a third rail.

Southern railroad interests finally met and adopted the standard gauge in 1886. On two days during the spring of 1886, the gauges were changed, converting the 5-foot gauge into the now-standard 4'8½" gauge on more than 11,000 miles of track in the South to match the northern standard. A belated victory for the North!

Many of the lessons from this experience remain relevant today.

- Incompatibilities can arise almost by accident, yet persist for many years.

- Network markets tend to tip toward the leading player, unless the other players coordinate to act quickly and decisively.

- Seceding from the standard-setting process can leave you in a weak market position in the future.

- A large buyer (such as the U.S. government) can have more influence than suppliers in tipping the balance.

- Those left with the less popular technology will find a way to cut their losses, either by employing adapters or by writing off existing assets and joining the bandwagon.

We will see these themes over and over again in current-day standards battles.

Battle of the Systems: AC versus DC Power

Another classic nineteenth-century standards battle concerned the distribution of electricity. Thomas Edison promoted a direct current (DC) system of electrical power generation and distribution. Edison was the pioneer in building power systems, beginning in New York City in 1882. Edison's direct current system was challenged by the alternating current (AC) technology developed and deployed in the United States by George Westinghouse. The key to the commercialization of AC was the development of the transformer, which permitted power to be transmitted efficiently at high voltages and then stepped down to lower voltages for local distribution and use. The AC technology permitted the distribution of electricity over far greater distances than did DC.

Thus was joined the "Battle of the Systems." Each technology had pros and cons. Direct current had, for practical purposes relating to voltage drop, a one-mile limit between the generating station and the user, but it was more efficient at generating power. Direct current also had two significant commercial advantages: a head start and Edison's imprimatur.

Unlike railroads, however, electricity was not in great need of standardization. Indeed, the two technologies initially did not compete directly but were deployed in regions suited to their relative strengths. DC was most attractive in densely populated urban areas, while AC made inroads in small towns.

Nonetheless, a battle royal ensued in the 1887–1892 period, a struggle that was by no means confined to competition in the marketplace but rather to the courtroom, the political arena, public relations, and academia. We can learn much today from the tactics followed by the rival camps.

The Edison group moved first with infringement actions against the Westinghouse forces, which forced Westinghouse to invent around Edison patents, including patents involving the Edison lamp. Edison also went to great lengths to convince the public that the AC system was unsafe, going so far as to patent the electric chair. Edison first demonstrated the electric chair using alternating current to electrocute a large dog, and then persuaded the State of New York to execute condemned criminals "by administration of an alternating current." The Edison group even used the term "to Westinghouse" to refer to electrocution by alternating current. But electrocution was not the "killer app" of the power industry: lighting was what people wanted.

Ultimately, three factors ended the Battle of the Systems. First and foremost, advances in polyphase AC made it increasingly clear that AC was the superior alternative. Second, the rotary converter introduced in 1892 allowed existing DC stations to be integrated into AC systems, facilitating a graceful retreat for DC. Third, by 1890 Edison had sold his interests, leading to the formation of the General Electric Company in 1892, which was no longer a DC-only manufacturing entity. In this context, Edison's efforts can be seen as an attempt to prevent or delay tipping toward AC, perhaps to obtain the most money in selling his DC interests. By 1893, both General Electric and Westinghouse were offering AC systems and the battle was over.

All of the tactics found in this historical episode are regularly used today. True, few high-tech companies rely on death row to gain competitive advantage, but they frequently attempt to influence consumer expectations. In network markets, expectations are crucial and can easily be self-fulfilling: the product or technology expected to prevail *does* prevail. Keep this in mind when we discuss the recent standards battle over 56k modems in Chapter 9.

The battle between Edison and Westinghouse illustrates other important points:

- Technologies can seek well-suited niches if the forces toward standardization are not overwhelming.

- Ongoing innovation (here, polyphase AC) can lead to victory in a standards war.

- A first-mover advantage (of DC) can be overcome by a superior technology (of AC) if the performance advantage is sufficient and users are not overly entrenched.

- Adapters can be the salvation of the losing technology and can help to ultimately defuse a standards war.

Telephone Networks and Interconnection

The story of how "Hello!" triumphed over "Ahoy!" is amusing but not very important. However, many quite serious compatibility and inter-connection issues arose in the early days of our telephone system. With the Internet emerging as a new form of network, and with the Telecommunications Act of 1996 mandating that telephone companies open up their networks to competition, we have much to learn from the early days of telephone competition and interconnection.

The story begins in the mid-1890s, when several key Bell patents expired and the country emerged from a depression, causing independent (non-Bell) companies to proliferate. By 1903, Bell companies controlled less than half of the phones in America. Independents and rural cooperatives had the majority. In fact, more than half of incorporated towns and cities had more than one service. Perhaps by 2003 we can achieve this level of competition again!

There was no obvious reason at that time why these many independent phone companies could not thrive in the twentieth century. Sure, head-to-head competition in a given locale might be ruinous, given the high fixed costs and low marginal costs associated with the telephone network. Traditional economies of scale would thus suggest consolidation at the local level. But what forces and strategies led to the emergence of a dominant *national* telephone company, the Bell System?

Oddly enough, the key was long-distance telephone service. We say "oddly" because long-distance service did not appear to be a decisive competitive advantage at the turn of the century. In 1900, a mere 3 percent of all calls were long distance. Evidently, most people did not care much about long-distance service, and many telephone companies did not even offer long-distance service; they made their money on short-distance toll service. Furthermore, long-distance capability was a technical problem of some magnitude.

But the handwriting was on the wall. Local phone companies were finding it very profitable to combine adjacent towns and extend their reach. And some businesses, especially in urban areas, were willing to pay a great deal for long-distance service.

The Bell System, with by far the most extensive long-distance network, thus faced a fundamental strategic issue: would it be better to restrict long-distance access to its affiliates or to open up its network to independents? At first, Bell allowed only its affiliates to have access to its long-distance network. After 1900, with the proliferation of independents, Bell hit upon the winning strategy: open up to *nonaffiliated* companies that met Bell's technical and operating standards and that were not direct local competitors. This strategy stimulated traffic throughout the Bell network, enhanced the value of Bell service by increasing the number of parties that could be reached, and made Bell stronger versus the independents where Bell faced local competition.

Soon, the Bell System's advantage based on its long-distance network reversed the tide of competition. The peak percentage of total telephones controlled by nonconnecting independent telephone companies, some 41 percent, was achieved in the year Bell implemented the loading coil in the system, which greatly enhanced its long-distance capabilities. Bell was able to charge more than rival independents for its local service but also remain attractive because of its ability to connect long-distance calls. The independents tried but failed to establish a national alternative to the Bell System, in part because Bell controlled key cities.

Over time, these advantages allowed the Bell System to grow into the dominant local and long-distance carrier that it remained, under the corporate name of AT&T, until its breakup in 1984. AT&T denied local rivals access to its long-distance network, arguing that interconnection with independents with inferior standards (driven by competition) could compromise the integrity of its entire network. More generally, AT&T pushed for a natural monopoly model for the telephone system. After 1907, AT&T bought out many of its local competitors, which presumably had been weakened by these tactics. AT&T's acquisitions were accepted to support universal service, at the expense of competition.

Many of today's companies face interconnection issues not unlike those facing AT&T a hundred years ago. Just as independent telephone companies complained then about their inability to offer long-distance service, independent software vendors today fear that Microsoft will provide its own programmers interface information that is superior (in quality or timing) to what they are provided. The economic lesson is timeless: if you control a key interface or bottleneck, you should open it up, but on your own terms and conditions. These include technical conditions necessary to preserve the integrity of your product and economic terms that compensate you for any foregone business. The early Bell System story also illustrates how control of certain key customers (for example, New York and Chicago) can be parlayed into a dominant market position in the presence of network effects.

Color Television

Our next historical example is considerably more recent: the adoption of color television in the United States. Television is perhaps the biggest bandwagon of them all. Some 99 percent of American homes have at least one television, making TV sets more ubiquitous than telephones or flush toilets.

The color television technology used in the United States is known as the National Television Systems Committee (NTSC) system. (Critics insist that NTSC really means "Never Twice the Same Color.") This system was formally adopted by the Federal Communications Commission in 1953. The story of this adoption is a sobering example of formal standard setting gone awry.

We begin our story with the inauguration of commercial black-and-white television transmission in the United States on July 1, 1941. At that time, RCA, the owner of NBC and a leading manufacturer of black-and-white sets, was a powerful force in the radio and television world. But the future of television was clearly to be color, which had first been demonstrated in America by Bell Labs in 1929.

Throughout the 1940s, CBS, the leading television network, was pushing for the adoption of the mechanical color television system it was developing. During this time RCA was busy selling black-and-white sets, improving its technology, and, under the legendary leadership of David Sarnoff, working on its own all-electronic color television system. As the CBS system took the lead in performance, RCA urged the FCC to wait for an electronic system. A major obstacle for the CBS system was that it was not backward-compatible: color sets of the CBS type would not be able to receive existing black-and-white broadcasts without a special attachment.

Despite this drawback, the FCC adopted the CBS system in October 1950, after a test between the two color systems. The RCA system was just not ready. As David Sarnoff himself said: "The monkeys were green, the bananas were blue, and everyone had a good laugh." This was a political triumph of major proportions for CBS.

The market outcome was another story. RCA and Sarnoff refused to throw in the towel. To the contrary, they redoubled their efforts, on three fronts. First, RCA continued to criticize the CBS system. Second, RCA intensified its efforts to place black-and-white sets and thus build up an installed base of users whose equipment would be incompatible with the CBS technology. "Every set we get out there makes it that much tougher on CBS," said Sarnoff at the time. Third, Sarnoff intensified RCA's research and development on its color television system, with around-the-clock teams working in the lab. The resulting technology literally was done with mirrors.

CBS was poorly placed to take advantage of its political victory. To begin with, CBS had no manufacturing capability at the time and had not readied a manufacturing ally to move promptly into production. Following the FCC decision, CBS did purchase a TV set maker, Air King, but it would be a few years before Air King could economically manufacture color sets in commercial quantities. As a result, the official premier of CBS color broadcasting, on June 25, 1951, featuring Ed Sullivan, among others, was largely invisible, seen only at special studio parties. There were about 12 million TV sets in America at the time, but only a few dozen could receive CBS color.

Luck, of a sort, entered into the picture, too. With the onset of the Korean War, the U.S. government said that the materials needed for production of color sets were critical instead for the war effort and ordered a suspension of the manufacture of color sets. Both CBS and RCA were secretly pleased. CBS was able to make sets anyhow. RCA was happy to delay the sales of color sets that would compete with its own black-and-white sets, welcomed the time to further advance its own technology, and was delighted to have time to further build an installed base of black-and-white sets incompatible with the CBS color system.

By the time the ban was modified in June 1952, the RCA system was ready for prime time. A consensus in support of the RCA system had formed at the NTSC. This became known as the NTSC system, despite the fact that RCA owned most of the hundreds of patents controlling it. This relabeling was a face-saving device for the FCC, which could be seen to be following the industry consortium rather than RCA. In March 1953, Frank Stanton, the president of CBS, raised the white flag, noting that with 23 million black-and-white sets in place in American homes, compatibility was rather important. In December 1953, the FCC officially reversed its 1950 decision.

But, yet again, political victory did not lead so easily to success in the market. In 1954, Sarnoff predicted that RCA would sell 75,000 sets. In fact, only 5,000 sets were purchased, perhaps because few customers were willing to pay $1,000 for the 12½″ color set rather than $300 for a 21-inch black-and-white set. With hindsight, this does not seem surprising, especially since color sets would offer little added value until broadcasters invested in color capability and color programming became widespread. All this takes time. The chicken-and-egg problem had to be settled before the NBC peacock could prevail.

As it turned out, NBC and CBS affiliates invested in color transmission equipment quite quickly: 106 of 158 stations in the top forty cities had the ability to transmit color programs by 1957. But this was of little import to viewers, since the networks were far slower in offering color programming. By 1965, NBC offered 4,000 hours of color, but CBS still showed only 800 color hours, and ABC 600. The upshot: by 1963, only about 3 percent of TV households had color sets, which remained three to five times as expensive as black-and-white sets.

As brilliant as Sarnoff and RCA had been in getting their technology established as the standard, they, like CBS, were unable to put into place all the necessary components of the system to obtain profitability during the 1950s. As a result, by 1959, RCA had spent $130 million to develop color TV with no profit to show for it. The missing pieces were the creation and distribution of the programming itself: content. Then, as now, a killer app was needed to get households to invest in color television sets. The killer app of 1960 was *Walt Disney's Wonderful World of Color*, which Sarnoff obtained from ABC in 1960. RCA's first operating profit from color television sales came in 1960, and RCA started selling picture tubes to Zenith and others. The rest is history: color sets got better and cheaper, and the NBC peacock became famous.

We can all learn a great deal from this episode, ancient though it is by Internet time. First and foremost, adoption of a new technology can be painfully slow if the price/performance ratio is unattractive and if it requires adoption by a number of different players. For color TV to truly offer value to viewers, it was not enough to get set manufacturers and networks to agree on a standard; they had to produce sets that performed well at reasonable cost, they had to create compelling content, and they had to induce broadcasters to invest in transmission gear. The technology was just not ready for the mass market in 1953, much less 1950. Interestingly, the Europeans, by waiting another decade before the adoption of PAL and SECAM, ended up with a better system. The same leapfrogging is now taking place in reverse: the digital HDTV system being adopted in the United States is superior to the system selected years before by the Japanese, as we explain in the next section.

Second, the collapse of the CBS standard shows that first-mover advantages need not be decisive, even in markets strongly subject to tipping. Since the CBS technology circa 1950 was not backward-compatible, market tested, or ready for commercialization, it never really got started. In the presence of a committed rival that would just not quit, the game was far from over after the 1950 FCC vote.

Third, the color television experience highlights the importance of building alliances. CBS had the political allies necessary to obtain FCC approval for its system in 1950, but this was a phyrric victory since CBS lacked the manufacturing capability, or a suitable ally, to start to pump out sets in commercial volumes. Then as now, winners must take greater risks, building the manufacturing capacity and even the hardware before a formal standard is set. Indeed, as we discuss later, flooding the market with equipment built to your own specs can be a way of tipping the standard-setting process in your favor. But this is not a strategy for the timid.

Fourth, the color TV example shows the dangers of sitting back and assuming that you can maintain market dominance just because you control the current generation of technology or have a large installed base. Sarnoff, visionary though he was, was naturally tempted to milk the cash cow of RCA's black-and-white business rather than rush forward with the introduction of color television. The FCC's adoption of the CBS color technology in 1950 was a wake-up call. Sarnoff was then able to snatch victory from the jaws of defeat only by taking risks and redoubling his efforts. In the end, CBS played a vital role in spurring RCA forward with the development of its color system.

High-Definition Television

Our last extended example is high-definition television, now sometimes referred to as digital television. The HDTV story is of course far more recent than our other examples. Still, plans to adopt HDTV in the United States have been unfolding for more than a decade, HDTV is the successor to the NTSC color television standard just discussed, and the HDTV experience bolsters our theme: the technology changes, as does the cast of characters, but not the underlying economics.

HDTV—when it finally arrives—will be a major improvement over today's broadcast television. HDTV proponents claim it offers picture quality equivalent to 35 millimeter film, with roughly twice the resolution of the NTSC standard, not to mention six-channel digital surround-sound. You may wonder then why a decade after the FCC established the Advisory Committee on Advanced Television Service to study HDTV standards, HDTV has yet to be launched in the United States.

Not only has HDTV been touted as the future of television. HDTV has also been held out as critical to the health of America's consumer electronics industry. Back in the late 1980s and early 1990s, one observer after another proclaimed that American industrial strength would be in peril if we were to "lose" the HDTV battle against the Japanese and the Europeans. These pundits noted, accurately, that the United States imports the vast majority of its TV sets and that it has been the slowest of the three regions to put into place a set of standards for HDTV.

In this context, calls for the federal government to take an active role in promoting HDTV grew sharper and more urgent. How, it was asked, could the "market" be relied on to coordinate the introduction of HDTV production equipment, HDTV programming, HDTV transmission systems, and HDTV receivers? Stay tuned.

Back in the 1970s, the Japanese government coordinated and subsidized the development of the various technologies needed to make HDTV work. The Japanese public broadcasting company, NHK, began experimental transmissions using its analog "Muse" system back in 1979. Japanese firms and the government spent as much as $1.3 billion to develop their HDTV technology. In 1986, the United States backed the

Japanese system as a global standard, an outcome that was only thwarted by European protectionism. By 1991, NHK was broadcasting eight hours per day. But sets remained extremely expensive, and the advantages of HDTV were evident only on the largest sets (36 inches and up).

An interesting episode in February 1994 shows how fragile standards bandwagons can be. A senior official in the Ministry of Posts and Telecommunications (MPT) stated that the Japanese government was considering abandoning the (analog) Muse system because "the world trend is digital." In a stunning demonstration of the importance of expectations and consumer confidence in standards battles, this statement alone threw the market into a turmoil. An executive at Matsushita remarked, "This is like pouring water in a sleeping person's ear." The very next day, the presidents of Matsushita, NEC, and Sony, along with top executives of eight other television manufacturers, held a news conference to defend the Muse technology, and the MPT official was forced to retract his statement. But the damage had been done: how could the retraction be credible?

In fact, sales of HDTV sets in Japan have remained sluggish for years. Given the Japanese penchant for gadgets, this may be more a matter of simple high prices than fear of being stranded with an incompatible piece of electronics. By 1994, the cheapest HDTV sets still cost $6,000, and only about 20,000 HDTV sets had been sold in Japan. Sales did accelerate in 1995, when 81,000 sets were sold; sales more than doubled in 1996, to 198,000 sets. Still, as of early 1997, cumulative sales came to only 330,000 sets, a drop in the bucket in the world of television, that most mass-market of products.

Today, the Japanese are banking on an all-digital, satellite-based system scheduled to go into service around the year 2000 (accelerated from 2007 to reflect the poor reception of the Muse system). The Japanese will not use the transmission system employed in the United States, somewhat reducing the scale economies available to set manufacturers. But, in a victory for the United States, the Japanese have adopted the same standard for producing and displaying digital video signals. Thus, the same cameras, monitors, and related equipment can be used in TV studios worldwide, and videotapes made in the United States will be able to play in VCRs around the world. The European, Japanese, and American digital television systems will all use the same MPEG-2 standard to compress images for transmission.

The Europeans were second in the "race" and fared no better. They formed an HDTV joint venture called Eureka 95 in 1986. Eureka 95 enjoyed European Commission funding of $180 million, along with the participation of Philips, Thomson, Bosch, and others. This project developed an analog system "HD-MAC" designed to facilitate the transition from Europe's existing PAL and SECAM systems. However, since HD-MAC signals could not be interpreted by existing sets, the EC pushed satellite broadcasters to use transitional systems (D-MAC and D2-MAC) in the early 1990s. Backward compatibility could be achieved only at a stiff price: broadcasters complained that the image quality of D-MAC and D2-MAC was little better than PAL's. By 1993, the Europeans had abandoned HD-MAC. Now the Europeans are planning to adopt an all-digital system similar, but not identical, to the Japanese system.

Meanwhile, the United States was far behind, in no small part because of the political power of broadcasters, who had little to gain from the arrival of HDTV. A technical standard was nowhere in sight in 1989, when NHK began regular HDTV broadcasting.

The United States chose a unique way to manage the transition from analog to digital television. Still burned by the debacle of the incompatible CBS color standard of 1950, and beholden as usual to broadcasting interests, the FCC decided to give away billions of dollars of valuable spectrum space to broadcasters to enable "simulcasting." Each broadcaster was allocated a second 6-MHz channel to simultaneously broadcast HDTV and NTSC signals for roughly a decade. After that, the broadcasters are supposed to return the extra spectrum, and owners of analog sets will need to purchase converters to receive HDTV broadcasts. This arrangement arose out of a clever lobbying ploy by broadcasters back in the 1980s: by scaring Congress with the prospect of the Japanese beating out the United States in HDTV, broadcasters were able to preserve for themselves vacant channel space in the UHF portion of the spectrum that was in danger of being reassigned to uses other than television. Remember this key point as the HDTV story unfolds: the broadcasters have long lusted after more (free) spectrum space but have never had much appetite for HDTV itself.

In 1988, the FCC helped establish an industry body to actually pick the HDTV transmission standard, based on performance tests. Twenty-three proposals were floated in 1988, but only six remained when the testing was to begin in the fall of 1991. The six systems were sponsored by four teams: (1) NHK, (2) Zenith and AT&T, (3) General Instrument and MIT (two proposals), (4) Philips, Sarnoff Research Labs, NBC, and Thomson (two proposals). In May 1993, after NHK had dropped out, the three remaining teams formed a "Grand Alliance," merging their technologies and agreeing to engage in cross-licensing. This effectively ended their rivalry in the standards battle. Finally, in February 1994, parts of the original Zenith system were picked over those of the General Instrument system. Despite the presence of the cross-licensing agreements, Zenith's stock soared on the news.

Ironically, the United States has now leaped into the lead precisely *because* it entered the fray belatedly. The U.S. system is all-digital, whereas the NHK and MAC systems were analog. This turn of events not only shows the perils of rushing ahead prematurely. It also illustrates the advantages of using competition, rather than central authority, to select technology. The reason the United States has an all-digital HDTV system is because, on the very last day for entries into the HDTV sweepstakes in May 1991, General Instrument entered an all-digital system. The other teams had previously questioned the feasibility of fitting an all-digital system into the 6-MHz bandwidth available. Stunned by General Instrument's example, all but NHK developed all-digital systems within a year.

In 1996, when the FCC was finally ready to issue the new HDTV standard, a group of computer companies and Hollywood honchos sought to change the specifications, arguing that they would impede convergence and competition between the TV and PC industries, disadvantaging them in the "war for viewers." When the broadcasters agreed to drop the objectionable specs in late 1996, a broad agreement on the digital TV standard was reached by the broadcasting, consumer electronics, and computer industries. On the day before Christmas, at long last, the FCC officially adopted an HDTV standard. In a victory for the computer industry, "the standard does not include requirements with respect to scanning formats, aspect ratios and lines of resolution."

The selection of the HDTV technical standard was hardly the end of the story, however. It was more like the crack of the starting gun in a bicycle race in which no rider desires to take the lead and fight the wind. Remember how the broadcasters were dragging their feet on HDTV early on, far more keen on spectrum space than HDTV as such? Well, sure enough, they fought hard for the right to use the new spectrum as they please, to take their time initiating digital transmissions, and to keep the extra spectrum for as long as possible.

Some of these issues were resolved in April 1997 when the FCC issued rules for the adoption of digital television. In what could be another blow for speedy introduction of HDTV, the FCC "will not require broadcasters to air 'high definition' programming or initially to simulcast their analog programming on the digital channel." And the "build-out" schedule agreed to by broadcasters as a quid pro quo for obtaining their new "digital channels" is hardly breathtaking. FCC rules require the affiliates of the top four networks and the top ten markets to be on the air with a digital signal by May 1, 1999. Affiliates of the top four networks in markets eleven to thirty must be on the air by November 1, 1999. So, about half of American households will be able to receive over-the-air digital signals by January 1, 2000. (The FCC has tentatively set a date of 2006 by which time broadcasters must return their second channel.)

What all this will mean for the sales of HDTV sets is far from clear, however. About 65 percent of U.S. households have cable TV, and so far none of the major cable operators has made plans to provide high-definition programming. Quite the contrary, many are trying to expand the number of programs they can offer by *reducing* the quality of each channel. TCI, for example, is implementing half-resolution images, known as VHS-quality pictures, since VHS recording leaves a picture only about half as clear as the original. This is a sobering development for HDTV. The satellite broadcast industry has announced no plans to offer high-definition programming, either. Digital TV is more likely to mean extra channels than high definition, at least for now, especially since HDTV sets are likely to sell for as much as $10,000.

Inevitably, then, a major fight is brewing between those who distribute video programming, notably the broadcasters, and those who sell television sets. The finger pointing is hot and heavy. No one wants to go first. But no one wants to appear to be holding back HDTV, either. The networks say they cannot put into place specific plans for the use of their new digital channels until television manufacturers make their intentions known. But the manufacturers made the same criticism of the broadcasters, resulting in a high-stakes game of chicken. Moreover,

Congress is feeling snookered by broadcasters, who got free spectrum with a promise of HDTV and now seek to use that spectrum for other purposes. We predict the fairly rapid emergence of *digital* television, with set-top boxes receiving digital signals and translating and relaying them to TV sets. But the prospects for significant sales of *high-definition* television sets remain bleak.

At times, HDTV just seems jinxed. In February 1998, when WFAA-TV in Dallas became one of the nation's first regular digital broadcasters, yet another obstacle to HDTV was discovered: the HDTV broadcasts interfered with heart monitors at two nearby hospitals. The hospitals were using a frequency that the FCC has now assigned to TV stations for HDTV broadcasts. No heart patients were harmed, but the incident was yet another reminder of the many costs of switching to a new television standard.

The HDTV story certainly shows how difficult and time consuming it can be to establish a new technology standard when so many pieces of the puzzle have to fit together for the picture to come into view. The tortured HDTV history highlights several other economic principles as well, which we will develop in the next chapter:

- Early leaders (Japan) can easily fall behind if they standardize on technology that is not a sufficient advance on previous generations to obtain critical mass.

- A powerful group (the computer industry) can upset the apple cart late in the day.

- It is often possible to make a truce in a standards war (the Grand Alliance) by merging technologies and agreeing to cross-license essential patents.

- It can be hard to hold a coalition together if some members (broadcasters) would rather delay or sabotage the new standard.

Just as a chain is only as strong as its weakest link, the pace of adoption can be set by the component supplier that is least interested in the new standard. This is a reminder that you must give your alliance partners incentives to push the technology forward if you are keener than they are to push for rapid adoption.

LESSONS

The information age is built on the economics of networks, not the economics of factories. Positive feedback is central to the network economy. Happily enough, some guiding principles are available to help us understand network economics. Better yet, many of the economic forces so powerful today in the network economy are not entirely new. They have been faced by several industries in the past, and we can learn much from their experience.

Following are the main lessons to take away from the economics of networks and positive feedback, from our analysis of the basic trade-offs and generic strategies in network markets, and from our historical case studies of the emergence of new technologies:

- **Positive feedback is the dynamic process by which the strong get stronger.** But there is a dark side to the force: positive feedback also makes the weak get weaker.

- **Adoption dynamics in the presence of positive feedback tend to follow a predictable pattern.** The typical pattern involves an S-shaped, or "logistic," growth path: a slow start, followed by explosive growth, then saturation.

- **Consumers value information technologies that are widely used, just as they value communications networks with broad reach.** The resulting demand-side economies of scale, or network externalities, are a major cause of positive feedback in the information economy.

- **Positive feedback works to the advantage of large networks and against small networks.** This principle applies to real networks, such as the telephone network or a network of compatible modems, and to virtual networks, such as the network of users of the Lotus 1-2-3 spreadsheet program.

- **Consumer expectations are vital to obtaining the critical mass necessary to fuel growth.** During the early stages of product introduction, expectations management is critical.

- **Firms introducing new products and technologies face a fundamental trade-off between performance and compati-**

bility. The evolution strategy involves a high degree of backward compatibility but limited performance improvement. The revolution strategy involves little or no compatibility with existing products but compelling performance.

- **Firms introducing new products and technologies also face a fundamental trade-off between openness and control.** Technologies that are made open are more likely to gain popularity, but the rewards from such success are far greater for an innovator that can retain control over the use and design of its technology.

- **There are four generic strategies for innovators in network markets: performance play, controlled migration, open migration, and discontinuity.** These strategies differ along the performance/compatibility and openness/control dimensions.

- **Many of the tactics for dealing with positive feedback and network externalities have been tried in the past.** We all have much to learn from historical examples, ranging from the early days of the telephone industry to the introduction of color television.

8 | Cooperation and Compatibility

Armed with an understanding of how positive feedback works and informed by historical precedent, we are now ready to explore in depth the different strategies for competing in network markets. This chapter focuses on the openness strategies, open migration and discontinuity, which are fundamentally based on cooperation with allies. The next chapter focuses on the control strategies, controlled migration and performance play, in the context of a battle between incompatible technologies.

Strategy in network markets is distinct from strategy in markets for information content, not to mention traditional industrial markets. Figuring out early on who are your allies, and who are your enemies, is especially important in network markets because of the winner-take-all nature of these markets. Do you really want an "open" standard? Do others? Which allies do you need to win, and how can you most effectively attract them? Can you assemble allies to launch your technology successfully while keeping some control over how it evolves? Should you fight a standards war or seek an early truce? And what should you do if you have a declining market share in a network industry? We will systematically look into these questions in the pages that follow.

Many commentators have likened cyberspace to the Wild West, where old patterns of behavior no longer apply and everything is up for grabs. Perhaps, but the lone cowboy approach rarely works in the information age. Network economics and positive feedback make cooperation more important than ever. Most companies need to cooperate with others to establish standards and create a single network of compatible users. But as soon as the ink is dry on the standards agreement, these same companies shift gears and compete head to head for their share of that network. The term *coopetition* captures the tension between cooperation and competition prevalent in network industries. When distinct components have to work together as a system, the paramount strategic questions involve cooperation and coordination: with whom should you cooperate, how broadly, and under what terms?

HOW STANDARDS CHANGE THE GAME

As you map out your strategy in the face of positive feedback and network effects, you will need to identify your natural allies early in the game. This can be a difficult process, since there are no clear battle lines in network markets. For example, you cannot take it on faith that the other market participants truly want to establish a standard. Rather, an incumbent supplier may prefer to see a new technology die from lack of standardization, hoping to prolong its profits from older technology. We doubt that Microsoft had much interest in seeing a unified Unix standard, or a unified Java standard for that matter, since these technologies pose far more of a threat to Microsoft than an opportunity. Beware of companies participating in the standard-setting process, formally or informally, that deep down have no interest in seeing a successful standard emerge.

When negotiating standards, beware of companies that deep down have no interest in the development of a successful standard.

Even if your allies all welcome a standard, they may disagree over how extensive or detailed that standard should be. As we saw, a big, if late-breaking, issue in the HDTV standards process was whether the standard would include specifications regarding scanning formats and line resolution. The scope of the standard is also under attack in DVD, with an apparent breakdown regarding the "write" part of the standard. The major players in the DVD industry have agreed to a "read" standard under the pressure of the content providers, who naturally prefer to provide content in a standardized format. But the content providers don't care about write standards. If anything, they would be happy to see incompatible standards, since it would make piracy more difficult. Without the harmonizing pressure from the content providers, the DVD manufacturers have succumbed to their natural instinct to use their own proprietary write formats.

To figure out who really wants a standard, and who doesn't, you need to envision how the market is likely to evolve with or without an agreed-upon standard. Standards alter the very nature of competition in several important ways.

Expanded Network Externalities

First and foremost, standards enhance compatibility, or interoperability, generating greater value for users by making the network larger. To illustrate, consider format standards for information media, such as the VHS standard for videotapes or the 3½″ standard for computer disks. These standards fuel beneficial network externalities in two ways. First, and most directly, the standard makes it possible to share information with a larger network (without the need to convert the data from one format to another). Second, and indirectly, the enhanced ability to share data attracts still more consumers using this format, further expanding the available network externalities. This analysis applies equally to real communications networks, like fax machines and ATM networks, and to virtual networks, such as users of compatible computer software or compatible disk drives. Either way, the larger network is a real boon to consumers.

If you ever lose sight of this basic tenet of network markets—that is, the fact that compatibility creates substantial consumer benefits, think of the Baltimore fire of 1904: when firemen from neighboring towns arrived to help fight the fire, many of their fire hoses did not fit into Baltimore's hydrants. The information age equivalent occurs when your wireless telephone fails to work in an incompatible distant PCS system, or when you cannot plug in your laptop or download your e-mail in a foreign country.

Reduced Uncertainty

Standards reduce the technology risk faced by consumers. This, too, accelerates acceptance of a new technology. A standard with many backers can go far to bolster the credibility of the technology, which then becomes self-fulfilling. In contrast, with incompatible products, consumer confusion and fear of stranding may delay adoption. Consumer confusion helped kill AM stereo radio a decade ago. More recently, the growth of the market for 56k modems was retarded until modem manufacturers could agree on a common standard.

We have stressed the importance of expectations as a driver of positive feedback in network markets: confidence breeds success, while doubt spells doom. One of the risks in a standards war is that the battle to win market share will undermine consumer confidence that *either* technology will prevail, resulting in a war with no victor. As each side strives to convince consumers that it will be the winner, consumers may take the easy way out and sit on the sidelines, especially if a serviceable older technology is already available and standardized. The same fate can easily befall a single new technology that lacks the support of sufficient market participants to become a standard.

Reduced Consumer Lock-In

If the standard is truly open, consumers will be less concerned about lock-in. They can count on future competition. This has worked nicely for CDs, where holders of patents essential to the CD standard, including Sony, Philips, and DiscoVision Associates, have charged only modest royalties. Likewise, consumers expected competition on the PC platform, owing to IBM's open approach. And competition they got—among hardware providers, that is, but not among operating systems, which became dominated by Microsoft.

Netscape is now touting the open nature of its product line to convince users that they will not be locked into a proprietary solution. Indeed, in June 1997 it even offered an "Open Standards Guarantee" on its Web site, and in early 1998 Netscape published the source code to its browser, Navigator. Even mighty Microsoft has been forced to move toward open standards such as XML in order to reassure its clientele that they will be able to exchange data with other users.

Competition for the Market versus Competition in the Market

Precisely because standards reduce lock-in, they shift the locus of competition from an early battle for dominance to a later battle for market share. Instead of competing *for* the market, companies compete *within* the market, using the common standards. Aggressive penetration pricing is far less likely under a common standard, but so is lock-in. One of the worst outcomes for consumers is to buy into a standard that is widely expected to be open, only to find it "hijacked" later, after they are collectively locked in. Motorola has been accused of precisely this tactic in promoting standards for public safety radio equipment and modems.

Dow Jones recently renegotiated contracts with firms that distributed quotes on the Dow Jones Industrial Average (DJIA), proposing to charge $1 per month per user for real-time quotes and 25 cents a month for quotes delayed by twenty minutes. (Note the versioned prices.) Dow Jones waited to announce these new charges until *after* a derivative securities market started that was based on the DJIA. The company argued that the new derivative securities made its quotes more valuable, but some providers of on-line financial services certainly felt that a formerly open standard had been slammed shut.

Competition on Price versus Features

Standards shift competition away from features and toward price, for the simple reason that many features are common across all brands. How many? This depends on how specific the standard is: the more detailed the standard, the harder it is for each producer to differentiate its product and still comply with the standard.

So, while a more extensive standard leads to fewer compatibility problems, and stronger network externalities, it also can reduce the ability of each supplier to differentiate its products, thereby intensifying price competition. For this very reason, consumers tend to seek more extensive standards than do suppliers.

It follows that rival manufacturers may all be better off living with some incompatibilities *and* with a smaller total market in order to deemphasize pricing competition and focus competition more on product features.

Competition to Offer Proprietary Extensions

Over time, there are strong incentives for suppliers to differentiate themselves by developing proprietary extensions, while still maintaining some degree of backward compatibility. This is one reason why hardware and software incompatibilities tend to crop up even on the relatively standardized PC platform. Competition to extend a standard can certainly be a boon to consumers, as new features are designed in a highly competitive race to offer improvements. But the resulting incompatibilities can be a major source of irritation.

The fruits and frustrations of competition to extend a standard technology can be blockaded by an owner of proprietary rights who uses these rights to control the evolution of technology. We described in Chapter 7 how a firm sponsoring an industry standard can control its evolution. Successful sponsors can commoditize certain components of the system, while making sure that network externalities are not lost over time owing to incompatibilities. Of course, the sponsor will seek to capture profits for itself. This is what Sony and Philips did, both by charging royalties to manufacturers of CD players and disks and by limiting the manufacture of certain enhanced CD players (such as players of interactive and high-density CDs). Sony and Philips made the decision that it was worth foregoing these improvements, which might have spurred sales of both players and disks, to avoid unfavorable publicity surrounding incompatibilities and thus preserve consumer confidence in the integrity of the standard.

Intel is taking a similar approach with the PC platform. Intel Labs is playing a major role in developing interfaces and standards such as "plug and play" and the "accelerated graphics port," then making them available to component manufacturers. Of all the players in the hardware side of PC world, Intel has the greatest interest in seeing that components interconnect smoothly and perform well. The faster, cheaper, and easier to use the components are, the more demand there is for Intel CPUs.

Component versus Systems Competition

Standards shift the locus of competition from systems to components. When Nintendo competes against Sega, consumers compare the Nintendo *system* of hardware and available software with the Sega system. The firm that can offer the superior *total* package stands to win. Compare this with audio and video equipment (stereo systems, televisions, and VCRs), where the various components are (by and large) compatible. A company can do well making the best or cheapest television, even if it sells no VCRs. Similarly, a different company can profit by selling stereo speakers, even if it makes no receivers or CD players. The same is true for PCs: HP has a very profitable printer business, even though its computer sales are modest. Sony has done well selling monitors, with essentially no presence in the PC box business, at least in the United States.

And so it goes. Specialists tend to thrive in the mix-and-match environment created by interface standards. Generalists and systems integrators tend to thrive in the absence of compatibility.

WHO WINS AND WHO LOSES FROM STANDARDS?

We have seen how standards change the nature of the game; here we examine how they affect the players.

Consumers

Consumers generally welcome standards: they are spared having to pick a winner and face the risk of being stranded. They can enjoy the greatest network externalities in a single network or in networks that seamlessly interconnect. They can mix and match components to suit their tastes. And they are far less likely to become locked into a single vendor, unless a strong leader retains control over the technology or wrests control in the future through proprietary extensions or intellectual property rights.

Standardization does have some downsides for consumers, however. The main one is a loss of variety: the standard may be poorly suited to some customers' needs, or it may just turn out to be an inferior technology, like QWERTY. Standardization can also deprive consumers of the benefits of aggressive penetration pricing during a standards battle. This loss is most likely to be significant for large or influential users that can play a pivotal role in the battle, like the large ISPs in the browser battle between Microsoft and Netscape. For consumers as a whole, however, penetration pricing is largely a down payment on future lock-in, so this factor should be of secondary concern.

Standards that "don't quite work" are the bane of customers. It used to be that you were never quite sure exactly which video cards would work with which sound cards; your PC maker added value by making sure that the components in the system you ordered all worked together. Nowadays, pretty much all PC hardware works together because of efforts by Intel and Microsoft to promulgate industry standards. This has been great for Intel and Microsoft but has partially commoditized the PC OEM business, in which competition is increasingly based on being the low-cost producer and distributor.

We're at the same point in software standards now that we were with PC hardware standards a decade ago—you're never quite sure what works together. The problem is that there isn't an industry player with enough clout to coordinate independent suppliers' efforts. Microsoft, naturally enough, pushes its own solutions; Sun, Oracle, and Netscape are trying to build an industry alliance around a different set of solutions, but seamless component integration just isn't here yet.

Complementors

Like consumers, sellers of complements welcome standards, so long as their products comply with the standard. AOL sells Internet access, a complement to modems. AOL benefits from the use of standardized, high-speed modems in that AOL itself does not need to maintain separate banks of modems with different formats. It follows that the demand for on-line services is stimulated when modem sales rise as a result of standards. In fact, influential complementors can affect the choice of a standard, just as can influential consumers. For example, content providers such as studios have been influential in the development of each generation of consumer electronics equipment.

The markets for audio and video entertainment illustrate just who the complementors are. Recording studios and retail music stores are complementors to music CDs and therefore beneficiaries of the CD standard. Phonograph manufacturers, on the other hand, offered a product that was a direct competitor to CD players. The CD was a grave threat to these companies; they had to learn to make CD players, a very different business from making phonographs, or go out of business.

In the case of the emerging DVD standard, content providers such as movie studios and software houses offer a complement to the new disks and stand to benefit from the new standard. Now it is makers of videocassette players that are in danger, since DVD players promise eventually to make VCRs obsolete. The impact of DVD on a distributor like Blockbuster is not as clear: as a distributor of video content, Blockbuster sells a complement to the DVD technology and stands to gain as higher-quality video images (with improved sound) become available. However, precisely because of the flexibility that DVD disks will allow, they are well suited to new channels of distribution, threatening to devalue Blockbuster's network of retail locations.

Incumbents

Product standards for new technologies can pose a grave threat to established incumbents. After all, if standards fuel the positive feedback cycle and help launch a new technology, they can easily cannibalize sales from an older technology. RCA, the leading maker of black-and-white television sets during the 1940s, was not eager to see a color television standard established that would challenge its leadership. Atari was none too happy when Nintendo managed to get positive feedback working for the Nintendo Entertainment System back in the mid-1980s.

Incumbents have three choices. First, an incumbent can try to deny backward compatibility to would-be entrants with new technology in the hope of blockading entry altogether, thereby extending the life of its own technology. This is what AT&T tried to do in the 1960s and 1970s when faced with demands that it permit various equipment, such as telephone handsets and PBXs, to interconnect with the AT&T system. Regulatory rules forced AT&T to open up its network to interconnection, first with equipment and later with other carriers, most notably MCI.

Second, an incumbent can rush to introduce its own new generation of equipment, perhaps with the unique advantage of backward compatibility, to win a standards war. This is what Atari did (unsuccessfully) when faced with Nintendo's entry into the U.S. video game market in the mid-1980s. Atari's second-generation equipment, the Atari 7800, could play games written for Atari's dominant first-generation system, the Atari 2600. Unfortunately for Atari, these older games held little

data protocols for multimedia conferencing. Whether you consider formal standard setting a necessary evil or a godsend, it is here to stay.

Formal standard setting is designed to be open to all participants and to foster consensus. This sounds good, but often results in a very slow process. The HDTV story is one example: it took roughly ten years to set a technical standard for digital television in the United States, and HDTV is yet to be adopted in the United States on a commercial scale.

A fundamental principle underlying the consensus approach to standards is that they should be "open," with no one or few firms controlling the standard. Thus, a quid pro quo for having one's technology adopted in a formal standard is a commitment to license any patents *essential* to implementing the standard on "fair, reasonable, and nondiscriminatory" terms. Note that this duty does *not* extend to *non*essential patents, which can lead to an amusing dance in which companies claim that their patents merely cover valuable enhancements to the standard and are not actually essential to complying with the standard.

The openness promise of a formal standards body is a powerful tool for establishing credibility. However, be aware that most standards bodies have no enforcement authority. Aggrieved parties must resort to the courts, including the court of public opinion, if they feel the process has been abused.

In the late nineteenth and early twentieth centuries, as part of the industrial revolution, formal standard setting focused on traditional manufacturing standards, such as those needed for interchangeable parts and mass production. As the twentieth century closes, the information revolution has shifted more and more formal standard setting into the high-tech and information areas.

TACTICS IN FORMAL STANDARD SETTING

If you are involved in setting a formal standard, it is important to determine your goal at the outset. If your goal is to quickly establish a standard incorporating your proprietary technology, you better not rely on formal standard setting. It's wise to participate, but you should be following a market-oriented track in parallel. If most network externalities occur at the national level, you can likely avoid the entanglements of the global standard-setting organizations. If you are not too picky about the actual standard, but want to make sure that no private entity controls the chosen standard, ANSI and ITU rules are well suited to your objectives. Very often, the most important rule is simply to show up at standard-setting meetings to make sure a "consensus" adverse to your interests does not form. Smaller companies sometimes find attendance burdensome, allowing larger firms to steer the process to their advantage. If you cannot spare someone to attend, consider teaming up with other small players whose interests are aligned with yours to send a representative.

Just showing up at a standards meeting can go a long way toward protecting your interests.

Formal standard setting often involves a dance in which companies negotiate based on quite different strengths. In setting the standard for 28.8k modems, for example, AT&T, British Telecom, and Motorola brought their patents to the table, Hayes and U.S. Robotics brought strong brand names to the table, and Rockwell brought its chipset manufacturing skills to the table, as they all negotiated the terms on which each company could manufacture these modems. Multiple patent holders jockeyed to get their patents built into the standard to ensure royalty income and to gain time-to-market advantages.

To navigate in this type of environment, you are well advised to gather information about the objectives of the *other* participants. This intelligence and analysis can be enormously helpful in targeting common interests, allies, and potential compromises. For example, if you can ascertain who is in a rush and who stands to gain from delay, you will be able to play the standards "game" far better.

Once you have assessed the strengths and objectives of the other players, you should apply the following principles of strategic standard setting:

Don't automatically participate. If you can follow a control strategy or organize an alliance outside the formal standard-setting process, you may be far better off: you can move more quickly, you can retain more control over the technology and the process, you will not be bound by any formal consensus process, and you need not commit to openly licensing any controlling patents. For example, Motorola did not participate in the ITU T.30 recommendation for facsimile equipment and later sought royalties from manufacturers of that equipment. This generated some ill will, since Motorola had previously agreed to license this same technology on reasonable terms for modems as part of the V.29 modem standard-setting process, but nonparticipation also generated significant royalty income for Motorola. To cite another example, the Federal Trade Commission sued Dell Computer over Dell's attempt to collect royalties on patents essential to the VESA bus standard, after Dell had previously represented that it held no such patents. In its defense, Dell asserted that it was unaware at the time that it held any such patents, but the case makes clear that participation brings with it real responsibilities.

Keep up your momentum. Don't freeze your activities during the slow standard-setting process. Actively prosecute any patent applications you have pending, keep up your R&D efforts, and prepare to start manufacturing. Remember how NBC was caught flat-footed, not ready to manufacture sets even after the FCC picked NBC's color TV standard.

Look for logrolling opportunities. The term *logrolling* refers to the trading of votes by legislators to obtain passage of favorable legislation. Logrolling has always been a part of the political process. The standard-setting process is a wild mix of politics and economics, including explicit side payments and side deals. Typically, such deals include agreements to incorporate pieces of technology from different players, as was done for HDTV in the United States and for modems at the ITU. Side deals can also involve agreements between those who have intellectual property rights (aka the "IPR club") such as patents to share those patents on a royalty-free basis, while imposing royalties on participants who are not members of the club. Whatever deals you offer to attract allies, make them selectively to the stronger players. But be sure to abide by the rules of engagement, including any nondiscrimination rules. Form or join an alliance, and make sure the other members do not defect.

Be creative about cutting deals. Figure out what key assets you bring to the table, and use those to assemble a coalition or to extract favorable terms when you pick sides. Consider low-cost licensing, second sourcing, hybrid standards, grantbacks of improvement patents, and commitments to participate in future joint development efforts. Whatever cards you have in your hand, play them when you are most likely to make a pivotal difference. Don't confine your deal making to the technology or product in question; think broadly of ways to structure deals that are mutually beneficial.

Beware of vague promises. The formal standard-setting process has a great deal of momentum. Don't count on vague promises of openness made early on; these may evaporate once a standard is effectively locked in. In the ITU, for example, individual companies are expected to support whatever position the State Department takes on behalf of the United States, since the department consults first with the industry. As a result, companies lose the ability to stop or steer the process once national positions are set; to do so would be regarded as treason. For just this reason, make sure early on that holders of key patents are explicit about their commitment to license for "reasonable" royalties. Reasonable *should* mean the royalties that the patent holder could obtain in open, up-front competition with other technologies, not the royalties that the patent holder can extract once other participants are effectively locked in to use technology covered by the patent. This is like the medieval concept of the "just price"; the just price of a horse was the price that would prevail at the open market at the annual fair, not the price that happens to emerge from a traveler in desperate need of a horse.

Search carefully for blocking patents. Beware of picking a standard that will require using a patent held by a company not participating in the standard-setting process. Suppose a standard is selected, production begun, and positive feedback is achieved. Then a company that did not participate in the standard-setting process suddenly appears and asserts that everyone complying with the standard is infringing on a patent held by that company. Remember, a nonparticipating patent holder is *not* required to license its patents on fair and reasonable terms. This is the nightmare of every participant, since the interloper can potentially control the entire market the participants have built. You cannot fully protect yourself from this contingency, but any technology not clearly in the public domain, or controlled by participants, should be thoroughly searched. Note that our advice to search for blocking patents is the flip side of our suggestion that some companies not participate in the process but instead seek to pursue a control strategy by establishing a proprietary standard with the aim of collecting substantial royalty payments.

Consider building an installed base preemptively. This is risky, and not always possible, but it can strengthen your bargaining position. Establishing manufacturing sources and building an installed base are akin to moving your troops into a stronger position while negotiating for peace. You might undermine the peace process and your efforts may go to waste, but flanking maneuvers are one way to kick-start a slow negotiation. U.S. Robotics/3Com and Rockwell/Lucent each marketed their modems actively, even while they negotiated under ITU auspices for the 56k modem standard. In this case, both camps offered free upgrades to the final ITU standard. The same thing happened in the previous generation of 28.8k modems. Rockwell offered "V.FC" ("fast class") modems in advance of the V.34 ITU standard, but then had to face infringement claims from Motorola. Among other things, Motorola asserted that its commitment to license patents essential to the V.34 standard did not apply until after the V.34 standard was formally in place.

BUILDING ALLIANCES

Whether you are participating in a formal standard-setting process or simply trying to build momentum behind your product, you need allies to ignite positive feedback. This requires identifying the companies that are your natural allies and then negotiating to obtain their support for your technology.

As you seek to build an alliance in support of a new standard, you should keep firmly in mind the competitive advantages you aim to retain for yourself. Promising sources of advantage include a time-to-market advantage, a manufacturing cost advantage, a brand-name advantage, and/or an edge in developing improvements. One or all of these competitive advantages can persist, even if the technology is freely available to all so you are barred from asserting IPRs to exclude competition. We've seen companies fight tooth and nail to have their technology included in a standard, even if they anticipate little or no royalty income as a result. In the HDTV story, Zenith's stock price surged after key components of its technology were selected for inclusion in the HDTV standard, even though Zenith had already agreed to extensive cross-licenses with General Instrument and others in the HDTV technical competition.

Assembling Allies

Look broadly for allies. Your allies can include your customers, your suppliers, your rivals, and the makers of complementary products. For each potential ally, try to figure out how your proposed standard will affect their fortunes, using the framework we developed earlier in this chapter for predicting how standards will alter competition.

What will it take to attract each ally? When is the opportune time to make an offer? Building a coalition is very much a political process. It is critical to understand both the concerns and the options of your potential partners to design a deal that will appeal to them.

Pivotal or influential customers should get special deals. For example, when Microsoft introduced Internet Explorer, it signed a deal with Dow Jones, giving Explorer users free access to the *Wall Street Journal*, a complementary product. As we mentioned in Chapter 3, many digital cameras are bundled with a stripped-down version of Adobe's Photoshop. The camera or scanner doesn't have big network externalities or switching costs, but Photoshop certainly does. It is a powerful and complex piece of software that has a wide following in the industry. Adobe has done a marvelous job of creating software that is easy to use out of the box and yet powerful enough to whet the consumer's appetite for the full-fledged version.

DigiMarc, initiator of the digital watermarking system described in Chapter 4, has partnered with providers of image manipulation software such as Adobe, Corel, and Micrografx, allowing them to include a low-end version of the DigiMarc system with their products in an attempt to get the bandwagon rolling for the DigiMarc standard.

It is tempting to offer very good deals to the early signers in an effort to get the bandwagon rolling. But if these deals cannot be extended to their competitors, you may have a hard time attracting other partners in the same industry because they would find themselves in an untenable competitive position. If you set a 10 percent royalty for the first firms to adopt your technology, it will be hard to get the later signers to accept a 20 percent royalty because they will find it difficult to compete with their lower-cost rivals. This is what happened to DiscoVision Associates, a company controlling key patents for the encoding and manufacturing of compact disks: after signing up a number of licensees on attractive terms early in the lifetime of the CD technology, DiscoVision was unable to raise its royalty rates to new licensees who had to compete in the low-margin CD replication business, even though the CD standard was by then well established.

A better strategy is to offer the early birds a *temporary* price break on the royalty. This gives them an incentive to climb on board, but it doesn't preclude higher rates for latecomers. One way to structure royalties to achieve this end is to offer a discounted royalty rate up to a certain cumulative output level, after which the royalty reverts to the "standard" rate. This is the opposite of the popular royalty structure in which rates decline with volume. Our proposed structure reduces the risks faced by early licensees, gives an advantage to early allies, and preserves more options for the licenser in the future.

Don't forget to address the question of who will bear the risk of failure if the bandwagon collapses. Will your partners be left holding the bag? In general, the costs of collapse should end up falling on those who are best positioned to prevent such a collapse and on those who can most easily absorb any unavoidable risk. Normally, both of these factors point to the larger firms, but not always. If smaller firms are in a better position to seek bankruptcy protection, it may be that they are better placed to absorb a lot of risk. Of course, in this case it's the creditors of the bankrupt firms that end up holding the bag.

Try to shift the risk of failure to a large customer or, even better, the government.

One clever approach is to shift some risk to a really big player, such as the government or a regulated monopolist. As we noted earlier, smart cards have not had much success in the United States but have done well in Europe. One reason is that the European state telephone monopolies mandated smart cards for pay phones. This was enough to build a critical mass for that technology. Other vendors felt comfortable adopting the technology, figuring that the government would support the system if necessary to prevent its failure.

There is nothing dishonorable about piggybacking on government efforts to establish a new standard. The U.S. Congress has mandated that U.S. benefit payments must be electronic by January 1, 1999. Smart cards may well play a role in such electronic benefit transfers, so the new government rules could significantly aid smart card deployment in the United States. Effectively, a very large and well-heeled customer is making a commitment to smart cards.

How much do you need allies? We discussed this in Chapter 7 when we compared the openness and control strategies. We identified three key assets that govern your ability to ignite positive feedback: existing market position, technical capabilities, and control over intellectual property rights. The stronger your position in terms of these three critical assets, the less important are allies and the more easily you can play those allies off against each other. In the mid-1980s, Nintendo had a distinctly superior system, strong copyright and patent protection for that system, and a solid installed base in Japan with which to attract game developers. Thus, Nintendo could afford to charge game developers for the right to put their games on the Nintendo system. No individual game created by these developers was crucial to Nintendo, but access to the Nintendo installed base was soon critical to each of them.

Be careful of building an alliance consisting of companies with very different interests; such unions can prove unwieldy. In consumer electronics, equipment manufacturers and content providers often come to loggerheads because they have very different interests regarding copying. The current standards war surrounding "write" technology for DVDs, mentioned earlier in this chapter, illustrates the problem.

Interconnection among Allies

We have emphasized that today's virtual networks of compatible users have much in common with the more familiar transportation and communications networks. We can exploit these similarities to learn from the experience of alliances in the more traditional network industries. Just as Apple agonized over the terms on which it permitted Macintosh clones to be built, flip-flopping several times, so too did railroads, telephone companies, and broadcast networks ponder interconnection terms in their day.

For as long as there have been networks, there has been interconnection: passengers or cargo brought by one network to its extremities are carried farther along by an adjacent network. National postal services developed interconnection procedures centuries ago, while telephone systems figured out interconnection roughly one hundred years ago. Airlines and railroads regularly exchange traffic. Over the years, smaller carriers have regularly complained about the terms on which larger carriers would interconnect with them. This issue is beginning to surface on the Internet, and it is endemic to the virtual networks that populate the information economy.

We can all learn much from historical interconnection agreements. While the technology underlying the Internet is new, the economic issues surrounding interconnection are not. Networks that deliver messages or physical goods typically involve four parties: the sender, the sender's carrier, the recipient, and the recipient's carrier. (More parties are involved if intermediate carriers handle the traffic; only three parties are involved if one carrier takes the message from end to end.) When you send a letter from the United States to France to your friend Jean, the four parties are you, the U.S. postal service, the French postal service, and Jean. (FedEx and DHL speed things up by routing traffic entirely over their own proprietary networks, reducing the transaction to three parties.) The same pattern applies to the Internet, with different carriers. Many of the economic issues surrounding interconnection that apply to the Internet today have been present in postal systems for centuries: how should payments be split between sender and recipient, and what "carrier-to-carrier" charges apply? In our example, who pays for the letter, you or Jean, and what payment, if any, must the U.S. postal service make to the French postal service as compensation for its delivery of the message to Jean?

Postal services have been dealing with these problems for centuries. Mail services arose more than two thousand years ago, initially to serve kings and emperors. Religious orders and universities also set up their own systems, with relay stations, and eventually permitted private individuals to send messages using their systems. Opening the systems to private customers was a way of spreading the fixed costs of these messenger systems over more users. Charges were based on the type of message, its size, and the distance traveled, and were generally paid by the recipient, not the sender. (In an unreliable system, both incentives and risk are better managed by making the recipient pay for the delivery of the message.)

Interconnection issues arose when one postal system sought to hand off mail to another for delivery. Bilateral agreements between European countries were negotiated in the seventeenth century to govern inter-connection. By the nineteenth century, most large European countries were party to at least a dozen of these treaties, requiring that multiple detailed accounts be kept. This complex and costly system was finally replaced in 1874 by the Treaty of Berne, which led to the Universal Postal Union, now a part of the United Nations. Then, as now, a multi-lateral agreement and a centralized clearinghouse greatly reduced inter-connection costs among "end-to-end" networks.

Interconnection became more strategic once networks began to compete against each other over the same routes: side-by-side networks rather than end-to-end networks. For as long as there have been com-peting networks, these networks have used interconnection terms and conditions to gain competitive advantage. For decades, U.S. telephone companies have been paying outrageous fees to foreign state-run tele-communications monopolies for completion of outbound calls in foreign countries. As we saw in Chapter 7, early in this century AT&T used its control over the long-distance telephone network to consolidate control over the majority of local telephone service in the United States.

All of these practices have their virtual equivalents in computer and information networks, virtual or real. Take the Apple Mac network. Apple limited "access" to its network by refusing to license independent manufacturers, so-called clones, until roughly a decade after the intro-duction of the Mac. Apple did not aggressively seek to establish the largest network or to connect with the PC network using adapters, the virtual equivalent of interlining. Rather, Apple was content at the outset to have a cool product with a loyal following in the education and graphics markets. But niche strategies are inherently dangerous in mar-kets with strong network externalities. Apple's strategy was akin to hav-ing a specialty fax network for the design and publishing industries, based on superior image resolution and color capabilities. This is fine until the makers of mass-market fax machines learn to match you in performance, and then you're dead before you know what hit you. To get on the right side of the positive-feedback curve requires a strategy based on broad appeal, along with a broad, compatible product line.

Only the impressive performance of the Macintosh and the technological sluggishness of Microsoft in matching the ease of use of the Macintosh have allowed Apple to survive as long as it has with its niche strategy.

> *If you control a key interface or bottleneck, you should open it up— but on your own terms and conditions.*

In the presence of strong network externalities, interconnection and network access strategies can make the difference between achieving critical mass and floundering. It is all too easy to try to retain tight control over your network by refusing to license critical technology or by manipulating interface specifications to disadvantage rival suppliers, only to find that this strategy has backfired by steering customers and suppliers to rival networks. In hindsight, this is where Sony went wrong with VCRs: it lost out to Matsushita's open licensing program. Today, many industry observers believe that Apple went wrong in personal computers by refusing to license its hardware and software, thereby losing out to IBM and its clones.

In assembling allies, we advise you to offer interconnection or compatibility, but on terms that reflect your underlying strength, and with limitations to reduce the risk that you will lose control over the network with time. Java gives us a sobering example of the dangers of losing control. Sun was eager to license Java to as many producers as possible and was even happy to offer a license to its fiercest competitor, Microsoft. But Microsoft cleverly retained the right to "improve" Java in the licensing agreement. Microsoft then proceeded to add its own "improvements" that worked only in the Windows environment! Microsoft critics called this a foul attempt to fragment a standard; Microsoft itself says it is only trying to give customers better performance. It's likely that both positions are correct—but it's still a big headache for Sun.

Negotiating a Truce

In standard setting as in diplomacy, alliances form between potential combatants as a means of preventing war, not merely to solidify common interests. In both situations, the alliance arising out of a negotiated truce can be a lifesaver, even though it is an uneasy union. We'll discuss standards wars in the next chapter; here we consider the rewards and perils of negotiating a truce to avoid such a war.

If you control one of two incompatible technologies competing for market ascendancy, you may well be better off negotiating a truce than fighting a costly and lengthy standards war. Ideally, these negotiations will take place not through the slow, formal standard-setting process but by fashioning a creative agreement between your camp and the rival camp.

A standards truce should be possible if both sides can make more money in peaceful coexistence than in a standards war. If cooperation increases the players' joint profits, there should be a way to structure a truce to make both sides happy. (Usually, such deals do not run afoul of antitrust laws; we'll consider the legal limits on standard setting in Chapter 10.)

There is plenty of reason to think a truce will normally lead to higher profits. Basically, if the total value created by the technology is enhanced by standardization, suppliers and customers should be able to divide up this value. If the pie is larger, everyone should be able to get a bigger piece, including consumers. But the hard part comes in dividing up the enlarged pie. This is where the standard-setting tactics listed above enter into the picture: picking a hybrid technology, licensing and cross-licensing, most-favored customer terms, commitments to openness, and so on.

As in any truce negotiations, both sides need to determine how they would fare if war were to break out. Based on the assets held by the two companies or coalitions, the negotiations can take one of three basic forms: (1) an inevitable standards war, (2) a game of chicken in which each side tries to assert its own technology over the other but will concede rather than fight, or (3) an unbalanced game between a strong team that would rather fight and a weak team that would rather negotiate a truce. These three possibilities are shown in Table 8.1.

First, it may be that both sides would rather fight than join forces. That is, they would rather compete to set their own standard rather than agree on a common standard. This happens when consumers put a high value on variety as well as network externalities, when price competition to sell a standardized product standard would erode profit margins, and when each side is confident it will win the war. The force of the "not invented here" syndrome should not be underestimated. If both key players would rather compete than agree on a standard, a standards battle is inevitable. Each team should start lining up allies for the fight

Table 8.1. The Standards Game

		Weak team's choices	
		Willing to fight	*Wants standard*
Strong team's choices	*Willing to fight*	Standards war	A tries to block B
	Wants standard		Voluntary standard

and moving troops into position. See Chapter 9 about tactics you can use to wage—and win—a standards war.

The second possibility is that each side would prefer to establish its own technology as a standard but is prepared to accept the other's technology as a standard rather than waging a ruinous winner-take-all battle. That is, each side prefers its own technology but would rather switch than fight. In this case, the standards negotiations are like a game of chicken: each side will try to convince the other that it is the more stubborn of the two. War may come, but the two sides are better off cutting a deal.

In the third scenario, one player is strong and confident of winning a standards battle. This player would prefer to compete with incompatible products. The other side is weak, and knows it. The weak player would like to adopt the strong player's technology to ensure compatibility and reduce or neutralize its disadvantages. The stronger firm may be able to prevent the weaker firm(s) from achieving full compatibility, either by asserting intellectual property rights or by changing interfaces frequently. In this third case, there will be a predictable dynamic in which the strong team tries to limit access to its network or at least charge for interconnection or compatibility. See Chapter 9 for advice on how to play the two roles in this game, those of the strong and the weak companies.

As with any negotiation, stubborn players can erode or destroy the gains from trade. Our advice: don't be proud. Be prepared to join, even with a bitter rival, to establish a standard if it helps you both. Of course, you need to stay on your guard in dealing with a direct rival. Will the standard picked give your rival an edge? Is the proposed standard really neutral now *and* in the future? Above all, remember that maximizing your return does *not* mean maximizing your control over the technology. As we said in Chapter 7:

> Your reward = Total value added to industry
> × your share of industry value

Avoiding a standards battle will increase the value to all firms operating in the industry if consumer confusion, fear of stranding, and lack of consensus would otherwise have stalled the technology. The critical issue you face is how much of that extra value you will be able to appropriate.

The imperative to find common ground, and the fact that savvy companies can get past their differences and cooperate to enable new technologies, can be seen in the dealings between Microsoft and Netscape. Much has been made of the browser wars between Netscape and Microsoft, which we discuss in some detail below. But focus for a moment on the spheres in which these two implacable enemies have agreed to follow a common standard.

First consider the problem of protecting privacy on the Internet. Consumer fears over loss of confidential information are clearly a drag on on-line commerce, to the detriment of both Microsoft and Netscape. Netscape took the first step, proposing the Open Profiling Standard (OPS) along with the Firefly Network and Verisign. The OPS employs profiles that enable personal computer users to control the information about themselves that is disclosed to a particular Web site. To get things rolling, Netscape lined up about forty other companies in support of the standard, including IBM and Sun Microsystems as well as some on-line publishers. Microsoft was conspicuously absent from the coalition. For a brief time, it looked like the two arch-rivals would promote different standards for privacy software. But they quickly avoided this mutually destructive approach. Just weeks after Netscape had made its move, Microsoft announced its support in June 1997 for the Netscape-sponsored standard. This standard will now become part of the Platform for Privacy Preferences (P3) being developed by the World Wide Web Consortium.

Neither company was proud, but both were cautious. Netscape has a policy of not inviting Microsoft into its standard-setting efforts too early, for fear of giving Microsoft the opportunity to use the process to gain a proprietary advantage. According to Mike Homer, Netscape's vice president for marketing, "Nobody tells Microsoft of these things if they want to gain a broad consensus." For its part, Microsoft stated that it would have supported the OPS earlier had Netscape agreed to share its specifications at that time.

A second arena in which Microsoft and Netscape were able to cooperate involved 3-D on the Internet. In August 1997, they agreed to support compatible versions of Virtual Reality Modeling Language (VRML), a 3-D viewing technology, in their browsers. Again, Microsoft was pragmatic rather than proud, adopting a language invented at Silicon Graphics. There is no doubt compatibility will create a larger pie to split: VRML had been slow to gain acceptance, both because it was embedded in incompatible browsers and because consumers had to download plug-in software for displaying the graphics. Problems still remain—3-D files are large and slow to download—but at least consumers will not have to worry whether their browser will work at a particular Web site. Both Navigator 4.0 and Internet Explorer 4.0 now contain VRML capability.

A third example of Microsoft and Netscape teaming up involves security for on-line transactions. In February 1996, Visa and MasterCard announced the Secure Electronic Transactions (SET) standard. SET was a method of protecting the security of electronic payments by encrypting credit card numbers sent to on-line merchants. It was backed not only by Visa and MasterCard but also by Microsoft, Netscape, and IBM.

That Visa and MasterCard could cooperate is less surprising on its face than the joint endorsement of Microsoft and Netscape: Visa and MasterCard are both controlled by roughly the same set of banks, and they cooperate extensively to route transactions between their two merchant acceptance and cardholder networks. But, again, Microsoft and Netscape were smart enough to figure out how *not* to compete, at least on this dimension. Such a dispute would undoubtedly delay widespread Internet commerce and work to the detriment of both firms as well as consumers.

The path to peace was rocky. Back in June 1995, MasterCard and Visa had said they would coordinate. But by the fall of 1995 a standards war was brewing: Microsoft and Visa proposed what they called Secure Transaction Technology, while MasterCard, Intuit, IBM, and Netscape pushed for a system called Secure Courier. The Microsoft/Visa proposal was touted by them as "open"—that is, available to any company—but the underlying computer software needed to create actual products was only to be made available through licenses from Visa or Microsoft. When it became clear that this wouldn't fly, the companies capitulated and settled on a truly open standard.

Alliances in Action

XEROX AND ETHERNET. The story of the Ethernet standard shows how you can use a formal standards body to establish credibility. Bob Metcalfe developed Ethernet at Xerox PARC in the late 1970s as a way to send vast amounts of data at high speed to the laser printers that Xerox was designing. Xerox patented Ethernet, and Metcalfe left PARC to start 3Com, a company dedicated to networking products.

His first client was Digital, which asked him to develop a new high-speed network standard that didn't infringe on Xerox's patents and that Digital could use to network its workstations. Metcalfe suggested that Digital talk to Xerox first; why reinvent the wheel if Xerox would license it on attractive terms?

Xerox realized, quite correctly, that it would have to offer an open networking standard to get computer manufacturers to adopt the Ethernet interface for their printers. If that same standard could be used for connecting computers, so much the better. Digital, Xerox, and 3Com recognized the value of having an open standard, and Metcalfe went to the National Bureau of Standards to try to set the process in motion. While there, he ran into an Intel representative who was looking for new technologies to embed in integrated circuits.

Digital, Intel, and Xerox subsequently recognized their common interest and formed the DIX group, named after the first letters of their names. (Metcalfe says it was spelled DI3X, but the 3 is silent.) The coalition convinced the IEEE, a highly respected and neutral industry-wide organization, to adopt Ethernet as an open standard, subject to the usual "fair and reasonable" licensing terms, and Xerox agreed to license Ethernet to all takers at a nominal $1,000 flat fee. Adoption by the IEEE did much to create self-fulfilling expectations that Ethernet would emerge as the accepted industry standard.

A few years later, IBM made its Token Ring an open standard on similar terms, but by that time Ethernet had such a large installed base that IBM wasn't able to catch up. Ethernet became the LAN standard because the DIX group recognized the value of openness from the beginning.

ADOBE POSTSCRIPT. Adobe PostScript is another wonderful example of opening up to establish a standard. Xerox had an earlier page description language called Interleaf that it kept proprietary. Interleaf ran only on Xerox hardware, dooming it to a small market share. John Warnock, the leader of the Interleaf team, left Xerox to create PostScript. He realized that PostScript would succeed only if it was open, so Adobe publicly announced that it was not restricting other uses of its page description language: anyone could write and market a PostScript interpreter. Adobe asserted no intellectual property rights to the language itself. Several vendors took Adobe up on the offer, and now there are several suppliers of PostScript interpreters, including GhostScript, a free PostScript interpreter from the GNU Project.

How did Adobe profit from this alliance strategy? Adobe was already far down the learning curve, and it managed to keep a few tricks to itself, including "font hints," which made Adobe PostScript look better on low-resolution devices. The strategy worked well. PostScript became a standard, and Adobe maintained a leading position in the page-description industry and managed to leverage this position in several complementary products in the publishing field.

Several years later Adobe managed to follow a similar strategy with its portable document format (PDF). The company allowed PDF to become an open standard but cleverly exploited the complementarities between creating and viewing a document. Adobe charged for the PDF creation software, while giving away the viewing software.

MICROSOFT'S ACTIVEX. A more recent example of giving away a technology is Microsoft's ActiveX protocols, which allow programs on one computer to communicate with programs on another remote machine. Microsoft did not just *say* it would make ActiveX open, it actually gave responsibility for managing ActiveX to the Open Group, an independent industry group. ActiveX is competing with a rival technology called CORBA, a much more sophisticated, cross-platform technology backed by nearly everyone else in the industry.

Microsoft reportedly spent more than $100 million to develop ActiveX and yet was willing to give it away, at least in part. Microsoft rightly recognized that the relevant question was not how much it cost to develop the technology but rather how much it would cost if Microsoft kept it proprietary. In that case, CORBA would be the only open standard for object calls, and Microsoft could find itself with an orphaned technology and stranded customers. Sunk costs are sunk—it is future costs that matter. But note that Microsoft will continue to make and sell its own *enhancements* to ActiveX, provided they meet the specifications that will be managed by the Open Group.

A key issue in ceding control of ActiveX is Microsoft's reputation. According to the *Wall Street Journal,* "In the past, some software developers were hurt when Microsoft unexpectedly changed key specifications for the technologies it controlled, including its mainstay, the Windows operating system. On occasion, Microsoft has also been able to get a head start on rivals by exploiting new technologies it has developed."[1] Merely announcing that ActiveX would be open would not be enough to convince people to use it—Microsoft actually had to give up some control of the system to make its claims credible.

Assigning control of a standard to a "neutral" industry group has its own dangers, both for the original sponsor of the technology and for users: who will invest in the technology, and how will the standard be improved over time? A modern version of the "tragedy of the commons" can be the sad result: just as few took the trouble to protect the common grazing land from overuse in the seventeenth century, few today will make major investments to advance a technology that is in the public domain. Indeed, for just this reason, an article in *Byte* magazine reported that Microsoft has in fact retained effective control over ActiveX/COM, just as Sun has retained effective control over Java: "Both leading object technologies—and the Java environment—are now controlled by single vendors. Our industry has finally learned a crucial lesson: Technologies controlled by slow-moving standards bodies can't keep up with rapidly changing markets."[2]

MANAGING OPEN STANDARDS

What happens once an open standard is accepted and successful?

Managing successful open standards can be especially tricky. Truly open standards face two fundamental threats. First, if there is no clear sponsor, who will be in charge of setting the direction in which the standard will evolve? Will the standard stagnate, or will crippling incompatibilities arise, since no one can exert control? Second, without a sponsor, who will invest the resources to make improvements and thus keep the standard from stagnating? Who will be willing to invest in the installed base by pricing below cost—penetration pricing—if that is needed to stave off a threat?

> **An open standard is endangered if it lacks a sponsor.**

Open standards are prone to "splintering," or "fragmentation." Splintering of a standard refers to the emergence of multiple, incompatible versions of a standardized technology.

The classic example of the perils of managing open standards, and the dangers of splintering, is the story of the Unix operating system. Unix was originally developed at Bell Labs as a research tool. AT&T gave away the source code to academic researchers for many years, and it became a standard in the research community.

When the minicomputer market took off in the 1970s, Unix was modified and sold by many different companies; the workstation boom of the 1980s led to more versions of Unix, and no industry standard was established. Several different hardware vendors, including IBM, Sun, Hewlett-Packard, Silicon Graphics, and Novell, in a desire to differentiate their products, to add value, and to make improvements, created their own flavors of Unix. None of them wanted to wait for formal approval of their improvements and thereby lose both a timing and a differentiation advantage.

Beginning in the mid-1980s there were efforts to agree on a standard, but these were hampered by infighting among hardware and software vendors. Even the growing and common threat of Windows NT was not sufficient to create harmony among the various Unix vendors in the early 1990s.

In March 1993 the major suppliers of Unix attempted yet again to adopt a common approach that would make it possible for Unix applications to look and work the same on different computers. This alliance consisted of several major players in the Unix industry, including Sun Microsystems, Novell, Santa Cruz Operation, IBM, and Hewlett-Packard. HP and IBM in particular had been direct rivals of Sun and had not generally collaborated on software matters with Sun. The threat posed by Windows NT helped spur these rivals to try to cooperate.

In June 1993, Novell tried to take on a leadership role in the Unix world by acquiring Unix System Laboratories from AT&T in a stock swap valued at about $320 million. Later that year, Novell freely gave away the Unix trademark. Novell's plan was to give the Unix name away to the X/Open Company, a London-based consortium of fourteen hardware and software companies founded in 1985 to promote standardized approaches to Unix. The idea was to let any company call its product *Unix* as long as it met the X/Open specifications.

How did Novell plan to gain from this? Novell continued marketing its own flavor of Unix, UnixWare, hoping that X/Open would give Unix new momentum and that UnixWare would get a decent share of a growing Unix market. Novell's plan ran into snags, however, as IBM, HP, Sun, and Santa Cruz Operation expressed concerns that Novell was attempting to make UnixWare the de facto Unix standard. They asserted that UnixWare was an inferior version of Unix. Meanwhile, Windows NT continues to make inroads in markets that were once the exclusive province of Unix.

Open standards can also be "hijacked" by companies seeking to extend them in proprietary directions, and thus in time gain control over the installed base. Microsoft has been accused of trying to extend both Java and HTML in proprietary directions.

The Standard Generalized Markup Language (SGML) is an open standard for storing and managing documents. Its best-known instance is HyperText Markup Language (HTML), but SGML goes far beyond HTML in its capabilities. SGML's development was pushed by the Department of Defense and other large agencies for whom multiple formats of documents are a huge headache. Despite its claim of being a lingua franca for documents, SGML has never taken off because no large firm has emerged to champion it. Recently there has been some excitement about the Extensible Markup Language (XML), which is a subset of HTML. The danger, of course, is that SGML will splinter in the same way Unix did, with multiple dialects being promulgated.

Sun faces this problem with Java. Sun's competitors and complementors would like to see Java open. However, Sun has been reluctant to give up control over the development of Java, fearful that without a champion, Java could fragment. This puts Sun in a difficult position with other players in the Java coalition.

A final warning on alliances: they can collapse, too. You need to worry not only about forming them but also about keeping them together. The Unix example of splintering is one way in which an alliance can come apart, but not the only way. The "grand alliance" of HDTV offers a good example of a shaky alliance; television manufacturers, broadcast networks, computer manufacturers, and software firms are all sniping at each other about various extensions of the original agreement. Many broadcasters, for example, are planning to use their new spectrum space to deliver multiple channels using digital signals, not to send HDTV signals. Set manufacturers, hoping to sell lots of pricey HDTV sets, are understandably distressed at this prospect. The cable TV networks, which were not involved in the original negotiations, are yet another wild card. They, too, are planning to use digital compression technology to offer more lower-quality channels rather than fewer high-quality channels.

LESSONS

We can distill from this chapter a number of lessons useful to any company participating in an alliance in support of a compatibility standard:

- **To compete effectively in network markets, you need allies.** Choosing and attracting allies is a critical aspect of strategy in the network economy. Competition thus becomes a mixture of politics and economics. You must assemble allies to promote a standard and then compete against these same companies once the standard is established.

- **To find your natural allies, you must determine how a proposed standard will affect competition. Standards alter competition in several predictable ways.** Standards expand network externalities, reduce uncertainty, and reduce consumer lock-in. Standards also shift competition from a winner-take-all battle to a more conventional struggle for market share, from the present into the future, from features to prices, and from systems to components.

- **Standards tend to benefit consumers and suppliers of complements at the expense of incumbents and sellers of substitutes.** Look for your allies among the groups that will benefit from a standard. Then be creative in finding ways to split the enlarged pie that results from a successful standard.

- **Formal standard setting is now being used to develop more standards than ever before.** Formal standard setting is slow, but it can give a new technology enormous credibility. Several key tactics will make you more effective in the formal standard-setting process. Don't slow down your competitive efforts just because you are engaged in formal standard setting. Look for opportunities to build alliances by cutting creative deals, such as licensing arrangements, with selected participants of the standard-setting effort. Beware of companies that hold key patents and are not participating in the process.

- **Find your natural allies and negotiate to gain their support for your technology.** Allies can include customers, complementors, suppliers, and competitors. Be prepared to offer special deals to early supporters; with positive feedback, a few visible early supporters can be enough to tip expectations in your favor, making it easier to attract more allies over time.

- **Before you engage in a standards battle, try to negotiate a truce and form an alliance with your would-be rival.** An agreed-upon standard may lead to a far bigger overall market, making for a larger pie that you can split with your partners. Don't be proud; be prepared to cut a deal even with your most bitter enemy.

- **Try to retain limited control over your technology even when establishing an open standard.** Without a champion, open standards can stagnate or splinter into incompatible pieces. Allies may be happy to let you guide the future evolution of the standard, so long as you have a lasting commitment to openness.

phonographs, cassette players, and reel-to-reel tapes. They were not in a battle with another new technology. They merely (!) had to convince consumers to take a leap and invest in a CD player and compact disks.

What is distinct about standards wars is that there are *two* firms, or alliances, vying for dominance, each one employing one of the four generic strategies discussed in Chapter 7 in the battle. One of the combatants may be an incumbent that controls a significant base of customers who use an older technology, as when Nintendo battled Sony in the video game market in the mid-1990s. Nintendo had a large installed base from the previous generation when both companies introduced 64-bit systems. Or both sides may be starting from scratch, as in the battle between Sony and Matsushita in VCRs.

The outcome of a standards war can determine the very survival of the companies involved. How do you win one?

CLASSIFICATION OF STANDARDS WARS

Not all standards wars are alike. A critical distinguishing feature is the magnitude of the switching costs, or more generally the adoption costs, for each rival technology. We can classify standards wars according to how compatible each player's proposed new technology is with the current technology.

If both your technology and your rival's technology are compatible with the older, established technology but incompatible with each other, we say the battle is one of *rival evolutions*. Competition between DVD and Divx (both of which will play CDs), the 56k modem battle (both types communicate with slower modems), and competition between various flavors of Unix (all of which run programs written for older versions of plain vanilla Unix) all fit this pattern.

If your technology offers backward compatibility and your rival's does not, we have evolution versus revolution. The evolution versus revolution war is a contest between backward compatibility, evolution, and superior performance, revolution. Evolution versus revolution includes the important case of an upstart fighting against an established technology that is offering compatible upgrades. The battle between Lotus 1-2-3 and Excel in the late 1980s and early 1990s in the market for spreadsheets followed this pattern. So did the contemporaneous strug-

Table 9.1. Types of Standards Wars

	Rival Technology	
Your Technology	*Compatible*	*Incompatible*
Compatible	Rival evolutions	Evolution versus revolution
Incompatible	Revolution versus evolution	Rival revolutions

gle between dBase IV and Paradox in the market for desktop database software. (The mirror image of this occurs if your rival offers backward compatibility but you do not: *revolution versus evolution.*)

Finally, if neither technology is backward-compatible we have *rival revolutions.* The contest between Nintendo 64 and the Sony PlayStation and the historical example of AC versus DC in electrical systems follows this pattern. These four types of standards battles are categorized in Table 9.1.

INFORMATION-AGE STANDARDS WARS

We start with three case studies of information-age standards wars. They illustrate several of the tactics that can be employed and some possible outcomes. One war, that over AM stereo radio, was mutually destructive. Another war, cellular telephones, has led to the continued use of two incompatible technologies. The third battle, over 56k modems, was resolved through a standards agreement.

AM Stereo Radio

Some wars have no winners. AM stereo is a good example. Never heard of AM stereo? Our point exactly. The failure of AM stereo radio to gain popularity in the 1980s resulted from a battle between rival revolutions that left no winners.

As early as 1959, petitions were filed with the FCC to adopt an AM stereo standard. By the late 1970s, several incompatible systems were competing for FCC endorsement, sponsored by Magnavox, Motorola, Harris, Belar, and Kahn. The FCC actually picked the Magnavox system in 1980, only to be met with a storm of protest. In an echo of the color television fiasco, the FCC reversed itself in 1982, voting 6 to 1 to let the "market" decide. Four of the five rival systems started to compete in the market, seeking to attract both radio broadcasters and receiver manufacturers.

Since the radio industry itself was quite fragmented, the pivotal player was General Motors' Delco Electronics Division, the largest dominant manufacturer of radio receivers. Delco picked the Motorola system. AM stereo was estimated to add $20 to $40 to the retail price of a car radio. But radio stations saw little reason to invest in equipment, especially in the face of uncertainty over which technology would prevail. Some 30 percent of radio stations cited "market confusion" as a reason for not broadcasting in stereo. The second most-cited reason was "insufficient audience," which is almost the same thing.

We see several lessons in this experience. First, it is a reminder that rival, incompatible approaches to a new technology can indeed kill or at least greatly retard the growth of that technology. Second, a new technology had better offer significant value-added to start a bandwagon rolling. Third, the AM stereo experience shows that adoption is especially difficult when multiple groups of buyers (automobile companies/drivers and radio stations) need to coordinate. Fourth, the example suggests that the best strategy was that adopted by Motorola, namely, to focus on the buyer group that was more concentrated, auto manufacturers, and specifically on Delco, potentially a pivotal buyer. Finally, we note with dismay that neighboring radio stations were unable to coordinate to at least pick the same technology in their own local geography, in part because the National Association of Broadcasters warned its members that this type of coordination might subject station owners to antitrust scrutiny.

Digital Wireless Telephones

Digital wireless telephones permit an interesting comparison of formal standardization in Europe with a standards war in the United States. As with HDTV, the United States has adopted a market-oriented approach, while Europe centralized the selection of new technology. As with HDTV, the U.S. system encouraged the emergence of a promising new technology initially backed by an upstart. Unlike with HDTV, however, the Europeans managed to adopt new digital wireless telephone technology more rapidly than in the United States. So far, at least, the U.S. standards battle has delayed adoption of a promising technology, without any evident benefit in terms of greater product variety.

In Europe, the Global System for Mobile Communications (widely known as GSM) is a well-established standard for digital wireless telephone service. GSM was officially endorsed back in 1992, and valuable spectrum was provided to support GSM implementation. As of 1997, some 40 million Europeans were using GSM. Worldwide, GSM is the dominant technology for digital wireless telephones, with 108 countries adopting it as a standard.

In the United States, by contrast, three systems are offering rival revolutions. The three incompatible technologies vying for leadership in the market for digital telephone systems are (1) GSM, (2) Time Division Multiple Access (TDMA, a close cousin of GSM), and (3) Code Division Multiple Access (CDMA), a radically different system sponsored by the company Qualcomm. The three systems are incompatible in the sense that consumers buying a phone for one system will not be able to switch to another without buying an expensive new phone. However, they are compatible in the sense that users of one system can make calls to users on another system. Fragmentation of the market not only raises consumer switching costs; it also undermines economies of scale in the manufacture of the telephones and gear.

As of 1997, TDMA was in the lead in the United States with more than 5 million subscribers; CDMA had about half that amount. GSM was a distant third with around a million subscribers. Older analog technology retains the lead in the U.S. cellular telephone industry, with nearly 50 million subscribers, but sooner or later analog will surely be displaced by either CDMA or TDMA. Some would say the United States is five years behind Europe in the adoption of digital wireless telephone service, but others argue that CDMA is technologically superior.

Since the buyers in this market, the cellular telephone and personal communication services (PCS) providers, are large, the three-way battle has led to an intricate mating dance between wireless carriers and manufacturers. Ericsson, the champion for TDMA, has AT&T Wireless, SBC, and BellSouth on board. Qualcomm, which created CDMA and has championed it, has signed up Primeco (a joint venture between Bell Atlantic, US West, and AirTouch), Sprint PCS, and most of the other PCS providers. This industry offers a good example of how large, pivotal buyers can obtain attractive terms and conditions if they are willing to make early commitments to specific technologies.

Qualcomm has aggressively pursued a performance play strategy. Qualcomm has been persistent in promoting CDMA, going back to a time when many industry observers dismissed its technology as futuristic but unrealistic. In 1990, when Bell Atlantic and Nynex picked CDMA, the industry was shocked. The Cellular Telephone Industry Association had endorsed TDMA in early 1989 (over Frequency Division Multiple Access, FDMA, a technology supported by Motorola and AT&T that has since disappeared), at which time Qualcomm had not even announced its technology. Many thought CDMA would not be workable for another decade. To this day, Qualcomm's assertions that CDMA has far greater capacity than GSM or TDMA are hotly disputed. Qualcomm managed to shake up this industry much as General Instrument did in the HDTV competition, stunning the larger players with an all-digital system. By bringing on board Bell Atlantic and Nynex, Qualcomm forced equipment manufacturers to make CDMA products.

The precise extent of network externalities is critical to the dynamics of this battle. Consider first the geographic scope of network externalities. If users stayed near their homes, network externalities would apply only within each cellular franchise territory. Consumers in one area would benefit if both cellular providers used the same system, so they could switch systems without buying new handsets. But these same consumers would care little about the technology used in other areas (apart from the chance of relocating to another area). Under these circumstances, there would be little reason to expect a single system to dominate the entire U.S. market. As roaming becomes more important to wireless telephone customers, however, national market shares matter and positive feedback becomes stronger. Moreover, there is always the prospect of positive feedback based on traditional (supply-side) economies of scale in the manufacture of equipment.

How large are the network externalities within a region? Strong, but not overwhelming. Customers need not worry very much about being stranded: if a local carrier has invested in a CDMA system, say, there is little danger that CDMA service will become unavailable (since the infrastructure investments are largely sunk and cannot be moved to other regions). Most important, a user of a CDMA system has no difficulty placing a call to a user of a GSM system. Still, with incompatible local systems, a consumer buying an expensive wireless telephone is locked in. The natural solution to this problem is for consumers to obtain discounts on telephones in exchange for signing service contracts. The conclusion: the market for digital wireless telephone systems is subject to consumer lock-in (wireless carriers are heavily locked into the technology they deploy, and subscribers are somewhat locked in when they buy a phone), but not especially prone to tipping.

What can we learn from this example? First, a decentralized, market-oriented approach may be slower, but it also gives smaller players a chance to succeed with revolutionary new technology. By contrast, picking new technology through a more political process tends to favor larger, established players, even if they are not as imaginative and do not take the same risks. Second, remember that not every market tips. There is surely some positive feedback in the digital wireless telephone market, both around the world and in the United States, but it is not a winner-take-all business. Third, we see Qualcomm successfully executing a performance play strategy based on enlisting large and influential customers, starting with Bell Atlantic and Nynex. We discuss preemption tactics in standards wars below. Even if CDMA is truly the superior technology (which many doubt), Qualcomm could not claim victory simply on technical grounds. Preemption and expectations management were critical to their success.

56k Modems

A standards battle involving two distinct sets of buyers recently played out in the market for 56k modems. The battle was waged between U.S. Robotics (now owned by 3Com) and a team led by Rockwell and Lucent. This was a battle over rival evolutions, since both versions of the modem communicate well with older, slower, standardized modems.

The fact that there *are* 56k modems is somewhat of a surprise, even to experienced modem engineers. For years the accepted wisdom was that modems simply could not operate faster than around 28.8 kbs over regular telephone lines; 28.8 kbs was close to the theoretical limit, and the corresponding ITU standard, V.34, was widely expected to be the "last" modem standard. Integrated Services Digital Network (ISDN) was seen as the only way to speed things up, but ISDN has been slow in coming and a tough sell for household adoption.

Well, theoretical limits just aren't what they used to be. Earlier modem standards had been designed for a roughly symmetric flow of inbound and outbound information. For downloading from the Internet, however, the flow is highly asymmetric: users receive information, and ISPs send it out. Using this idea to redesign modems has led to the 56k category (although performance is highly sensitive to conditions on the telephone line and the higher speeds only apply to downloading).

Everyone knew there was tremendous pent-up demand for faster modems, with consumers impatient with the sluggish pace of downloading information from the Internet at 28.8k. The available market has been estimated at more than $5 billion per year. So the 56k technology represented a major market opportunity, made all the more attractive because backward compatibility with 28.8k modems (and lower) was available to all under ITU specifications.

U.S. Robotics, the leader of one camp, controlled roughly 25 percent of the market for modems, enjoyed strong brand-name recognition, and asserted control over patents crucial to the 56k technology. Rockwell was the leader of the rival team. Rockwell's chief advantage was that it manufactures most of the chipsets that are the electronic heart of modems. But neither player could move forward smoothly without the other, and, in any event, a formal ITU recommendation is widely seen as critical for the legitimacy of any modem standard.

U.S. Robotics attempted to preempt with its "x2" products. The company signed up most ISPs, including America Online, Prodigy, MCI, and CompuServe. In doing this, it attacked the most concentrated part of the demand side, which is an excellent way to execute a preemption strategy in a standards battle, so long as pivotal buyers like America Online do not capture all of the profits from the new technology. This strategy is in harmony with the key assets of U.S. Robotics as a leading modem maker with strong ties to ISPs. 3Com's acquisition of U.S. Robotics only strengthened its hand vis à vis ISPs. U.S. Robotics was also poised to take the lead in building an installed base, exploiting what looked in early 1997 like a genuine time-to-market advantage.

But Rockwell and Lucent were not sitting on their hands. First, since Rockwell and Lucent are leading manufacturers of modem chipsets, they were well placed to control the actual implementation of 56k technology by modem manufacturers. Second, Rockwell accelerated its efforts and successfully narrowed the timing gap with U.S. Robotics by coming to market with its own "K56flex" brand. Perhaps most important, Rockwell and Lucent boldly adopted an alliance strategy, assembling an impressive coalition of modem manufacturers, computer OEMs, and networking equipment manufacturers such as Ascend Communications and Cisco Systems. Computer OEMs are increasingly key, since more and more consumers now purchase computers already fitted with a modem than ever before. In February 1997 the "Open 56k Forum" was unveiled to great fanfare (expectations management), consisting of companies that sell 70 percent of the modems worldwide.

Both sides in this battle worked hard to manage expectations and instill an aura of inevitability to their approach. One ad for Ascend 56k modems used the headline "If you are going to take sides in the 56k battle, make sure you choose the right one." Knowing that consumers, afraid of being stranded, would try to pick the winner, each side claimed it was capturing a large share of the market. At one point, the Rockwell team claimed that 93 percent of ISPs were using Rockwell-based hardware, while U.S. Robotics asserted that 80 percent of ISPs supported its design. While jarring, these claims were not necessarily inconsistent, since many ISPs were indeed supporting both protocols in order not to lose business.

The battle for users' minds—or at least their modems—was also waged on the Internet. Rockwell/Lucent and U.S. Robotics both maintained Web sites touting their products. In August 1997, Rockwell/Lucent listed 650 supporters on its Web site and U.S. Robotics listed around 500. *PC World* contacted the eighteen ISPs listed on the K56flex Web site that "supported and planned to deploy" this standard and found that only three actually offered the service, while eight others planned to do so. The U.S. Robotics site was a little better; fourteen of the twenty-one ISPs on the x2 list of supporters actually offered x2 support, and four others said they planned to do so.

At times, it looked like this standards battle would play out in a crazy way, with ISPs largely choosing U.S. Robotics x2 technology and households mostly buying Rockwell/Lucent technology. With this adoption pattern, no one would be able to take advantage of the higher speeds! An outcome with consumers using one standard and ISPs using another would not be a happy one, nor would it be sustainable.

Fears over incompatibility surely slowed down the market during 1997. Pressure mounted on ISPs to offer separate dial-in lines for each of the two protocols. But in the end, this was a standards battle in which consumers were not badly burned. Crucially, both camps promised free upgrades that would make their modems compatible with the ultimate ITU standard. This eased consumer fears to some degree, but consumers were rightly wary of "patches" meant to solve compatibility problems down the line, and were uncertain in any event whether they would see improved performance right away.

The battle wound down in early December 1997, when a working committee of the ITU announced that 3Com and Rockwell had reached a tentative agreement on a compromise standard now known as the ITU V.90 standard. 3Com stock jumped dramatically on the news, with Rockwell's stock making more modest gains. The new international standard encompasses technical aspects of both transmission methods. Each side claimed victory. Industry observers agreed that the accord would spur modem sales: Dataquest estimated that sales of 56k modems would rise from 10.8 million in 1997 to 33 million in 1998.

KEY ASSETS IN NETWORK MARKETS

Just what does it take to win a standards war? Your ability to successfully wage a standards war depends on your ownership of seven key assets: (1) control over an installed base of users, (2) intellectual property rights, (3) ability to innovate, (4) first-mover advantages, (5) manufacturing abilities, (6) strength in complements, and (7) brand name and reputation. What these assets have in common is that they place you in a potentially unique position to contribute to the adoption of a new technology. If you own these assets, your value-added to other players is high.

The very same assets that bolster your position in a standards war also strengthen your hand in standards negotiations. For just this reason, we have already noted some of the key assets in network markets in our treatment of standard setting in Chapter 8. Here we offer a more complete list of assets, noting that some companies have used these assets to fight standards wars, while others have used them to help establish standards favorable to their interests.

1. **Control over an installed base of customers.** An incumbent firm, like Microsoft, that has a large base of loyal or

locked-in customers, is uniquely placed to pursue an evolution strategy offering backward compatibility. Control over an installed base can be used to block cooperative standard setting and force a standards war.

2. **Intellectual property rights.** Firms with patents and copyrights controlling valuable new technology or interfaces are clearly in a strong position. Qualcomm's primary asset in the digital wireless telephone battle was its patent portfolio. The core assets of Sony and Philips in the CD and DVD areas were their respective patents. Usually, patents are stronger than copyrights, but computer software copyrights that can be used to block compatibility can be highly valuable.

3. **Ability to innovate.** Beyond your existing IPRs, the ability to make proprietary extensions in the future puts you in a strong position today. In the color TV battle, NBC's R&D capabilities were crucial. If you have a crackerjack R&D group, it may be worth some current sacrifices if you think you can outrun your competitors in the long haul. Hewlett-Packard's engineering skills are legendary in Silicon Valley; it is often in HP's interest to compromise on standards since it can out-engineer the competition once the standard has been defined, even if it has to play some initial catch-up.

4. **First-mover advantages.** If you already have done a lot of product development work and are farther along the learning curve than the competition, you are in a strong position. Canon is a good example. It created the personal laser printer market and has continued to dominate the manufacture of the engines in laser printers, in part by exploiting the experience curve to keep costs lower and quality higher than its competitors. Netscape obtained stunning market capitalization based on its ability to bring new technology to market quickly.

5. **Manufacturing abilities.** If you are a low-cost producer, owing to either scale economies or manufacturing competence, you are in a strong position. Cost advantages can help you survive a standards war or capture share competing to sell a standardized product. Compaq and Dell have both pushed hard in

driving down their manufacturing costs, which gives them a strong competitive advantage in the PC market. Rockwell has lower costs than its competitors in making chipsets for modems. These companies benefit from open standards, which emphasize the importance of manufacturing skills.

6. **Strength in complements.** If you produce a product that is a significant complement for the market in question, you will be strongly motivated to get the bandwagon rolling. This, too, puts you in a natural leadership position, since acceptance of the new technology will stimulate sales of the other products you produce. The larger your gross margins on your established products, the stronger this force is. Intel's thirst to sell more CPUs has driven in its efforts to promote new standards for other PC components, including interfaces between motherboards and CPUs, busses, chipsets, and graphics controllers.

7. **Reputation and brand name.** A brand-name premium in any large market is highly valuable. But reputation and brand name are especially valuable in network markets, where expectations are pivotal. It's not enough to have the best product; you have to convince customers that you will win. Previous victories and a recognized name count for a lot in this battle. Microsoft, HP, Intel, Sony, and Sun each have powerful reputations in their respective domains, giving them instant credibility.

Don't forget that *customers* as well as technology suppliers can control key assets, too. A big customer is automatically in "control" of the installed base. America Online recognized this in the recent 56k modem standards battle. Content providers played a major role in the DVD standards battle. IBM was pivotal in moving the industry from 5¼" diskettes to 3½" disks. Most recently, TCI has not been shy about flexing its muscle in the battle over the technology used in TV set-top boxes.

No one asset is decisive. For example, control over an older generation of technology does not necessarily confer the ability to pick the next generation. Sony and Philips controlled CDs but could not move unilaterally into DVDs. Atari had a huge installed base of first-generation video games in 1983, but Nintendo's superior technology and hot new games caught Atari flat-footed. The early leader in modems, Hayes, tried to buck the crowd when modems operating at 9600 kbps were introduced and ended up in Chapter 11 bankruptcy.

TWO BASIC TACTICS IN STANDARDS WARS

Whichever generic strategy you are pursuing in a standards battle, there are two basic marketplace tactics that you will need to employ: preemption and expectations management.

Preemption

The logic of preemption is straightforward: build an early lead, so positive feedback works for you and against your rival. The same principle applies in markets with strong learning-by-doing: the first firm to gain significant experience will have lower costs and can pull even farther ahead. Either way, the trick is to exploit positive feedback. With learning-by-doing, the positive feedback is achieved through lower costs. With network externalities, the positive feedback comes on the demand side; the leader offers a more valuable product or service.

One way to preempt is simply to be first to market. Product development and design skills can be critical to gaining a first-mover advantage. But watch out: early introduction can also entail compromises in quality and a greater risk of bugs, either of which can doom your product. Recall the examples of CBS in color television and Japan in HDTV. The race belongs to the swift, but that speed should be gained by R&D, not by marketing an inferior system.

Being first to market can backfire if superior technology will soon arrive.

In addition to launching your product early, you need to be aggressive early on to build an installed base of customers. Find the "pioneers" (aka gadget freaks) who are most keen to try new technology and sign them up swiftly. Pricing below cost—that is, penetration pricing—is a common tactic used to build an installed base. Discounting to attract large, visible, or influential customers is virtually unavoidable in a standards war.

In some cases, especially for software with a zero marginal cost, you can go beyond free samples and actually *pay* people to take your product. As we see it, there is nothing special about zero as a price, as long as you have multiple revenue streams to recover costs. Some programmers pay cable operators to distribute their programming, knowing that a larger audience will augment their advertising revenues. In the same fashion, Netscape is prepared to give away its browser or even pay OEMs to load it on new machines in order to increase the usage of Navigator and thus direct more traffic to the Netscape Web site.

The big danger with negative prices is that someone will accept payment for "using" your product but then not really use it. This problem is easily solved in the cable television context, where programmers simply insist that cable operators actually carry their programming once they are paid to do so. Likewise, Netscape can check that an OEM loads Navigator (in a specified way) on new machines and can conduct surveys to see just how the OEM configuration affects use of Navigator. Manufacturers do the same thing when they pay "slotting allowances" to supermarkets for shelf space by checking that their products are actually displayed where they are supposed to be displayed.

Before you go overboard by giving your product away or paying customers to take it, you need to ask three questions. First, if you pay someone to take your product, will they really use it and generate network externalities for other, paying customers? Second, how much is it really worth to you to build up your installed base? Where is the offsetting revenue stream, and when will it arrive? Third, are you fooling yourself? Beware the well-known winner's curse, in which the most optimistic participant wins a bidding war only to find that the other bidders were more realistic.

Penetration pricing may be difficult to implement if you are pursuing an openness strategy. The sponsor of a network can hope to recoup the losses incurred during penetration pricing once it controls an established technology. Without a sponsor, no single supplier will be willing to make the necessary investments to preempt using penetration pricing. For precisely this reason, penetration pricing can be particularly effective when used by a company employing a control strategy against a rival adopting an openness strategy.

New technologies require champions willing to invest early to build an installed base.

Another implication is that the player in a standards battle with the largest profit streams from related products stands to win the war. We have seen this with smart cards in Europe. They were introduced with a single application—public telephone service—but soon were expanded to facilitate other transactions involving small purchases. Eventually, many more applications, such as identification and authentication, will be introduced. Visa, MasterCard, and American Express are already jockeying for position in the smart card wars. Whichever player can figure out the most effective way to generate multiple revenue streams from an installed base of smart card holders will be able to bid most aggressively, but still profitably, to build up the largest base of customers.

Expectations Management

Expectations are a key factor in consumer decisions about whether or not to purchase a new technology, so make sure that you do your best to manage those expectations. Just as incumbents will try to knock down the viability of emerging new technologies, so will those very entrants strive to establish credibility.

Vaporware is a classic tactic aimed at influencing expectations: announce an upcoming product so as to freeze your rival's sales. In the 1994 antitrust case brought by the Justice Department against Microsoft, Judge Sporkin cited vaporware as one reason he found the proposed consent decree insufficient. In an earlier era, IBM was accused of the same tactic. Of course, drawing the line between "predatory product pre-announcements" and simply being late bringing a product to market is not so easy, especially in the delay-prone software market. Look at what happened to Lotus in spreadsheets and Ashton-Tate in database software. After both of these companies repeatedly missed launch dates, industry wags said they should be merged and use the stock ticker symbol "LATE." And we must note with some irony that Microsoft's stock took a 5.3 percent nosedive in late 1997 after announcing a delay in the launch of Windows 98 from the first to the second quarter of 1998.

The most direct way to manage expectations is by assembling allies and making grand claims about your product's current or future popularity. Sun has been highly visible in gathering allies in support of Java, including taking out full-page advertisements listing the companies in the Java coalition, showing how important expectations management is in markets with strong network externalities, WordPerfect even filed a court complaint against Microsoft to block Microsoft from claiming that its word processing software was the most popular in the world. Barnes & Noble did the same thing to Amazon, arguing that its claim to being the "world's largest bookstore" was misleading.

ONCE YOU'VE WON

Moving on from war to the spoils of victory, let's consider how best to proceed once you have actually won a standards war. You probably made some concessions to achieve victory, such as promises of openness or deals with various allies. Of course, you have to live with those, but there is still a great deal of room for strategy. In today's high-tech world, the battle never really ends. So, take a deep breath and be ready to keep moving.

Staying on Your Guard

Technology marches forward. You have to keep looking out for the next generation of technology, which can come from unexpected directions. Microsoft, with all its foresight and savvy, has had to scurry to deal with the Internet phenomenon, trying to defuse any threat to its core business.

You may be especially vulnerable if you were victorious in one generation of technology through a preemption strategy. Going early usually means making technical compromises, which gives others that much more room to execute an incompatible revolution strategy against you. Apple pioneered the market for personal digital assistants, but U.S. Robotics perfected the idea with Palm Pilot. If your rivals attract the power users, your market position and the value of your network may begin to erode.

The hazards of moving early and then lacking flexibility can be seen in the case of the French Minitel system. Back in the 1980s, the French were world leaders in on-line transactions with the extensive Minitel computer network. The network is sponsored and controlled by France Telecom. Before the Internet was widely known, much less used, millions of French subscribers used the Minitel system to obtain information and conduct secure on-line transactions. Today, Minitel boasts more than 35 million French subscribers and 25,000 vendors. One reason Minitel has attracted so many suppliers is that users pay a fee to France Telecom each time they visit a commercial site, and a portion of these fees is passed along to vendors. Needless to say, this business model is quite different from what we see on the Web.

Nonetheless, the Minitel system is beginning to seem limited when compared with the Internet, and France is lagging behind in moving onto the Internet. Just as companies that invested in dedicated word processing systems in the 1970s were slow to move to more generalized PCs in the 1980s, the French have been slow to invest in equipment that can access the Internet. Only about 3 percent of the French population uses the Internet, far short of the estimated 20 percent in the United States and 9 percent in the United Kingdom and Germany. Roughly 15 percent of French companies have a Web site, versus nearly 35 percent of U.S. businesses. Only in August 1997 did the French government admit that the Internet, not Minitel, was the way of the future rather than an instrument of American cultural imperialism. France Telecom is now planning to introduce next-generation Minitel terminals that will access the Internet as well as Minitel.

What is the lesson here? The French sluggishness to move to the Internet stems from two causes that are present in many other settings. First, France Telecom and its vendors had an incentive to preserve the revenue streams they were earning from Minitel. This is understandable, but it should be recognized as a choice to harvest an installed base, with adverse implications for the future. Milking the installed base is sometimes the right thing to do, but make this a calculated choice, not a default decision. Second, moving to the Internet presents substantial collective switching costs, and less incremental value, to French consumers in contrast with, say, American consumers. Precisely because Minitel was a success, it reduced the attractiveness of the Internet.

The strategic implication is that you need a migration path or roadmap for your technology. If you cannot improve your technology with time, while offering substantial compatibility with older

Offer your customers a migration path to fend off challenges from upstarts.

versions, you will be overtaken sooner or later. Rigidity is death, unless you build a really big installed base, and even this will fade eventually without improvements.

The key is to anticipate the next generation of technology and co-opt it. Look in all directions for the next threat, and take advantage of the fact that consumers will not switch to a new, incompatible technology unless it offers a marked improvement in performance. Microsoft has been the master of this strategy with its "embrace and extend" philosophy of anticipating or imitating improvements and incorporating them into its flagship products. Avoid being frozen in place by your own success. If you cater too closely to your installed base by emphasizing backward compatibility, you open the door to a revolution strategy by an upstart. As we discussed in Chapter 7, this is precisely what happened to Ashton-Tate in databases, allowing Borland and later Microsoft to offer far superior performance with their Paradox and FoxPro products. Your product roadmap has to offer your customers a smooth migration path to ever-improving technology, and stay close to, if not on, the cutting edge.

One way to avoid being dragged down by the need to retain compatibility with your own installed base is to give older members free or inexpensive upgrades to a recent but not current version of your product. This is worth doing for many reasons: users of much older versions have revealed that they do not need the latest bells and whistles and thus are less likely to actually buy the latest version; the free "partial" upgrade can restore some lost customer loyalty; you can save on support costs by avoiding "version creep," and you can avoid being hamstrung in designing your latest products by a customer-relations need to maintain compatibility with older and older versions. To compromise the performance of your latest version in the name of compatibility with ancient versions presents an opening for a rival to build an installed base of more demanding users. Happily, this "lagged upgrade" approach is easier and easier with distribution so cheap over the Internet. Lagged upgrades also tie in well with the versioning approach to software we described in Chapter 3.

Microsoft did a good job handling this problem with migration to Windows 95. Politely put, Windows 95 is a kludge, with all sorts of special workarounds to allow DOS programs to execute in the Windows environment, thereby maintaining compatibility with customers' earlier programs. Microsoft's plan with Windows 98 is to move this consumer version of Windows closer to the professional version, Windows NT, eventually ending up with only one product, or at least only one user interface. It will still want to version its operating system's capabilities for all the reasons described in Chapter 3.

Commoditizing Complementary Products

Once you've won, you want to keep your network alive and healthy. This means that you've got to attend not only to your own products but to the products produced by your complementors as well. Your goal should be to retain your franchise as the market leader but encourage a vibrant and competitive market for complements to your product.

This can be tricky. Apple has flipped back and forth on its developer relations over the years. First it just wanted to be in the computer business and let others develop applications. Then it established a subsidiary, Corbis, to do applications development. When this soured relations with other developers, Apple spun Corbis off. And so it went—a back-and-forth dance.

Microsoft faced the same problem, but with a somewhat different strategy. If an applications developer became successful, Microsoft just bought it out! Or tried to—Microsoft's intended purchase of Intuit was blocked by the Department of Justice. Nowadays a lot of new business plans in the software industry have the same structure: "Produce product, capture emerging market, be bought by Microsoft."

Our view is that you should try to maintain a competitive market in complementary products and avoid the temptation to meddle. Enter into these markets only if (1) integration of your core product with adjacent products adds value to consumers or (2) you can inject significant additional competition to keep prices low. If you are truly successful, like Intel, you will need to spur innovation in complementary products to help fuel growth.

> *Enter adjacent markets only if integration adds value for consumers.*

Competing with Your Own Installed Base

You may need to improve performance just to compete with your installed base, even without an external threat. How can you continue to grow when your information product or technology starts to reach market saturation? One answer is to drive innovation ever faster. Intel is pushing to improve hardware performance of complementary products and to develop applications that crave processing power so as to drive the hardware upgrade cycle. Comptition with one's own installed base is not a new problem for companies selling durable goods. The stiffest competition faced by Steinway in selling pianos is that from used Steinways.

One way to grow even after you have a large installed base is to start discounting as a means of attracting the remaining customers who have demonstrated (by waiting) that they have a relatively low willingness to pay for your product. As we saw in Chapters 2 and 3, this is a good instinct, but be careful. First, discounting established products is at odds with a penetration pricing strategy to win a standards war. Second, if you regularly discount products once they are well established, consumers may learn to wait for the discounts. The key question: can you expand the market and not spoil your margins for traditional customers?

Economists have long recognized this as the "durable-goods monopoly" problem. Ronald Coase, recent winner of the Nobel Prize in economics, wrote twenty-five years ago about the temptation of a company selling a durable product to offer lower and lower prices to expand the market once many consumers have already purchased the durable good. He conjectured that consumers would come to anticipate these price reductions and hold off buying until prices fall. Since then, economists have studied a variety of strategies designed to prevent the resulting erosion of profits. The problem raised by Coase is especially severe for highly durable products such as information and software.

One of the prescriptions for solving the durable goods monopoly problem is to *rent* your product rather than sell it. This will not work for a microprocessor or a printer, but rapid technological change can achieve the same end. If a product becomes obsolete in two or three years, used versions won't pose much of a threat to new sales down the line. This is a great spur for companies like Intel to rush ahead as fast as possible in increasing the speed of their microprocessors. The same is true on the software side, where even vendors dominant in their

Once you've sold to everyone, you need improvements to drive upgrade sales.

category, such as Autodesk in computer-aided design, are forced to improve their programs to generate a steady stream of revenues.

Protecting Your Position

A variety of defensive tactics can help secure your position. This is where antitrust limits come in most sharply, however, since it is illegal to "maintain a monopoly" by anticompetitive means. We'll discuss those limits further in Chapter 10.

One tactic is to offer ongoing attractive terms to important complementors. For example, Nintendo worked aggressively to attract developers of hit games and used its popularity to gain very strong distribution. This tactic can, however, cross the legal line if you insist that your suppliers or distributors deal with you to the exclusion of your rivals. For example, FTD, the floral network, under pressure from the Justice Department, had to cancel its program giving discounts to florists who used FTD exclusively. Since FTD had the lion's share of the floral delivery network business, this quasi-exclusivity provision was seen as protecting FTD's near-monopoly position. Ticketmaster was subjected to an extensive investigation for adopting exclusivity provisions in its contracts with stadiums, concert halls, and other venues. And the Justice Department has attacked Microsoft's contracts with OEMs for having an effect similar to that of exclusive licenses.

A less controversial way to protect your position is to take steps to avoid being held up by others who claim that your product infringes on their patents or copyrights. Obviously, there is no risk-free way to do this. But it makes a great deal of sense to ask those seeking access to your network to agree not to bring the whole network down in an infringement action. Microsoft took steps along these lines when it launched Windows 95, including a provision in the Windows 95 license for OEMs that prevented Microsoft licensees from attempting to use certain software patents to block Microsoft from shipping Windows 95. Intel regularly asks companies taking licenses to its open specifications to agree to offer royalty-free licenses to other participants for any patents that would block the specified technology. This "two-sided openness" strategy prevents *ex post* hold-up problems and helps to safely launch a new specification.

Leveraging Your Installed Base

Once you have a strong installed base, basic principles of competitive strategy dictate that you seek to leverage into adjacent product spaces, exploiting the key assets that give you a unique ability to create value for consumers in those spaces. We discussed such leveraging in Chapter 6, but some new wrinkles come up in the network context. For example, control over an interface can be used to extend leadership from one side of the interface to the other.

But don't get carried away. As we have just seen in this chapter, you may be better off encouraging healthy competition in complementary products, which stimulates demand for your core product, than trying to dominate adjacent spaces. In acquiring companies selling neighboring products, you should be driven by true synergies of bringing both products into the same company, not simply by a desire to expand your empire. Again, legal limits on both "leveraging" and on vertical acquisitions can come into play. For example, the FTC forced Time Warner to agree to carry on its cable systems a rival news channel when Time Warner acquired CNN in its merger with Turner.

Geographic expansion is yet another way to leverage your installed base. This is true for traditional goods and services, but with a new twist for network products: when expanding the geographic scope of your network, make sure your installed base in one region becomes a competitive advantage in another region. Just don't build a two-way bridge to another region where you face an even stronger rival; in that case, more troops will come across the bridge attacking you than you can send to gain new territory.

Geographic effects were powerful in the FCC auctions of spectrum space for PCS services, the successor to the older cellular telephone technology. If you provide personal digital assistance (PDA) wireless services in Minneapolis, you have a big advantage if you also provide such services in St. Paul. The market leader in one town would therefore be willing to outbid rivals in neighboring locations. In the PCS auctions, bidders allegedly "signaled" their most-preferred territories by encoding them into their bids as an attempt to avoid a mutually unprofitable bidding war. The Department of Justice is investigating these complaints. Our point is not to offer bidding strategy but to remind you that geographic expansion of a network can be highly profitable. Network

was concerned about this when it dropped the PC Jr. in the mid-1980s. Apart from consumer goodwill, retaining a presence in the market can be vital in keeping up customer relations and brand identity, even if you have little prospect of making major sales until you introduce a new generation of products. Apple faces this problem with its new operating system, OS X. How does it maintain compatibility with its loyal followers while still building a path to what it hopes will be a dramatic improvement in the operating environment?

Adapters and Interconnection

A tried and true tactic to use when falling behind is to add an adapter or to somehow interconnect with the larger network. This can be a sign of weakness, but one worth bearing if the enhanced network externalities of plugging into a far larger network are substantial. We touched on this in our discussion of how to negotiate a truce; if you are negotiating from weakness, you may simply seek the right to interconnect with the larger network.

The first question to ask is whether you even have the right to build an adapter. Sometimes the large network can keep you out. Atari lacked the intellectual property rights to include an adapter in its machines to play Nintendo cartridges because of Nintendo's lock-out chip. In other cases, you may be able to break down the door, or at least try. Discover Card wanted the right to issue Visa cards; American Express hoped to offer cards that could be used as Visa cards if a cardholder went to a merchant that did not accept American Express. Discover sued Visa, but did not gain the right to issue Visa cards. However, in Canada, the dominant ATM network, Interac, was compelled to let nonmember banks interconnect. In the telephone area, the FCC is implementing elaborate rules that will allow competitive local exchange carriers to interconnect with the incumbent monopoly telephone networks.

The most famous legal case of a less-popular network product maneuvering to achieve compatibility is the battle between Borland and Lotus in spreadsheets. To promote its Quattro Pro spreadsheet as an alternative to the dominant spreadsheet of the day, Lotus 1-2-3, Borland not only made sure that Quattro Pro could import Lotus files but copied part of the menu structure used by Lotus. Lotus sued Borland for copyright infringement. The case went all the way to the Supreme

Court, where the vote was deadlocked, so Borland prevailed based on its victory in the First Circuit Court of Appeals. This case highlights the presence of legal uncertainty over what degree of imitation is permissible; the courts are still working out the limits on how patents and copyrights can be used in network industries.

If you fall behind, target a market niche or interconnect with the larger network.

There are many diverse examples of "adapters." Conversion of data from another program is a type of adapter. Translators and emulators can serve the same function when more complex code is involved. Converters can be one-way or two-way, with very different strategic implications. Think about WordPerfect and Microsoft Word today. WordPerfect is small and unlikely to gain much share, so it benefits from two-way compatibility. Consumers will be more willing to buy or upgrade WordPerfect if they can import files in Word format *and* export files in a format that is readable by users of Word. So far, Word will import files in WordPerfect format, but if Microsoft ever eliminates this feature of Word, WordPerfect should attempt to offer an export capability that preserves as much information as possible.

The biggest problem with adapters, when they are technically and legally possible, is performance degradation. Early hopes that improved processing power would make emulation easy have proven false. Tasks become more complex.

Digital's efforts with its Alpha microprocessor illustrate some of the ways in which less popular technologies seek compatibility. The Alpha chip has been consistently faster than the fastest Intel chips on the market. Digital sells systems with Alpha chips into the server market, a far smaller market than the desktop and workstation markets. And Digital's systems are far more expensive than systems using Intel chips. As a result, despite its technical superiority, the Alpha sold only 300,000 chips in 1996 compared with 65 million sold by Intel. This leaves Digital in the frustrating position of having a superior product but suffering from a small network. Recognizing that Alpha is in a precarious position, Digital has been looking for ways to interconnect with the Intel (virtual) network. Digital offers an emulator that lets its Alpha chip run like an Intel architecture chip, but most of the performance advantages that Alpha offers are neutralized by the emulator. Hoping to improve the performance of systems using the Alpha chip, Digital and Microsoft announced in January 1998 an enhanced Alliance for Enterprise Computing, under which Windows NT server-based products will be released concurrently for Alpha- and Intel-based systems. Digital also has secured a commitment from Microsoft that Microsoft will cooperate to provide source-code compatibility between Alpha- and Intel-based systems for Windows NT application developers, making it far easier for them to develop applications to run on Alpha-based systems in native mode.

Adapters and converters among software programs are also highly imperfect. Converting files from WordStar to WordPerfect, and now from WordPerfect to Word, is a notoriously buggy process. Whatever the example, consumers are rightly wary of translators and emulators, in part because of raw performance concerns, and in part because of lurking concerns over just how compatible the conversion really is: consider the problems that users have faced with Intel to Motorola architectures, or dBase to Paradox databases.

Apple offers a good example of a company that responded to eroding market share by adding adapters. Apple put in disk drives that could read floppy disks formatted on DOS and Windows machines in the mid-1980s. In 1993 Apple introduced a machine that included an Intel 486 chip and could run DOS and Windows software along with Macintosh software. But Apple's case also exposes the deep tension underlying an adapter strategy: the adapter adds (some) value but undermines confidence in the smaller network itself.

Finally, be careful about the large network changing interface specifications to avoid compatibility. IBM was accused of this in mainframe computers. Indeed, we suggested this very tactic in the section above on strategies for winners, so long as the new specifications are truly superior, not merely an attempt to exclude competitors.

Survival Pricing

As we saw in Chapter 2, the marginal cost of producing information goods is close to zero. This means that you can cut your price very low and still cover (incremental) costs. Hence, when you find yourself falling behind in a network industry, it is tempting to cut price to spur sales, a tactic we call *survival pricing*.

This temptation should be resisted. Survival pricing is unlikely to work. It shows weakness, and it is hard to find examples in which it has made much difference. Our very first case study of the *Encyclopedia Britannica* versus *Encarta* illustrated this problem.

Survival pricing doesn't work; it just signals weakness.

Computer Associates gave away Simply Money (for a $6.95 shipping and handling fee), but this didn't matter. Simply Money still did not take off in its battle against Quicken and Money. On the other hand, Computer Associates got the name and vital statistics of each buyer, which was worth something in the mail list market, so it wasn't a total loss. IBM offered OS/2 for as little as $50, but look at the result. Borland priced Quattro Pro very aggressively when squeezed between Lotus 1-2-3 and Microsoft Excel back in 1993.

The problem is that the purchase price of software is minor in comparison with the costs of deployment, training, and support. Corporate purchasers, and even individual consumers, were much more worried about picking the winner of the spreadsheet wars than they were about whether their spreadsheet cost $49.95 or $99.95. At the time of the cut-throat pricing, Borland was a distant third in the spreadsheet market. Lotus and Microsoft both said they would not respond to the low price. Frank Ingari, Lotus's vice president for marketing, dismissed Borland as a "fringe player" and said the $49 price was a "last gasp move."

Survival pricing—cutting your price after the tide has moved against you—should be distinguished from penetration pricing, which is offering a low price to invade another market. Borland used penetration pricing very cleverly in the early 1980s with its Turbo Pascal product. Microsoft and other compiler companies ignored Turbo Pascal, much to their dismay later on.

Legal Approaches

If all else fails, sue. No, really. If the dominant firm has promised to be open and has reneged on that promise, you should attack its bait-and-switch approach. The Supreme Court in the landmark *Kodak* case, discussed in Chapter 6, opened the door to antitrust attacks along these lines, and many companies have taken up the invitation. The FTC case against Dell Computer also fits into the category of reneging on promises of openness. All of this corresponds with our earlier admonition: get clear and explicit protections early on, if you can, or else give serious thought to fighting a standards war.

CAPSTONE CASE: MICROSOFT VERSUS NETSCAPE

We conclude our discussion of strategic standard setting by applying our framework to one of the most widely watched and reported standards wars of the last several years: the Battles of the Browsers. During one heated skirmish in this war, interest was so intense that *Business Week* reported that President Clinton queried Netscape chief executive James L. Barksdale about his strategy. "That the contest caught even the President's eye underscores just how seminal it is: This battle is for nothing less than the soul of the Internet."[1]

In one corner we have the company that popularized the very idea of an Internet browser: the Internet pioneer, darling of the stock market, and still reigning champion in the browser category, Netscape Communications Corporation. In the other corner we have the heavyweight of high tech: the world's largest software supplier, dominant on the desktop, grimly intent on catching the Internet wave, none other than the mighty Microsoft.

For the past three years, Microsoft has been pulling out the stops to overtake Netscape, trying to displace the Netscape Navigator with its own Internet Explorer. Each company has brought to bear substantial competitive assets. When Microsoft went on the attack, Netscape had a far superior product and a substantial installed base of satisfied users. Microsoft, however, had its brand name, a history of dominating one software application after another, control over the underlying operating system, and seemingly limitless financial resources at its disposal.

Let's follow the steps laid out in the last few chapters.

The first step is to gauge the importance of positive feedback in the browser category. Are strong network externalities present for browser users? To date, we would say the network externalities are modest, not strong. First, there appears to be little by way of training needed for someone to effectively use a browser. Indeed, one of the attractions of the Netscape Navigator is that many people find it simple and intuitive. Nor do most users have any "data" in a Navigator-specific format. To the contrary, Navigator relies on HTML, which is quite open, and bookmark files are easily transferred between browsers. So individual switching costs are not large.

What about collective switching costs? Are there strong forces stopping any one user from employing an unpopular browser? Not yet. So far at least, either brand of browser can view the vast majority of Web pages with equal effectiveness. This is not universally true, so network externalities are present to some degree, but they remain small so far. Indeed, some observers have expressed concern that Microsoft will find a way to strengthen the network externalities, through control over software for servers, if and when it has a stronger position on the client/browser side. If Microsoft is able to get the majority of servers to display material in a superior fashion for the Internet Explorer, strong positive feedback might kick in. However, the most popular product in the Internet server market is Apache, which enjoys a 47 percent market share and is completely open. Microsoft and Netscape servers have 22 percent and 10 percent of the market, respectively.

In fact, the relatively weak network externalities explain in part why the browser war has turned into trench warfare, not a blitzkrieg. Netscape's position is hardly impenetrable, and Microsoft, especially with its offsetting advantages, could credibly stay in the game with a market share around 30 percent of shipments during 1997.

What are the market shares in the browser war, anyhow? An unusual but handy aspect of the browser market is that market shares can be measured in terms of *usage* rather than purchases of the product, since Web sites can determine the browser used by a visitor. For the purposes of assessing network externalities, usage is far more important than purchase: the "active" installed base is what matters. Products given away for free but not used just don't matter. Recent data indicate that Netscape Navigator's share of usage is 54 percent, with Microsoft's Internet Explorer weighing in at 33 percent. (Cyberdog, for the Macintosh, is a distant third with around 5 percent of hits.)

The browser wars involve rival evolutions. Consumers bear little of the costs of adopting either brand of browser. So far at least, both browsers are compatible with existing hardware and software systems. If Microsoft were ever to design Windows to make Navigator *incompatible* with Windows, they will have converted the war into evolution versus revolution. We doubt this will happen, however, so long as the Justice Department remains alert.

Most of the action involves four of the tactics for waging a standards war that we have discussed above: (1) preemption, (2) penetration pricing, (3) expectations management, and (4) jockeying for allies. Let's look at these in turn.

Preemption

Netscape enjoyed a big head start with Navigator, which was introduced in 1995. Microsoft licensed the original source code for Mosaic from Spyglass and rushed Internet Explorer to market. Microsoft's haste showed, and Internet Explorer was widely regarded as a joke until Internet Explorer 3.0 was released in August 1996. By that time, many firms and individuals had already installed Netscape Navigator. With technology moving so rapidly, however, and in the absence of substantial consumer lock-in, an ongoing race developed to bring out new and improved versions ahead of the competition. As in other software categories, sales surge with the release of a new version, then drift until the cycle repeats itself.

Preemption and leapfrogging play out differently in different distribution channels. The primary channels are (1) direct distribution to consumers, either over the Internet or through retail outlets, (2) sales to OEMs for placement on new machines, and (3) indirect distribution through ISPs. Once a user has downloaded one browser, there is little reason to use another unless it offers superior functionality. OEMs can and do place multiple browser icons on the desktop to give their customers a choice when they turn on their new machine. In this channel, preemption can still occur if one browser supplier obtains exclusive rights to have its browser on that OEM's desktop, or if the OEM is given an incentive not to load the rival browser on its machines. So far, browser software does not occupy so much disk storage space as to crowd out another browser, and antitrust oversight makes it risky for Microsoft to sign exclusive deals with OEMs.

Preemption is also possible through the ISP channel. Microsoft structured deals with America Online, CompuServe, Prodigy, AT&T Worldnet, Netcom, and MCI, among others, that made Internet Explorer the "preferred browser" for those ISPs. Since many consumers are inclined to follow the advice of their ISP in picking their browser, these bundled offerings can have a material affect on market shares. Precisely for this reason, the Justice Department has scrutinized Microsoft's contracts with ISPs, and in early 1998 Microsoft modified these contracts to permit ISPs to promote rival browsers.

Penetration Pricing

Both Netscape and Microsoft are masters at penetration pricing, each in its own way.

Netscape led the way in making its software available free of charge over the Internet. As we saw in Chapter 4, one of the wonderful things about the Internet is that it can serve as an extremely efficient, low-cost means of distributing information products, be they content or tools such as software. So, even while Netscape sold Navigator in retail stores for $49, with printed documentation, the same software was generally available free on-line. Of course, many users who were new to the whole on-line world were not sophisticated enough to download Navigator without the use of the Navigator software itself.

Netscape also pioneered the idea of plug-ins, software written by third parties that enhance the functionality of the basic Navigator program. Netscape provided links to these publishers from its Web site to make it easy for users to customize their browser. Making quality enhancements available free is a variant on penetration pricing. In this way, Netscape was able to build up a network of software developers tied to its technology.

For a while, Netscape tried to charge customers who were downloading Navigator. This attempt was half-hearted, however: Navigator 4.0 was available free for a trial period, after which Netscape requested that users pay if they wished to keep using the software. In early 1998, Netscape went way beyond simply offering Navigator for free. It released the source code for Navigator, so people can now both use it freely *and* modify it at will.

Microsoft's first step was to make Internet Explorer available free on-line. This tactic made a lot of sense as part of Microsoft's catch-up strategy. In fact, Microsoft has gone even further, actually *paying* OEMs and ISPs to give preference to Internet Explorer over Navigator, by making Internet Explorer the "default" browser. The company has also publicly stated that Explorer will be free "now and in the future," an obvious attempt at expectations management.

Why are both companies willing to engage in such aggressive penetration pricing? These giveaways are taking a toll on Netscape: revenues from "client licenses" declined from more than half of Netscape's revenues in 1996 to less than 40 percent in the second quarter of 1997. Our discussion in Chapter 2 raises one possibility: competition has driven the price of this information good down to marginal cost, which is tiny. But this explanation is incomplete. Clearly, each company sees longer-term strategic benefits of increased use of its browsers. What are these benefits, and how do they relate to the giveaways? To answer that question, we have to follow the money: what revenues are at stake in this standards war?

Start with Netscape. The key is that placements of Navigator help Netscape earn revenues from its other products. For example, Netscape's Web site is one of the most heavily accessed pieces of real estate on the Net, in large part because many of the 65 million users of Navigator have never changed the default setting on their browsers. This gives Netscape a very attractive platform for advertising. Netscape is clearly moving to establish its Web site as a major "portal" to the Internet. This will bring Netscape more directly into competition with Yahoo! and Excite, while helping to wean it of the need for browser revenues.

Beyond that, Netscape recently released its push-media software, Netcaster, which is piggybacking on Netscape's browser: as customers download the browser, they have the option of taking the whole package. The more people use Navigator and Netcaster, the more of users' time and attention Netscape has to sell to its advertisers, and the more revenue Netscape can earn by selling space on Netcaster. Yahoo!, for example, recently announced that it will be paying $4.7 million for the rights to the Netscape Guide button. Not surprisingly, advertising revenues are a growing share of Netscape's total revenues.

Netscape's grander plan is to offer an entirely new user interface. The new Netscape Constellation is nothing less than a complete user environment, centered around the browser. Constellation thus can serve as a layer between users and the existing operating system, just as Windows initially was a layer between the user and the aging DOS. In addition, this user interface is a gateway to the Internet. Viewed this way, the browser wars are but a skirmish in the larger battle over users and gateways to the Internet, which is, of course, a major threat to Microsoft. Who cares about access to the desktop if someone else controls access to the Internet?

Microsoft's motives are also based on augmenting revenue streams "adjacent" to the browser itself. As we noted above, Microsoft has publicly stated that it intends *never* to charge consumers for a stand-alone browser. Microsoft's plan is to tie the browser into its operating system, replacing the Windows 95 user interface with an interface much more like that of today's stand-alone browsers. Viewed in this way, it is easier to see why Microsoft is willing to invest so heavily in building up the installed base of Internet Explorer users: it will both ease the transition to Windows 98 and deny Netscape the chance to challenge Microsoft's control over the user interface. Control of the user interface is enormously valuable because it gives Microsoft access to that most valuable item in the information age: human attention. Indeed, one of Microsoft's weaknesses is that many people fear that it will use its browser to somehow control on-line sales. These fears were fueled by a statement by Microsoft's Nathan Myrhvold that Microsoft hoped to earn a "vig" or vigorish, on every transaction over the Internet that uses Microsoft's technology. However, testifying before Congress, Bill Gates denied that this was Microsoft's goal.

Expectations Management

Netscape has stated recently that it plans to place its browser on as many as 100 million desktops. The company also announced that one hundred industry partners will package the Navigator browser with their products. Trumpeting grand plans for future sales, as well as extensive distribution agreements, is a classic method of building favorable expectations in the hope that they will be self-fulfilling. The very name of Netscape's recent marketing campaign for Navigator says it all: "Netscape Everywhere."

Microsoft is not pulling its punches, either, in attempts to convince consumers that Internet Explorer is the browser of the future. Microsoft stated clearly and at an early stage that it planned to further integrate Internet Explorer into its Windows operating system. By doing so, Microsoft is simultaneously making it more difficult for any operating-system challenger to offer dramatic improvements in the user interface, guaranteeing enormous distribution for Internet Explorer and making it harder for Netscape to convince consumers that they need Navigator.

Alliances

Allies are especially important to Netscape, given its small size and young age. Netscape and Sun Microsystems are strong allies, with Netscape supporting Sun's Java and Sun helping lend credibility to Netscape. Arthur Andersen's support has helped Netscape make big inroads into the corporate intranet market. Netscape has also made arrangements with publishers to distribute on-line material to Navigator users and with Internet service providers to offer Navigator to their customers.

As already noted, Microsoft has assembled its share of allies by offering attractive financial terms to content providers, ISPs, and OEMs. Indeed, even Microsoft's 1997 investment in Apple was designed to promote Internet Explorer by increasing the distribution of the browser on Macintosh machines. Oddly, most of the press reports at the time missed this important aspect of the new Microsoft/Apple accommodation.

LESSONS

- **Understand what type of standards war you are waging.** The single most important factor is the compatibility between the dueling new technologies and established products. Standards wars come in three forms: rival evolutions, rival revolutions, and revolution versus evolution.

- **Strength in the standards game is determined by ownership of seven critical assets.** The key assets are (1) control of an installed base, (2) intellectual property rights, (3) ability to innovate, (4) first-mover advantages, (5) manufacturing abilities, (6) presence in complementary products, and (7) brand name and reputation.

- **Preemption is a critical tactic during a standards war.** Rapid design cycles, early deals with pivotal customers, and penetration pricing are the building blocks of a preemption strategy.

- **Expectations management is also crucial to building positive feedback.** Your goal is to convince customers and complementors that you will emerge as the victor; such expectations can easily become a self-fulfilling prophecy. To manage expectations, you should engage in aggressive marketing, make early announcements of new products, assemble allies, and make visible commitments to your technology.

- **When you've won your war, don't rest easy.** Cater to your installed base and avoid complacency. Don't let the desire for backward compatibility hobble your ability to improve your product; doing so will leave you open to an entrant employing a revolution strategy. Commoditize complementary products to make your systems more attractive to consumers.

- **If you fall behind, avoid survival pricing.** A better tactic is trying to interconnect with the prevailing standard using converters and adapters.

10 | Information Policy

Your leading rival sues you for infringing several key patents. Do you countersue, using your own patent portfolio as a weapon, negotiate a cross-license, or straight-out acquire the rival? You are facing low-priced competition from gray-market imports of your own discounted products intended for markets in Asia. Can you block these imports to support higher prices in the United States? Seeing consolidation coming, and hoping to support a larger R&D program, you seek to acquire one of your direct competitors. Will the antitrust authorities block your deal? You introduce a new version of your product, and rivals threaten to sue you under the antitrust laws because you have altered the interface they rely on for their products to work with yours. Are you at risk of a large, treble-damage award?

Sooner or later, probably sooner, you will face issues like these, where strategic choices are driven by the rules of engagement in the information economy: just what do government antitrust and regulatory rules permit, and what do they prohibit? In this chapter, we describe the government's information policy as it relates to the strategies we have discussed so far. By and large, the information sector continues to operate under long-standing rules of engagement designed for the entire economy. We explain these rules, emphasizing the key dimensions for most readers of this book: antitrust and government regulation. We show how these rules operate in practice and identify areas where the old rules are proving inadequate. Finally, we will suggest changes that could be made so that the government supports, rather than impedes, the growth of the information economy.

Our analysis here is a departure from previous chapters, where we have been primarily concerned with information strategy in private, for-profit companies. However, the same economic analysis we have used to examine strategic choices in the private sector can be used to analyze public policy choices. The focus, of course, is a bit different. Instead of looking at strategies to increase profitability, we look at strategies to increase the net social benefits. Luckily, as Adam Smith taught us long ago, competitive pressures between producers will often induce them to make choices that maximize the general welfare. This is as true for Smith's butchers and bakers as for today's programmers and chip fabricators: the "corporate centric" view and the "policy centric" view are often not as far apart as one might think.

Since the government's rules inevitably affect industry participants, no executive in the network economy can afford to be ignorant of government information policy. As Jim Barksdale, CEO of Netscape, puts it: "Netscape joined the Technology Network because as an Internet company, we've observed first hand how government can help or hinder the technology industry. We've learned that working with the government is far more productive than trying to ignore it."[1]

POLICY OVERVIEW

We have developed three major themes in this book, each of which raises questions for government policy:

- **Differentiation of products and prices.** The high first-copy costs of information and information technology inevitably lead to price and product differentiation. Strategies involving mass customization, differential pricing, personalized content, and versioning are natural outcomes in such industries. However, these strategies raise antitrust issues about fair competition. Is it discriminatory to charge different users different prices for essentially the same product?

- **Lock-in.** Since information products work together in systems, switching any single product can be very costly to users. The lock-in that results from such switching costs confers a huge competitive advantage on firms that know how to take advantage of it. This leads to concerns about the nature of competition. What tactics are counted as "fair" and "unfair" competition with lock-in? Will you be branded an aftermarket monopolist under antitrust law if you are the sole supplier to some locked-in customers? If you are such a "monopolist," how will your strategic choices be limited?

- **Positive feedback.** Positive feedback based on network externalities is ubiquitous in the information economy. Winner-take-all competition and standards battles are common as rivals vie for temporary market control. If you agree to cooperate with your rivals to establish standards, you run the risk of violating laws against cartels and of collusion. Alternatively, if you compete and win, you may be guilty of monopolization, depending on the tactics you employed to gain or keep control over the market. Even if you avoid antitrust entanglements, you may have to deal with regulatory agencies such as the FCC. The FCC has a long and extensive history of regulating the telephone industry to promote universal service, to impose various cross-subsidies, and to limit monopoly power. Will regulation of these types encroach on the Internet and beyond into networking, or even computer hardware and software more generally?

Your ability to fashion a strategy in each of these areas is directly affected by government rules.

PRICE DIFFERENTIATION

In Chapter 2 we argued that differential pricing was a natural way to recover the high fixed costs of information and information technology. However, the Robinson-Patman Act of 1936 says that such price discrimination is illegal if it "effectively lessens competition," and many antitrust cases have been brought on these grounds. For example, a group of pharmaceutical drug manufacturers has been facing a massive antitrust action the past several years in part because they each set drug prices lower for hospitals and HMOs than for retail drug stores. The

Robinson-Patman Act has been widely criticized on both legal and economic grounds, but it's the law.

Don't panic. Clearly, differential pricing is standard operating practice for information products. There are three primary legal arguments that render the vast majority of price differentiation immune from successful legal challenge:

- You are allowed to set lower prices that result from lower costs.

- You are allowed to set differential prices to meet the competition.

- Differential pricing is only questionable if it "lessens competition."

How can you, or the courts, tell if your pricing will lessen competition? Certainly, differential pricing itself should not be taken as prima facie evidence of anticompetitive behavior. It is true that *in some cases* differential pricing can serve as an anticompetitive strategy, but price discrimination for information goods is often positively beneficial to groups receiving discounts. Furthermore, as we saw earlier in the book, price discrimination may be a necessary strategy to recover costs and thus to support the creation of content in the first place.

From the economic point of view, the critical question to ask is whether differential pricing allows the producer to sell to markets that otherwise would not be served. In many of the cases we examined in Chapter 3, the answer is clearly yes. If film producers had to set one price for first-run movies in all countries, only the high-income countries could afford to go to the movies. When they can set high prices for high-income countries and low prices for low-income countries, they are able to serve groups of consumers who would otherwise not be able to purchase the product.

COMPETITION POLICY

Most competition laws are pretty vague. The Sherman Act (1890) makes it illegal to "monopolize" a market. The Clayton Act (1914) prevents mergers likely to "substantially lessen competition." FCC regulations refer to the "public interest." To make sense of these laws, and the ways they are enforced, we need to consider the philosophy behind them.

Principles of Competition Policy

The underlying principle guiding antitrust law is the protection of competition as a *process*. If a single firm is victorious and gains a monopoly position based on offering low prices and superior product quality, the competitive process has worked just fine. Congress's judgment in passing the Sherman Act in 1890 was that this competitive process would ultimately be best to spur economic growth and protect consumers' interests. The famous antitrust enforcer Thurmond Arnold likened the role of the Justice Department's Antitrust Division to that of a referee in a boxing match, whose job it is to make sure the fight is fair.

Competition policy is intended to ensure a fair fight, not to punish winners or protect losers.

The competitive process can easily lead to a concentrated industry structure, with one or a few firms dominating the market, at least for a time, until they, too, are toppled. This is especially common in information industries, because of the economies of scale involved in creating information and because of the positive feedback and network externalities we explored earlier. The fact is, it can be highly efficient for one or a few companies to supply the entire market. For example, if the minimum efficient scale of operation is large relative to the overall size of the market, a single large firm may be more cost-effective than several small ones. Under these conditions, supporting several firms is very costly, perhaps more costly than working with a sole supplier. The Defense Department has certainly learned this lesson during the past several years as it has tolerated, and at times encouraged, consolidation of its supplier base.

Fair enough. But how does the government and legal system respond when our cherished free market economy spawns a powerful monopolist? Broadly speaking, there are three answers.

First, the government can sit back and do nothing, recognizing that there are economies of scale on the supply and demand sides of the market and hoping that market forces will in time erode the monopoly power. Remember, it is not illegal to have a monopoly, only to "monopolize." If you obtain a monopoly position fair and square, you are free to reap the benefits that come with market dominance. That much is pretty clear. But be careful: even if you obtained your monopoly position legally, you can and likely will be accused of defending or maintaining it through anticompetitive tactics.

Second, the government (or private parties) can attack the monopoly as illegally obtained. Monopolies obtained through acquisition, predatory pricing, exclusive dealing, or tying and bundling can be subject to challenge. In extreme cases, the monopolist can be broken up; more likely the suspect practices will be prohibited in the future or an acquisition or merger blocked.

Third, the government can directly regulate the monopoly. This is the approach that has been taken for decades to the local telephone business as well as other utilities such as electricity. Regulation makes the most sense when the monopoly is unlikely to be eroded by entry or technological change. In theory, the regulation will wither away when no longer needed. In practice, as revealed by the Interstate Commerce Commission in railroads and the Civil Aeronautics Board in the airlines, to name just two, regulatory agencies create their own constituencies and often outlive their usefulness. So far, at least, no one is advocating the establishment of an Internet Commerce Commission.

Thankfully, large swaths of the information sector of our economy are subject to little or no regulation. In these industries, the rules of conduct are set by the antitrust laws in the United States and abroad. Every manager in the network economy is well advised to have a general understanding of the types of business practices likely to run afoul of the antitrust laws. But you should not think of antitrust merely as something to *defend* against; you may also be able to use antitrust *offensively* to prevent other firms from engaging in predatory conduct or from consummating a merger that would harm you as a buyer or exclude you from the market. In other words, you can also profit by knowing when your suppliers or competitors are breaking the rules so you can blow the whistle on them.

Implications for Strategy

As the public debate over Microsoft's business practices illustrates, the line between aggressive competition and predatory conduct in the information economy is none too bright. Victory in the information economy, with its winner-take-all tendencies, inevitably generates ill will among the losers. Consumers, too, will complain if they feel locked in. Fortunately, such griping alone does not prove that a company has violated the law. What, then, are the legal limits on strategies involving lock-in, networks, and standards? What policies has the government pursued to promote competition in network markets? This section is a quick guide to fair play in the information economy.

The first rule to bear in mind is that monopolists are prohibited from employing certain strategies, even if the very same strategies are widely used and perfectly legal when employed by firms facing more competition. Microsoft tried to gloss over this point, suggesting that the Justice Department was threatening to interfere with every software company's right freely to design its own products. Not so. At most, the Justice Department policies would limit the ability of *monopoly* software companies to modify their products where the effect is to extend the realm of the monopoly or reduce the choices available to customers.

> *Monopolists are prohibited from using some tactics others may employ.*

All the same, you should not conclude that only leading companies such as Microsoft, Intel, and Cisco need concern themselves with competition policy. The fact is, each and every company in the information sector needs to be cognizant of antitrust rules and to fashion strategy with these rules in mind. For example, Iomega, the maker of those Zip drives that store seventy times as much as floppies, having successfully created a market for its product, has faced antitrust inquiries around the world relating to its product design, distribution practices, and enforcement of intellectual property. Iomega, a relatively small company, hardly imagined being confronted with these problems when it launched the Zip drive just a few years ago.

You are far better off anticipating legal challenges and planning your strategy to meet or avoid them than becoming enmeshed in complex and costly litigation and being forced to alter strategy as a result. The true sign of success may be that call from the Justice Department, concerned that you have monopolized your market. But once the excitement wears off, you will want to make sure you can justify your practices as legitimate competitive efforts rather than predatory or exclusionary.

Even if you think you are nowhere near having a monopoly, you still need to pay careful attention to how antitrust rules affect your industry.

There are three unpleasant surprises that firms operating in information technology businesses commonly face:

1. Virtually any acquisition or merger will be reviewed by the antitrust authorities. If you are joining forces with a rival, making your case will require careful planning, antitrust lawyers, and detailed economic analysis.

2. Antitrust sensitivities are raised whenever you meet and talk with your rivals—for example, for standard-setting purposes. This argues for carefully documented and managed meetings and negotiations.

3. You may be accused of being a monopolist, especially if some of your consumers are locked in. To defend yourself, you will need to establish either that you lack genuine and lasting monopoly power or that your conduct was legitimately competitive, not exclusionary or predatory.

Mergers and Joint Ventures

Mergers and joint ventures that "may substantially lessen competition" are illegal. The vast majority of mergers are perfectly legal, but mergers involving direct rivals are typically subjected to antitrust review by the Justice Department or the FTC. The two laid out their basic approach to analyzing mergers in 1992 in their "Horizontal Merger Guidelines." Mergers will be blocked if they are found to harm consumers, owing to either higher prices or lower quality.

Three areas of strategy can bring antitrust scrutiny: mergers and acquisitions, cooperation with rivals to set standards, and market dominance.

In our view, there is no need for special laws to handle mergers in information industries. The antitrust agencies are very sophisticated in their merger reviews and have developed substantial expertise in many high-tech industries, including telephones, cable television, and computer software and hardware. For example, the Justice Department conducted an extensive review of the proposed Worldcom/MCI merger, looking at various Internet markets as well as long-distance telephone service. Both the Justice Department and the FTC recognize that certain high-tech industries are highly dynamic, making any monopoly power transitory. They are unlikely to challenge mergers in these industries because of the low entry barriers in these rapidly changing environments.

On the other hand, there is no antitrust immunity for software mergers, and the Justice Department and the FTC correctly recognize that entry may be difficult because of high consumer switching costs and the intellectual property rights of incumbents. Several software mergers have indeed been challenged and then either abandoned or modified as a result: Adobe/Aldus in graphics software, Microsoft/Intuit in personal financial software, Silicon Graphics/Alias/Wavefront in high-end software for graphics workstations, Computer Associates/Legent in utility software for IBM mainframes, and Cadence/CCT in electronic design automation software. We believe government policy in this area is well developed and works from a sound basis.

Cooperative Standard Setting

Price fixing, collusion, cartels, and bid rigging are per se illegal in the United States and can constitute a criminal violation. This policy is not controversial. Collusion will be investigated and acted on by antitrust authorities. The problem comes in the gray area between "collusion" and "cooperation."

Adam Smith once said that "people of the same trade seldom meet together, even for merriment and diversion, but the conversation ends in a conspiracy against the public, or in some contrivance to raise prices." We wonder what he would have thought of standards negotiations, which require firms to "meet together." The public policy concern is that participants will use the opportunity of meeting to stifle competition. Federal antitrust authorities must ask themselves: is this a standard-setting process, or is it a cartel?

In the area of information technology, we are most concerned about actual and perceived limits on firms agreeing to establish product standards. Product standards, interfaces, and compatibility are critical to the efficient flow of information and introduction of information technologies. It would be ironic, and troubling, if the antitrust laws, in the name of protecting competition and consumers, discouraged the creation and adoption of new products and technologies simply because they entail cooperation and agreements by competing firms.

While the antitrust authorities generally don't like rivals getting together to negotiate product characteristics, it is clear that the public interest is very often enhanced by standards agreements. The question the antitrust authorities must ask themselves is whether the technology would be developed expeditiously without any standard-setting process. If the answer is that technological development would be slowed down or impeded entirely, or that consumers would lose important compatibility benefits, then the antitrust authorities should condone, and even encourage, the standard setting. Widespread participation or support by consumers will defuse, if not entirely forestall, any antitrust challenge to a standards agreement.

However, the antitrust authorities and the courts are likely to look with disfavor on negotiations that go beyond an agreement on product standards. Agreeing on product standards is a far cry from agreeing on the prices or terms at which the products will be sold. To use a sports analogy, the standard-setting process should be thought of as forging an agreement on the rules of play—the size of the playing field, the type of ball used, and so on. But once the rules of play have been established, you have to go out onto the field of play and compete vigorously and independently.

Fortunately, we believe that companies honestly engaged in efforts to establish new compatibility standards have little to fear from antitrust laws. Historically, antitrust law has placed only modest limits on the ability of competing firms to establish product standards. During the 1980s, the Supreme Court affirmed two antitrust judgments against companies setting performance standards. In one case, several manufacturers of steel conduit for electrical cable conspired to block an amendment of the National Electric Code that would have allowed the use of plastic conduit. The steel group was found to have hired people to pack the standard-setting meeting. In a second case, a trade association was involved in misrepresenting its standards, with the effect of declaring a rival company's products unsafe.

Although some might see these cases as warnings for those who would meet to set standards, we think the greater danger is for companies to overreact and miss opportunities for beneficial cooperation.

First, we consider the distinction between performance standards and compatibility standards significant. Plaintiffs in both of the cited cases were companies whose products were branded as unsafe. Open compatibility standards cannot have such an effect. Second, both of these cases involved abuse of the standard-setting process rather than any attack on the legitimacy of standard setting itself.

A good example of a standard that passed antitrust muster is that of the Motion Picture Expert Group (MPEG). The group was formed in 1988 to design technical standards for compressing digital video and audio data. The current version of the MPEG standard, MPEG-2, is used in digital TV, DBS, digital cable systems, personal computer video, DVD, interactive media, and CDs. MPEG-2 was developed under the auspices of the ISO, the IEC, and the ITU. On seeing everyone getting onto the bandwagon, Microsoft decided to include MPEG in Windows 95. MPEG-2 is now arriving for personal computers.

In June 1997, the Department of Justice approved a plan of eight companies, along with Columbia University, to combine twenty-seven MPEG patents into a single portfolio and license the inventions centrally. The eight companies are Fujitsu, General Instrument, Lucent, Matsushita, Mitsubishi, Philips, Scientific-Atlanta, and Sony. They researched some 9,000 patents to look for those essential to the MPEG-2 standard, since it was important to cite in the antitrust review that there were no practical alternatives to these patents.

Trade associations have been dealing with antitrust rules for decades, so the rules of the road are pretty clear when it comes to most cooperation. Consider, for example, the recent formation of IOPS.org. This is an industry group of large ISPs that "will focus primarily on resolving and preventing network integrity problems, addressing issues that require technical coordination and technical information-sharing across and among ISPs. These issues include joint problem resolution, technology assessment, and global Internet scaling and integrity."[2]

The telecommunications industry and the Internet, in particular, require interconnection, standardization, coordination, and other sorts of cooperation with competitors. Meeting with competitors can raise antitrust concerns, but we think that so long as the companies stick to their stated goals, it is highly unlikely that their activities will be judged illegal.

Having said this, the fact remains that many companies are spooked by the antitrust laws and are wary of negotiating with actual or potential rivals on product specifications or protocols. Inasmuch as these companies may be subjected to private lawsuits, both from aggrieved competitors and from class-action lawyers, potentially facing treble-damage claims, this wariness is understandable. We are aware, for example, of an ongoing lawsuit claiming that Sony, Philips, and others violated U.S. antitrust laws by agreeing to establish a standard format for compact disks. U.S. firms face greater legal exposure in collectively setting product standards than do their foreign counterparts, because the United States uniquely permits private antitrust actions combined with class actions and treble damages. Recent legislation has removed treble damages for certain research and production joint ventures. Further protection for participation in standard-setting activities may well be warranted.

Agreements to promote a common standard often go hand in hand with agreements to share patents and technology that enable the standard. Thus, the legal treatment of standard setting is tightly wrapped up with the treatment of cross-licenses, grantbacks, and patent pools. While the courts and the antitrust enforcement agencies clearly recognize the pro-competitive aspects of both standards and the sharing of intellectual property, they are also actively looking for abuses of the process, situations in which the participants have gone too far, stifling competition under cover of a standards agreement. While we hesitate to offer legal advice, the general principle here is that parties to a standards agreement need to be prepared to argue that their overall agreement benefits consumers and the public interest, not just their own interests, and that the scope of their agreement is not overly broad to achieve its beneficial purpose.

Finally, companies forming networks and setting standards must determine the conditions on which others will be permitted to interconnect with or join their network. These issues have been faced repeatedly by banks joining to form an ATM or a credit card network. Although these networks are rarely challenged as naked price fixing, rules limiting the addition of new members to the network have been challenged, as in Discover's lawsuit against Visa. Visa won, but the Justice Department has an ongoing investigation of the credit card industry, especially into the practices of Visa and MasterCard.

We recognize that both real and virtual networks can wield substantial economic power, because consumers often place great value on using a predominant standard. Even so, we tend to take the view that a group of firms forming a network has the right to choose with whom they will interconnect and on what terms they do so. We are more skeptical of exclusivity rules that limit network members from participating in other networks, especially when these rules are promulgated by ventures with significant monopoly power. Indeed, rules insisting that members not belong to other networks have been blocked, as in the Justice Department action against FTD, the floral network, and the European Union's action against Visa striking down its exclusivity rules.

Single-Firm Conduct

Mergers, joint ventures, and standard setting all involve more than one firm. Unilateral conduct can also run afoul of the antitrust laws, if it constitutes "monopolization." The hard part is distinguishing the firm that successfully competes, and thus gains a very large market share, from the firm that somehow crosses the line and gains a monopoly using tactics that are unfair, inefficient, or harmful to consumers, and thus illegal.

Certain commercial practices are a red flag to antitrust authorities. *Exclusive dealing* provisions are in this category: a monopolist who insists that its customers not deal with its competitors is in for some tough questions. *Tying* is another suspect practice: a monopolist who insists that customers take another product if they want the monopolized item are likely to be challenged. This sounds simple, but it can be devilishly hard to determine whether there really are two products involved instead of one. Was it tying for Ford to ship all of its cars with tires on them? Was it tying when Ford decided to put radios in its cars, thus posing a grave threat to the independent companies that had previously sold radios for installation into Ford cars? Ford was in fact challenged for changing the design of its dashboards—that is, the interface between cars and radios. We predict that these issues will become even more important in the years ahead because so many high-tech products interconnect with each other to form a system.

The most visible recent example of a tying problem has been the battle between the Department of Justice and Microsoft over Internet Explorer. The legal discussion has focused on whether Internet Explorer is a separate product or merely part of an "integrated" operating system. It is unfortunate that this almost metaphysical issue has become the focus of the debate, since the much more important question is Microsoft's conduct vis à vis OEMs, content suppliers, and other providers of complementary goods and services. How Microsoft fares with Justice may ultimately turn on whether or not Microsoft's contracts are exclusionary. As we noted earlier, Microsoft has already abandoned some restrictive licensing practices in the face of antitrust scrutiny both in the United States and in Europe.

This is not the first time that the computer industry has provided the field on which antitrust and high technology have collided. All during the 1970s, the Justice Department fought IBM, only to drop its suit in the early 1980s, even as IBM's power was subsiding due to market forces. During the 1990s, Microsoft has been the test case. Did Microsoft gain its monopoly over desktop operating systems by legitimately competing on the merits, or through anticompetitive tactics? In 1994, the Justice Department concluded that Microsoft had violated the antitrust laws in the way it structured its contracts with computer manufacturers, and Microsoft agreed to modify those contracts. The Microsoft case has evoked a great deal of commentary on both sides: those who say antitrust should keep its nose out of the dynamic computer industry, and those who say Microsoft is a dangerous monopolist that got away with a slap on the wrist.

We will hardly resolve the debate over Microsoft here. We believe a cautious approach toward antitrust policy and enforcement is called for in high-technology industries, in part because technological change does tend to erode monopoly power and in part because much of the conduct at issue has at least some claim on increasing consumer welfare. For example, when Netscape complains that Microsoft will drive Netscape from the market by incorporating its own browser, Internet Explorer, into Windows, one must ask whether consumers will indeed benefit from a greater integration of the browser and the operating system. In other words, assessing whether practices such as bundling the browser into the operating system are pro- or anticompetitive is a difficult, fact-specific process that involves a balancing of competing concerns. We can say no more, except to question whether these disputes are best handled in the courtroom with a lay jury or through some more sophisticated forum for dispute resolution.

DIRECT GOVERNMENT INTERVENTION

Direct government regulation of prices, quality, interconnection, and entry is a necessary evil to be used when the competitive process, supplemented and protected by antitrust law, breaks down. The obvious piece of the information economy currently subject to this type of regulation is the telephone system.

The big news of the past few years in regulating the information infrastructure must be the Telecommunications Act of 1996. We heartily endorse Congress's intention to break down artificial barriers between various telecommunications markets and to open local telephone markets to competition. The irony behind the act, however, is that the goal of local telephone competition, and thus the demise of regulation, can be achieved only with the help of a massive new set of regulations. Competitive local exchange carriers cannot get a foothold in the market without the cooperation of incumbent carriers in a myriad of ways: interconnecting to complete calls, enabling customers to keep their telephone numbers when switching carriers, leasing pieces of the incumbent's network to would-be competitors, and much more. As one of us put it in a speech last year: "Regulation: The Path to Deregulation."

Government regulators, including the FCC and state public utility commissions, should move aggressively to ensure that the conditions necessary to allow local telephone competition to flourish are indeed put into place. Competition will create pressures for companies to offer attractive packages of existing services, such as wireless and long distance, and new services, such as residential broadband and improved Internet access.

We welcome regulatory policies designed to control monopoly pricing, but we are even keener on policies that help transform monopoly markets into competitive ones, where technology permits. We caution that such a transformation of the telephone industry will take place only very gradually, however, making regulation necessary for many years to come. We also must note that regulation brings its own dangers: a regulatory structure created to control monopoly power can easily be used to serve other purposes, in particular, to support a system of cross-subsidization. Inevitably, the services that are providing the cross-subsidies are stifled: long-distance telephone calling has long been burdened by such cross-subsidies, which are the enemy of an efficient telecommunications policy.

Cable television regulation reveals another set of dangers associated with regulating information industries. In principle, municipal awards of cable franchises should work well, with municipal officials looking out for the interests of their subscriber/citizens. In practice, the federal government has become heavily involved, lurching from the Cable Act of 1984, which made it harder for municipalities to control their franchisees or replace them, to the Cable Act of 1992, which instructed the FCC to develop rates for basic cable services.

Congress has also legislated various rules governing the vertical relationships in the television industry. Congress imposed "must carry" rules on cable operators, requiring them to carry certain local television stations (these were recently upheld by the Supreme Court as constitutional). Congress, always keen to keep broadcasters happy, also has mandated that cable operations obtain "retransmission consent" from broadcasters before carrying their programming. So-called "program access" rules regulate the terms on which vertically integrated cable operators must make their programming available to direct broadcast satellite rivals. In addition, the FCC has imposed limits on how much "affiliated" programming cable operators may carry. These are not unlike the widely criticized "financial syndication rules" that long limited the ability of broadcast networks to take a financial interest in programming.

Regulations governing vertical relationships should fade away as competition grows.

Regulations like these, which control and circumscribe the vertical relationships between those who produce content and those who distribute it, are increasingly out of place as the creation of content and the distribution of information become more and more competitive. Surely, whatever power CBS, NBC, and ABC had in the 1950s has been eroded with the arrival of Fox and the many cable networks. Hopefully, the monopoly power enjoyed by cable operators will also erode as direct broadcast satellite becomes a stronger force and as telephone companies enter into multichannel video distribution. In this setting, regulations on vertical relationships in the information sector may well serve to benefit certain special interests rather than the public interest.

Our rule of thumb for regulation in the information sector is simple: government regulation should focus on controlling genuine monopoly power when it will not be eroded by competitive pressures. Regulation of basic cable rates by municipalities, or of basic telephone rates by state public utility commissions, fits this description. So do rules to force open monopoly markets, such as those required by the Telecommunication Act of 1996 as a quid pro quo for allowing local Bell telephone companies into long distance. But the government should refrain from imposing rules that limit the ways in which companies in the information industry deal with those in adjacent markets, unless these rules have a direct and clear role in limiting horizontal monopoly power.

Government regulators can also take steps to encourage new entry into monopoly markets by awarding government franchises to new entrants. The FCC took a step in this direction in the early 1980s by setting up two cellular telephone carriers rather than giving local telephone companies complete control of the cellular business. More recently, through the PCS auctions, the FCC has moved strongly to inject far more competition into the wireless telephone business. In many cities, several PCS licensees will soon compete with the incumbent cellular providers. FCC policies prohibiting cellular providers from bidding on in-region PCS licenses helped ensure that new competition would truly emerge. Similar issues arise in the awarding of satellite slots for direct broadcast satellite, which is turning into a true competitor for cable companies in multichannel video distribution.

The Government's Role in Achieving Critical Mass

The government does more than just impose regulatory rules as a way of promoting competition and innovation. The government can affirmatively finance, endorse, and adopt technologies to speed their widespread use. Of course, this is common in the defense sector, where the Pentagon is often the sole customer of a weapons system, but the same principles apply to the government as merely a large and influential buyer of a commercial system.

We saw in Chapter 7 that information and communications technologies often exhibit network externalities. There is a long, slow increase in their use until some critical mass is reached, after which the growth rate explodes. Once network goods obtain sufficiently wide use, the market may be an effective way to provide them. However, there may be a government role in helping such industries obtain critical mass. The Internet is a prime example. It is unlikely that the Internet would have achieved its current level of popularity without early subsidization by the government. Demonstration projects can help an industry achieve critical mass. Yet some would blanch at the notion of the government ultimately deciding which of several rival technologies will succeed in the market. Thankfully, the private sector is not saddled with the same computer system used by the Internal Revenue Service!

The government can provide critical mass to ignite positive feedback, but it should be cautious about picking winners.

In other words, one should not jump to the conclusion that an active government role is needed to kick-start an emerging technology. Do not underestimate the ingenuity of the private sector to find ways to solve the chicken-and-egg problem. Many highly successful technologies would not have been viable had the private sector not been able to achieve the necessary coordination to build critical mass. In the consumer electronics area, the private sector regularly organizes itself to solve chicken-and-egg problems. Video cassettes and VCRs are strong complements and are subject to indirect network effects: the demand for VCRs depends on the availability of video cassettes and vice-versa.

In the early 1980s, private video rental stores managed to achieve critical mass by renting out VCRs along with the cassettes. This allowed the video stores to achieve sufficient market penetration to stimulate the demand for the purchase of VCRs. Similar factors arise for video game machines, compact disk players, and the new digital video disk players. There are strong incentives for private parties to internalize network externalities, either through integration (as when Nintendo sold an entire system, consisting of a machine and proprietary games) or contract (as when Sony and Philips agreed to license their CD technology widely to get the CD bandwagon rolling).

Thus, we see a government role primarily in cases where network externalities are *difficult* to internalize, as when basic technology must be shown to be technologically feasible. We also see an important role for the government as a large, and perhaps pivotal, user of certain new technologies. The government, in lending its support to a particular technology or standard, can and should take into account private interests, not merely its own interests as a consumer of technology.

Universal Service

Since the value of the network depends on the total number of people connected to it, one often hears arguments that network goods should be universally provided. The mantra of universal service has long been part of telephone policy, and there are those who argue that universal service is now an appropriate public policy goal for Internet access.

We quite agree that widespread availability is desirable for many kinds of networked goods. However, it is a large leap from there to say that such access should occur only through government provision or subsidies. After all, many goods with network externalities are provided by the private sector, including our original example, fax machines, and the VCR/video cassette market discussed above.

Basic telephony service has long been regarded as a good that required a deliberate policy effort to achieve universal access. However, a close reading of history raises doubts. Empirical studies suggest that penetration of basic telephony services could easily be comparable with today's rates, even if there had been no policies of subsidized access. Various comments to the FCC in its recent docket on universal service reform indicated that the current structure of pricing in telephony is costing the United States billions of dollars in inefficiency, with very little impact on penetration rates for basic telephone service. To support universal service, prices of long-distance calling have been kept well above cost to support below-cost prices for basic telephone service. Studies clearly show that customers are far more sensitive to price in their long-distance calling patterns than they are in the use of basic service. As a result, the pricing patterns supporting universal service are in direct violation of basic economic principles of efficient pricing to cover joint and common costs, which call for markups to be lowest on services for which customers are the most price sensitive. In addition, the FCC recently admitted that its plans to provide subsidies to wire schools and libraries around the country will cost far more than originally estimated.

Advocates of universal service for Internet or telephony typically make their case on grounds of geography or income. One can well see why interested parties might argue for geographic subsidization: economic theory suggests that most of the benefits of offering services to an isolated area will be captured by those who own property in the area. Land with electricity service, telephone service, and road service is certainly more valuable than land with none of these features, and it is, of course, appealing to those who own the land to get someone else to pay for such improvements.

What is forgotten in this discussion is that those who live in rural areas have many advantages over urban dwellers. Crime rates are lower, housing is cheaper, and parking is inexpensive. What is the point of charging urbanites a price higher than cost for telephony service in order to subsidize access by rural dwellers, if all these other "inequities" persist? Overall, it makes more sense to have people face the true cost of their location decisions: if choosing clean air and low crime carries with it a higher cost of telephony service, so be it.

The case with respect to income is not so clear cut. Economists use the term *merit goods* to designate certain goods that are so important that they should be provided for everyone. However, we think that basic necessities such as food, shelter, and health care are much better candidates for merit goods than telephone service or Internet access. In any event, if universal service subsidies are to be provided, they should be limited to those with low incomes and to services that have been demonstrated to generate significant network externalities. Even if basic telephone service meets this test, second lines, for example, would not. Even though each of us has several lines in our home, we are pleased to see that the FCC recently made moves to raise the price of second lines (and business lines) closer to cost.

It is also important to understand clearly the reasons that the poor do not have access to goods such as telephone service. One study found that a higher fraction of low-income households in Camden, New Jersey, had VCRs than had telephones. The most important reason that people chose not to have telephones was that their friends and relatives would make long-distance calls and stick them with the bill! The monthly charge for basic access was not a significant factor in their choice of whether or not to purchase telephone service. Such a finding, if generally true, suggests a need for policies designed to achieve universal service very different from those that have been used in the past.

LESSONS

No executive in the technology sector can ignore the government's role in the information economy. And no government policy maker can fashion intelligent policy without a sound understanding of competitive strategy in the network economy. Here are our observations and predictions about government information policy:

- **Don't expect the government's role to diminish.** Information technology is subject to large increasing returns to scale on both the demand and the supply side. Market outcomes in such industries will inevitably tend to be somewhat concentrated and require industry standardization and coordination. The resulting monopolies and standards will continue to attract the attention of government antitrust enforcers, both in the United States and abroad. Nor will telephone regulation soon wither away. To the contrary, the Internet infrastructure is bound to become more regulated in the years ahead.

- **Every company needs to know the rules of competition.** You are far better off anticipating antitrust challenges, both from private parties and from the government, when you first fashion your strategy or plan an acquisition than you are having to adjust strategy later. Understanding competition policy also helps you to protect your interests when other companies are breaking the rules.

- **Companies have considerable freedom to engage in differential pricing.** Versioning and differential pricing are effective tools for cost recovery in industries with large fixed costs and small marginal costs and are only rarely subject to antitrust attack.

- **Competition policy is intended to ensure a fair fight, not to punish winners or protect losers.** If you manage to dominate your market by offering lower prices and better products, you have nothing to fear from the antitrust laws. By the same token, if you lose out in a fair fight, don't expect the antitrust laws to provide you with any comfort.

- **Mergers and acquisitions involving direct competitors are subjected to careful review by the Justice Department and the Federal Trade Commission.** To close your deal you need to convince these agencies that your acquisition will not harm consumers.

- **Don't be afraid of cooperating with other companies to set standards and develop new technologies, so long as your efforts are designed to bring benefits to consumers.** If you steer well clear of the antitrust hot-button areas of pricing and product introduction, and are genuinely working to establish and promote new and improved technologies, you are on solid ground and should be well protected from any antitrust challenge.

- **If you are fortunate enough to gain a leading share of the market, be sure to conduct an audit of your practices.** This audit should encompass your pricing, bundling, and distribution practices as well as any exclusivity provisions in contracts with customers or suppliers. You will then be well prepared to deal with antitrust challenges, should they arise.

- **Don't expect government regulation in the telecommunications sector to diminish any time soon.** Telephone regulation is meant to wither away as competition takes root; don't hold your breath. And Congress has repeatedly shown a hearty appetite for regulating the broadcasting and cable television industries. Internet, watch out.

Further Reading

This book draws heavily on the economics literature devoted to price discrimination, switching costs, standards, and networks. Our understanding of these issues has benefited greatly from the contributions of our fellow economists. Here we provide pointers to a few of the major articles in these areas, along with references to various facts cited in the text. The "InfoRules Website," at http://www.inforules.com, contains a more extensive listing of work in these areas.

CHAPTER 1   THE INFORMATION ECONOMY

See Arrow (1997) for a discussion of the unique properties of information as an economic good. The concept of an "experience good" was first developed by Nelson (1970). The reference to Herb Simon's work on the "economics of attention" is from Simon (1997). The figures for the Amazon-AOL deal are taken from Sandberg (1997). The Wal-Mart story is reported in the *Wall Street Journal,* October 7, 1997, "Wal-Mart Uses TV-Set Displays for Ad Network." The importance of "systems competition" for information technology was emphasized by Katz and Shapiro (1985, 1986a, b). See Kelly (1998) for an overview of the network economy.

CHAPTER 2   PRICING INFORMATION

Material on *Britannica* is based on Melcher (1997). Microsoft's gross profit margin is taken from Bank (1997). CD phone book history is described by Bulkeley (1995). The table of ad rates is based on that in Lesk (1998). Search engine spamming is discussed in Livingston (1997). More on Reuters and Bloomberg can be found in Hayes (1996) and Goldstein (1998), respectively. The figures on the *New York Times* are taken from Allbriton (1998). A. C. Pigou's classification of differential pricing is in Pigou (1920). The HFS case is described in Bigness (1997). The history of video we outline was drawn from Lardner (1987).

For an advanced survey of the economics of price discrimination see Varian (1989).

CHAPTER 3   VERSIONING INFORMATION

The economics of self-selection and quality discrimination are described in a number of economics books. See Varian (1996b), Chapter 24, for an elementary treatment and Wilson (1993) for an advanced discussion. Spence (1976) is one of the earliest treatments, Maskin and Riley (1984) provide a nice unified treatment, and Tirole (1988) contains a good, modern treatment of the theory.

Denerke and McAfee (1996) describe how quality reduction can be used strategically in designing product lines. Goldilocks pricing is described by Simonson and Tversky (1992) and Smith and Nagle (1995), though not under that name.

Bundling was first described by Adams and Yellen (1976). Its application to information goods was noted by Varian (1995) and extensively developed by Bakos and Brynjolfsson (1998). In particular, they show that consumer valuations of bundles tend to be less dispersed than the consumer values of their components owing to the classical "law of averages" effect. This reduced dispersion, in turn, allows for more value extraction, as described in the text. See Varian (1980) for a model of promotional pricing.

CHAPTER 4   RIGHTS MANAGEMENT

The success of the National Academy of Science Press and MIT Press in offering on-line versions was described in Winkler (1997). The Barney saga is described in Blumenthal (1992). The quote from Disney attorney John J. Tormey is from Bulkeley (1994). The treatment of McAfee software is taken from Angwin (1997).

The data about professional record producers being unable to distinguish second-generation analog copies is from http://www.eklektix. com/dat-heads/FAQ, item 63.

The comparison of circulating libraries and video stores was developed by Varian and Roehl (1997) based on a number of historical sources. Watt (1957) was especially valuable, though recent work by Doody (1996) argues that the English novel was more a reinvention than an invention.

CHAPTER 5   RECOGNIZING LOCK-IN

Extensive economics literature is available on relationship-specific capital and various forms of lock-in. Williamson (1975) is a classic reference in this field. A recent overview of the literature on switching costs is provided in Klemperer (1995). Many formal economic models of competition for consumers with switching costs can be found in the literature, including Klemperer (1987) and (1989), and Farrell and Shapiro (1988) and (1989). Beggs and Klemperer (1992) provide a rigorous analysis showing how a firm with a large installed base will tend to set higher prices, and thus gradually cede share to a rival with a smaller installed base.

The description of the Bell Atlantic lock-in is based on the public record in the case *Bell Atlantic and DSC Communications v. AT&T and Lucent*. The facts on Computer Associates are taken from the Justice Department's complaint against Computer Associates and Legent Corporation filed July 28, 1996. The Hotmail purchase is described in Wingfield (1997). Information on the Amazon and Barnes & Noble loyalty programs is from Wagner (1997). Details on the FCC rules for number portability can be found at the FCC Web site.

CHAPTER 6   MANAGING LOCK-IN

The quote about TCI and Microsoft comes from the article by Banks in the December 16, 1997, issue of the *Wall Street Journal*. Also refer to the article by Steve Hamm in the February 2, 1998, issue of *Business Week*.

The point that partial protection may result in lower quality was made in Farrell and Shapiro (1989). Various facts about Cisco are described in Lawson (1997). See Ausubel (1991) on competition in the credit card market. Recent work by Fudenberg and Tirole (1997) explores the use of contracts both to lock in customers and to lure them away from rivals.

CHAPTER 7   NETWORKS AND POSITIVE FEEDBACK

Network externalities were first defined and discussed in Rohlfs (1974). The idea was dormant for several years until Katz and Shapiro (1985) recognized its importance for strategy and Farrell and Saloner (1986) explored the dynamics of installed base competition. Arthur (1989, 1994) has emphasized the role of positive feedback in the economy. See Katz and Shapiro (1994) for a survey of recent work.

Several of our historical examples were taken from Friedlander (1995a, 1995b, 1996), Nesmith (1985), and Bunn and David (1988). Hilton (1990) gives a comprehensive history of narrow gauge railroads, including their ultimate demise. On QWERTY, see David (1985, 1986), and for the contrarian view, Leibowitz and Margolis (1990). Lucky (1998) describes both sides of the debate. Mueller (1996) gives a revisionist view of AT&T's early history. The early story of television is based in part on Fisher and Fisher (1997). Color television adoption data and much of the early HDTV story is from Farrell and Shapiro (1992). The HDTV data comes from the *New York Times*, March 11, 1997.

Two important on-line resources in this area are Hal Varian's "Information Economy" page at http://www.sims.berkeley.edu/resources/infoecon and Nicholas Economides' "Economics of Networks" page at http://raven.stern.nyu.edu/networks/.

CHAPTER 8   COOPERATION AND COMPATIBILITY

For a good overview of the economics of standards see Besen and Farrell (1994). See Farrell and Saloner (1988) for a theoretical comparison of standardization through committees versus markets, and Farrell and Saloner (1992) for a discussion of the impact of converters. See Farrell, Monroe, and Saloner (1997) for analysis of how compatibility shifts competition from the level of systems to the level of components.

For background on ActiveX see Chappell and Linthicum (1997). The quote about "Microsoft's reputation" is Zeigler and Clark (1996). The logic of "co-opetition" is thoroughly explored in Brandenburger and

Nalebuff (1996). A detailed discussion of the Unix-OSF history may be found in Saloner (1990).

Microsoft's and Netscape's standardization dance about OPS is described in the *New York Times* and the *Wall Street Journal* on June 12, 1997. Their negotiations over VRML are described in the *Wall Street Journal* of August 4, 1997.

A great deal of information about formal standard-setting organizations is available on-line. These organizations list their rules and procedures, as well as the scope for their activities and their various working groups. We can't help plugging one of our favorite Web sites: the Acronym and Abbreviation Server at http://www.ucc.ie/info/net/acronyms/acro.html. This site is immensely useful in sorting through the alphabet soup of Internet organizations.

CHAPTER 9   WAGING A STANDARDS WAR

The account of AM stereo radio is based on Besen and Johnson (1986). Numbers about cellular phones are taken from the *Wall Street Journal* article of September 11, 1997, "Cordless Confusion." The quote from Frank Ingari is taken from the *New York Times* of September 5, 1993. Figures on Apache, Microsoft, and Netscape's server shares are from the June 2, 1997, issue of *Tech Wire*.

See Farrell and Saloner (1992) and Economides and White (1996) for a treatment of one-way and two-way compatibility.

Ronald Coase (1972) discussed the fact that a company selling a durable product must compete against its own installed base. Bulow (1982) developed these ideas in a more formal model. Recent work by Fudenberg and Tirole (1998) explores the durable-goods monopoly problems in the context of product improvements.

For more information about Web sites that can only be viewed partially using one of the rival browsers, see Steve Lohr, "'Browser War' Limits Access to Web Sites: Netscape-Microsoft Duel Curbs Internet Growth," *New York Times*, December 8, 1997, p. D1.

CHAPTER 10   INFORMATION POLICY

The Barksdale quote is from http://www.kpcb.com/whatsnew/article5.html. See Varian (1985, 1996a) for a more detailed discussion of the welfare effects of price discrimination. The recent Supreme Court case involving gray markets is *Quality King Distributors v. L'Anza Research International,* No. 96-1470, decided March 1998.

For a discussion of the Department of Justice reasoning behind the Microsoft Consent Decree, see Richard Gilbert (1998), "Networks, Standards, and the Use of Market Dominance: Microsoft" (1995), in J. Kwoka and L. White, eds., *The Antitrust Revolution: The Role of Economics* (Oxford University Press, forthcoming). See Carl Shapiro, then deputy assistant attorney general for antitrust, "Antitrust in Network Industries," for a statement of Department of Justice policy toward network industries. For a current statement of the Justice Department's broader policy toward high-technology industries, see Joel I. Klein (1998), "The Importance of Antitrust Enforcement in the New Economy," available at www.usdoj.gov/atr/speeches. The Federal Trade Commission staff recently issued an extensive report that covered some of these very topics: "Competition Policy in the New High-Tech, Global Marketplace," May 1996. See Lemley and McGowan for a broader discussion of how network effects are treated in the law. Joel Klein, the assistant attorney general for antitrust, published a speech on cross-licensing and patent pools, "Cross-Licensing and Antitrust Law," May 2, 1997.

In today's global economy, complying with U.S. antitrust laws is not enough. Both IBM and Microsoft, not to mention Boeing, have had run-ins with the European competition authority. Generally speaking, European Union competition policy imposes more restrictions on monopolists than does U.S. law, under the doctrine of "abuse of dominance."

The 1992 Horizontal Merger Guidelines are available at the FTC and Department of Justice Web sites. They were slightly revised in 1997 to allow companies more room to argue that their merger should not be blocked because it would generate efficiencies. The Defense Department's view on defense mergers is summarized in two reports by defense science board task forces: "Antitrust Aspects of Defense Industry Consolidation," April 1994, and "Vertical Integration and Supplier Decisions," May 1997.

See Anton and Yao (1995) and Kattan (1993) for analysis of antitrust policy in standards setting. The two Supreme Court cases on standard setting are *Allied Tube & Conduit Corp. v. Indian Head, Inc.,* 486 U.S.

492, 1988, and *American Society of Mechanical Engineers v. Hydrolevel Corp.*, 456 U.S. 556, 1982, respectively. The case against Sony and Philips is *Disctronics Texas, Inc., et al. v. Pioneer Electronic Corp. et al.* Eastern District of Texas, Case No. 4:95 CV 229, filed August 2, 1996, at 12.

Evidence on the telephone usage patterns with and without universal service subsidies is provided in Mueller (1996). Mueller and Schement (1996) examined telephone usage patterns in Camden, New Jersey.

Notes

CHAPTER 2

1. Coleman, "Supermarkets Move into '90s."
2. Ung, "End of Concurrent Licensing Could Be Costly."

CHAPTER 3

1. Hamilton, "Microsoft Refutes Claim."
2. Sesit, "New Internet Site to Offer Risk-Analysis for Investors," C1.
3. Simonson and Tversky, "Choice in Context," 281–295.
4. Smith and Nagle, "Frames of Reference and Buyers' Perception."

CHAPTER 4

1. Barlow, "The Economy of Ideas," 85.
2. Watt, *The Rise of the Novel,* 200.
3. Knight, *The Old Printer and the Modern Press,* 284.
4. Ibid., 284.

CHAPTER 6

1. Bank, "TCI Uses Hi-Tech 'Layer Cake.'" See also Hamm, "Dance, He Said," 118.

CHAPTER 8

1. Ziegler and Clark, "Microsoft Gives Technology Away."
2. Chappell and Linthicum, "ActiveX Demystified," 56.

CHAPTER 9

1. Hof, Rebello, and Cortese, "Cyberspace Showdown," 34.

CHAPTER 10

1. "Leading Technology Executives Form Industry Political Service Organization."
2. "Internet Service Providers Team to Form Internet Operators Group."

Bibliography

Adams, William James, and Janet L. Yellen. "Commodity Bundling and the Burden of Monopoly." *Quarterly Journal of Economics,* 90, no. 3 (1976): 475–498.

Allbriton, Chris. "The Future of the Web? Two Men's Paths Tell Tale." *Contra Costa Times,* 4 January 1998, D8.

Angwin, Julia. "McAfee Sweeps Away Viruses," *San Francisco Chronicle,* 14 August 1997.

Anton, James, and Dennis Yao. "Standard-Setting Consortia, Antitrust, and High-Technology Industries." *Antitrust Law Journal* 64 (1995): 247–265.

Arrow, Ken. "Economic Welfare and the Allocation of Resources for Invention." In Donald M. Lamberton, ed., *The Economics of Communication and Information.* Cheltenham, U.K.: Edward Elgar, 1997.

Arthur, Brian W. "Competing Technologies, Increasing Returns, and Lock-In by Historical Events." *Economic Journal* 99, no. 397 (1989): 116–131.

———. *Increasing Returns and Path Dependence in the Economy.* Ann Arbor, Mich.: University of Michigan Press, 1994.

Ausubel, Lawrence M. "The Failure of Competition in the Credit Card Market." *American Economic Review* 81, no. 1 (1991): 50–81.

Bakos, J. Y.; and Erik Brynjolfsson. "Aggregation and Disaggregation of Information Goods: Implications for Bundling, Site Licensing, and Micropayment Systems." In D. Hurley, B. Kahin, and H. Varian, eds., *Internet Publishing and Beyond: The Economics of Digital Information and Intellectual Property.* Cambridge: MIT Press, 1998.

Bank, David. "Microsoft's Profit Tops Analysts' Expectations," *Wall Street Journal,* 21 October 1997.

———. "TCI Uses Hi-Tech 'Layer Cake' to Ward Off Microsoft." *Wall Street Journal,* 16 December 1997, B4.

Barlow, John Perry. "The Economy of Ideas." *Wired,* March 1994, 85. [On-line], 17 pages. Available: http://www.hotwired.com/wired/2.03/features/economy.ideas. html.

Beggs, Alan, and Paul Klemperer. "Multi-Period Competition with Switching Costs." *Econometrica* 60, no. 3 (1992): 651–666.

Besen, Stanley, and Joseph Farrell. "Choosing How to Compete: Strategies and Tactics in Standardization." *Journal of Economic Perspectives* 8 (1994): 117–131.

Besen, Stanley M., and Leland Johnson. *Compatibility Standards, Competition, and Innovation in the Broadcasting Industry.* Santa Monica, Calif.: Rand, 1986.

Bigness, Jon. "CUC-HFS Merger May Form a Giant in Direct-Marketing." *Wall Street Journal,* 29 May 1997.

Blumenthal, Karen. "How Barney the Dinosaur Beat Extinction, Is Now Rich." *Wall Street Journal,* 28 February 1992.

Brandenburger, Adam M., and Barry J. Nalebuff. *Co-opetition.* New York: Doubleday, 1996.

Bulkeley, William. "Finding Targets on CD-ROM Phone Lists," *Wall Street Journal,* 22 March 1995.

———. "Little Guy Sues Corporate Giant over a Mickey Mouse Sweatshirt." *Wall Street Journal,* 10 February 1994.

Bulow, Jeremy. "Durable-Goods Monopolists." *Journal of Political Economy* 90, no. 2 (1982): 314–332.

Bunn, Julie Ann, and Paul David. "The Economics of Gateway Technologies and Network Evolution: Lessons from Electricity Supply History." *Information Economies and Policy* 3, no. 2 (1988): 165–202.

Chappell, David, and David S. Linthicum. "ActiveX Demystified." *BYTE,* September 1997, 56.

Coase, Ronald. "Durability and Monopoly." *Journal of Law and Economics* 15, no. 1 (1972): 143–149.

Coleman, Calmetta Y. "Supermarkets Move into '90s, Cutting Back on Sales and Ads." *Wall Street Journal,* 29 May 1997.

Cortese, Amy. "Computer Associates: Sexy? No. Profitable? You Bet." *Business Week,* 11 November 1996.

David, Paul. "Clio and the Economics of QWERTY." *American Economic Review* 75, no. 2 (1985): 332–337.

———. "Understanding the Economics of QWERTY: The Necessity of History." In William Parker, ed., *Economic History and the Modern Economist.* Oxford: Basil Blackwell, 1986.

Denerke, R., and Preston McAfee. "Damaged Goods." *Journal of Economics and Management Strategy* 5, no. 2 (1996): 149–174.

Doody, Margaret Anne. *The True Story of the Novel.* New Brunswick, N.J.: Rutgers University Press, 1996.

Economides, Nicholas, and Lawrence J. White. "One-Way Networks, Two-Way Networks, Compatibility and Antitrust." In David Gabel and David Weiman, eds., *Opening Networks to Competition: The Regulation and Pricing of Access.* Boston: Kluwer Academic Press, 1998.

Farrell, Joe, and Carl Shapiro. "Optimal Contracts with Lock-In." *American Economic Review* 79, no. 1 (1989): 51–68.

Farrell, Joseph, Hunter K. Monroe, and Garth Saloner. "The Vertical Organization of Industry: Systems Competition versus Component Competition." University of California at Berkeley, 1997.

Farrell, Joseph, and Garth Saloner. "Installed Base and Compatibility: Innovation,

Product Preannouncement, and Predation." *American Economic Review* 76, no. 4 (1986): 940–955.

———. "Coordination Through Committees and Markets." *Rand Journal of Economics* 19, no. 2 (1988): 235–252.

———. "Converters, Compatibility, and the Control of Interfaces." *Journal of Industrial Economics* 40, no. 1 (1992): 9–36.

Farrell, Joseph, and Carl Shapiro. "Dynamic Competition with Switching Costs." *Rand Journal of Economics* 19, no. 1 (1988): 123–137.

———. "Standard Setting in High-Definition Television." *Brookings Papers on Economic Activity: Microeconomics,* 1992: 1–93.

Fisher, David E., and Marshall Jon Fisher. "The Color War." *Invention & Technology* 12, no. 3 (1997): 8–18.

Friedlander, Amy. *Emerging Infrastructure: The Growth of Railroads.* Arlington, Va.: CNRI, 1995(a).

———. *Power and Light: Electricity in the U.S. Energy Infrastructure: 1870–1940.* Arlington, Va.: CNRI, 1995(b).

———. *Natural Monopoly and Universal Service: Telephones and Telegraphs in the U.S. Communications Infrastructure.* Arlington, Va.: CNRI, 1996.

Fudenberg, Drew, and Jean Tirole. "Customer Poaching and Brand Switching." Department of Economics, Harvard University, Boston, Mass., 1997.

———. "Upgrades, Trade-Ins, and Buy-Backs." *Rand Journal of Economics"* (in press).

Gilbert, Richard. "Networks, Standards, and the Use of Market Dominance: Microsoft 1995." In *The Antitrust Revolution: Economics, Competition, and Policy,* edited by John Kwoka and Laurence White (New York: Oxford University Press, 1998).

Goldstein, Jon. "Michael Bloomberg's Wired World." *Time Digital,* 23 March 1998, 64–67.

Grove, Andrew S. *Only the Paranoid Survive: How to Exploit the Crisis Points That Challenge Every Company and Career.* New York: Currency Doubleday, 1996.

Hamilton, Annette. "Microsoft Refutes Claim of NT Server, NT Workstation Similarities." *ZD Anchordesk,* 11 September 1996. [On-line], 2 paragraphs. Available: http://www.zdnet.com/Anchordesk/story/story_321.html [5 June 1998].

Hamm, Steve. "Dance, He Said: How TCI's Malone Played Gates Off Against McNealy." *Business Week,* 2 February 1998, 118.

Hayes, John R. "Acquisition Is Fine, But Organic Growth Is Better." *Forbes,* 30 December 1996, 52–56.

Hilton, George W. *American Narrow Gauge Railroads.* Palo Alto, Calif.: Stanford University Press, 1990.

"Internet Service Providers Team to Form Internet Operators Group." IOPS.ORG Press Release, 20 May 1997. [On-line], 6 paragraphs. Available: http://www.iops.org/iops-release.html [5 June 1998].

Kattan, Joseph. "Market Power in the Presence of an Installed Base." *Antitrust Law Journal* 62, no. 1 (1993): 1–21.

Katz, Michael L., and Carl Shapiro. "Network Externalities, Competition, and Compatibility." *American Economic Review* 75, no. 3 (1985): 424–440.

————. "Product Compatibility Choice in a Market with Technological Progress." *Oxford Economic Papers, Special Issue on the New Industrial Economics,* 1986.

————. "Systems Competition and Network Effects." *Journal of Economic Perspectives* 8, no. 2 (1994): 93–115.

————. "Technology Adoption in the Presence of Network Externalities." *Journal of Political Economy* 94, no. 4 (1986): 822–884.

Kelly, Kevin. *New Rules for the New Economy.* New York: Viking Press, 1998.

Klein, Joel. "The Importance of Antitrust Enforcement in the New Economy." Technical report [On-line]. U.S. Department of Justice, 1998. Available: www.usdoj.gov/atr/public/speeches [August 1998].

Klemperer, Paul. "Markets with Consumer Switching Costs." *Quarterly Journal of Economics* 102, no. 2 (1987): 375–394.

————. "Price Wars Caused by Switching Costs." *Review of Economic Studies* 56, no. 3 (1989): 405–420.

————. "Competition When Consumers Have Switching Costs: An Overview with Applications to Industrial Organization, Macroeconomics, and International Trade." *Review of Economic Studies* 62, no. 4 (1995): 515–539.

Knight, Charles. *The Old Printer and the Modern Press.* London: John Murray, 1854.

Lardner, James. *Fast Forward.* New York: W. W. Norton & Co., 1987.

Lawson, Stephen. "Cisco Feels the Squeeze." *InfoWorld* 19, no. 31 (1997): 1.

"Leading Technology Executives Form Industry Political Service Organization; John Doerr and Jim Barksdale to Co-Chair the Technology Network—Focus on Education and Legal Reform." *Business Wire,* 8 July 1997. [On-line], 14 paragraphs. Available: http//www.kpcb.com/whatsnew/article5.html [5 June 1998].

Leibowitz, S. J., and Stephen Margolis. "The Fable of the Keys." *Journal of Law and Economics* 33, no. 1 (1990): 1–26.

Lesk, Michael. "Projections for Making Money on the Web." In Deborah Hurley, Brian Kahin, and Hal R. Varian, eds., *Internet Publishing and Beyond.* Cambridge: MIT Press, 1998.

Livingston, Brian. "More on Finding, or Not Finding, Your Special Web Site." *InfoWorld,* 10 November 1997.

Lucky, Robert. *Silicon Dreams: Information, Man, and Machine.* New York: St. Martin's Press, 1989.

Melcher, Richard A. "Dusting Off the Britannica." *Business Week,* 20 October 1997, 143–146.

Mueller, Milton. *Universal Service: Interconnection, Competition, and Monopoly in the Making of the American Telephone System*. Cambridge: MIT Press, 1996.

————, and Jorge Schement. "Universal Service from the Bottom Up: A Study of Telephone Penetration in Camden, New Jersey." *Information Society* 12, no. 3 (1996): 273–291.

Nelson, Phillip. "Information and Consumer Behavior." *The Journal of Political Economy* 78, no. 2 (1970): 311–329.

Nesmith, Achsah. "Arduous March Towards Standardization." *Smithsonian*, March 1985, 176–194.

Pigou, A. C. *The Economics of Welfare*. London: Macmillan, 1920.

Rohlfs, Jeffrey. "A Theory of Interdependent Demand for a Communications Service." *Bell Journal of Economics* 5, no. 1 (1974): 16–37.

Saloner, Garth. "Economic Issues in Computer Interface Standardization." *Economics of Innovation and New Technology* 1, no. 1–2 (1990): 135–156.

Sandberg, Jared. "Retailers Pay Big for Prime Internet Real Estate." *Wall Street Journal*, 8 July 1997, B7.

Sesit, Michael R. "New Internet Site to Offer Risk-Analysis for Investors." *Wall Street Journal*, 23 July 1997, C1.

Simon, Herbert. "Designing Organizations for an Information-Rich World." In Donald M. Lamberton, ed., *The Economics of Communication and Information*. Cheltenham, U.K.: Edward Elgar, 1997.

Simonson, Itamar, and Amos Tversky. "Choice in Context: Tradeoff Contrast and Extremeness Aversion." *Journal of Marketing Research* 29 (1992): 281–295.

Smith, Gerald E., and Thomas T. Nagle. "Frames of Reference and Buyers' Perception of Price and Value." *California Management Review* 38, no. 1 (1995): 98–116.

Spence, M. "Nonlinear Prices and Welfare." *Journal of Marketing Research* 8 (1976): 1–18.

Ung, Gordon Mah. "End of Concurrent Licensing Could Be Costly to Microsoft Customers." *Computerworld*, 7 November 1997.

Varian, Hal R. "Differential Prices and Efficiency." *First Monday* 1, no. 2 (1996). [Online]. Available: http://www.firstmonday.dk.

————. *Intermediate Microeconomics*. New York: W. W. Norton & Co., 1996.

————. "A Model of Sales." *American Economic Review* 70 (1980): 651–659.

————. "Price Discrimination." In *Handbook of Industrial Organization*, edited by Robert Schmalensee and Robert Willig (Amsterdam: North Holland Press, 1989).

————. "Price Discrimination and Social Welfare." *American Economic Review* 75, no. 4 (1985): 870–875.

————. "Pricing Information Goods." In Research Libraries Group, ed., *Scholarship of the New Information Environment Proceedings*. Washington, D.C.: Research Libraries Group, 1995.

———, and Richard Roehl. "Circulating Libraries and Video Rental Stores." Technical report, University of California, Berkeley, 1997. [On-line]. Available: http://www. sims.berkeley.edu/~hal.

Wagner, Mitch. "Online Retailers Buddy Up." *Wall Street Journal,* 15 September 1997.

Watt, Ian. *The Rise of the Novel.* Berkeley: University of California Press, 1957.

Williamson, Oliver E. *Markets and Hierarchies: Analysis and Antitrust Implications.* New York: The Free Press, 1975.

Wilson, Robert B. *Nonlinear Pricing.* New York: Oxford University Press, 1993.

Wingfield, Nick. "Microsoft Says It Will Buy E-Mail Start-Up in Stock Deal." *Wall Street Journal,* 1998.

Winkler, Karen. "Academic Presses Look to the Internet to Save Scholarly Monographs," *The Chronicle of Higher Education,* 12 September 1997.

Ziegler, Bart and Don Clark. "Microsoft Gives Technology Away to Beat Rival." *Wall Street Journal,* 2 October 1996, B1.

Index

About the Authors

Carl Shapiro is the Transamerica Professor of Business Strategy at the Haas School of Business at the University of California at Berkeley. He is also director of the Institute of Business and Economic Research and professor of economics at UC Berkeley. He earned his Ph.D. in economics at M.I.T. in 1981 and taught at Princeton University during the 1980s. He has been editor of the *Journal of Economic Perspectives* and a fellow at the Center for Advanced Study in the Behavioral Sciences.

Professor Shapiro served as Deputy Assistant Attorney General for Economics in the Antitrust Division of the U.S. Department of Justice during 1995–1996. He is a founder of the Tilden Group, an economic consulting company. He has consulted extensively for a wide range of clients, including Bell Atlantic, DirecTV, General Electric, Intel, Iomega, Kodak, Rockwell, Silicon Graphics, Sprint, Time Warner, and Xerox, as well as the Federal Trade Commission and the Department of Justice.

Professor Shapiro has published extensively in the areas of industrial organization, competition policy, the economics of innovation, and competitive strategy. His current research interests include antitrust economics, intellectual property and licensing, product standards and compatibility, and the economics of networks and interconnection.

His homepage is at http://www.haas.berkeley.edu/~shapiro.

Hal R. Varian is the dean of the School of Information Management and Systems at UC Berkeley. He is also a professor in the Haas School of Business, a professor in the economics department, and holds the Class of 1944 Chair at Berkeley. He received his S.B. degree from M.I.T. in 1969 and his M.A. (mathematics) and Ph.D. (economics) from UC Berkeley in 1973. He has taught at M.I.T., Stanford, Oxford, Michigan, and several other universities around the world.

Dean Varian is a fellow of the Guggenheim Foundation, the Econometric Society, and the American Academy of Arts and Sciences. He has served as co-editor of the *American Economic Review,* and as an associate editor of the *Journal of Economic Perspectives* and the *Journal of Economic Literature.*

Professor Varian has published numerous papers in economic theory, industrial organization, public finance, econometrics and information economics. He is the author of two major economics textbooks that have been translated into ten languages. His current research involves the economics of information technology. In particular, he is investigating strategic issues in technology management, the economics of intellectual property, and public policy surrounding information technology.

His homepage is at http://www.sims.berkeley.edu/~hal.